Blue Diamond Journey

The Healing of a Reluctant Seer

By

Esther Supernault

Order this book online at www.trafford.com
or email orders@trafford.com

Most Trafford titles are also available at major online book retailers.

Author of 3 other books, editor of three more

Printed in the United States of America.

ISBN: 978-1-4269-4115-3 (sc)

Library of Congress Control Number: 2010912051

Trafford rev. 04/20/2011

www.trafford.com

North America & international
toll-free: 1 888 232 4444 (USA & Canada)
phone: 250 383 6864 ♦ fax: 812 355 4082

Other Books written by Esther Supernault

****The following two books are used as University texts in Social Work classes across Canada. The Nishnawbe Aski Nation from Thunder Bay, Ontario, rated them as **number one** in family violence healing texts they researched from across Canada. American healing centres claim the lengthy bibliography and easy to read text offers assistance to students, staff and clients alike.

A Family Affair

****©1992, 2005 by Native Counseling Services of Alberta (NCSA), Edmonton, Non-Fiction ISBN: 1-895963-00-1 Price: $15.00

This book addresses the historical and cultural reasons for family violence in Canada's Native communities. Seven traditional Native principles about relationships are documented then tracked through drastic changes under European influence. These seven principles thus outline the solutions for healing violence in a community-based treatment program.

A Warrior's Heart (for our men)

****©1995, 2005 by Native Counseling Services of Alberta, Edmonton, Non-Fiction ISBN: 1-895963-01-X   Price: $20.00

This book offers a personal pathway for our men or women to stop and heal the violence in their lives. No distinction is made between victim and perpetrator. Using Native traditional ways, the book introduces the warrior within, helping people find their own answers in a good way that harms no one. Personal quotes, poems, laughing memories and heart-felt humility from people who have already completed their healing journey are added for encouragement. Using the medicine wheel of healing, a pathway of understanding is opened through teachings about spiritual, physical, emotional and intellectual development. One Aboriginal man said, "This is the first book that makes sense to me."

When We Still Laughed

©2001 by Esther Supernault, Fiction Novel
ISBN: 0-9730176-0-0   Price: $20.00

This well-researched historical novel portrays a hot-tempered young Irishman and a fiery Cree warrior traveling across the prairies from Fort Garry (Winnipeg, Manitoba) to Fort Edmonton (Alberta) in 1863. One man carries the legacy of Celtic knighthood and Catholicism, the other of ancient warriors and Mother Earth wisdom. Their quest is enriched by the teachings of a swampy earth spirit called Mud Woman. A refreshing, often hilarious perspective of both cultures echoes through classical legends, tall tales, myths and prophecies passed down through an eccentric cast of people the two men encounter in their travels. A powerful feminine influence weaves through the antics of mischievous Native grandmothers, warrior women and pioneer wives. From the stark image of the "Warrior's Last Trail" comes a spiritual answer of death, rebirth and rejuvenation - a powerful message for today's society.

Readers have called it "enlightening, entertaining while educational, humorous, tragic, fascinating, the best book I ever read, a Masterpiece that needs more marketing!" Many read it twice!

Understanding Abuse

© 2006   Price: $25.00

A 43-page training package for a community-based Family Violence Awareness presentation. It offers historical background for abuse; its symptoms; types and examples of abuse; profiles of victim and abuser as well as solutions for community workers.   The Appendix of colourful summaries of the course can be used to create transparencies for **overheads** or **power point presentations**. Esther is a facilitator/trainer so she wrote what she wanted for such a presentation.

Books Co-written and Edited by Esther Supernault

Heartbeat Angels

© 2001 by Pauline Newman of Newman Publishing, Non-Fiction
Edited by Esther Supernault ISBN: 9688594-0-2 Price: $20.00

This collection of seventy short stories is written by people who encountered or experienced the uplifting presence of angels or spiritual messages at crucial times in their lives. These honest, heartwarming testimonials offer comfort and inspiration to all. The threads of similar incidents woven through these stories, from people who have never met, prove there is something more than their imaginations at work. Esther included a story of her 'angel".

In the Works by Esther: *Wind Walker*, Fiction Novel (editing stage)

A young scribe struggles to record stories, without her judgement or interpretation, about the hidden creatures of Earth, as they tell it word for word. Her evolution from a novice mage to an elder is constantly challenged by a half-caste warrior magician. When their attraction ends in tragedy, their antagonism finds hilarious resolutions. Meet a wild, funny cast of dancing gardener sprites, quarrelling tree spirits, singing rocks, swaggering griffins, witty Yeti, sombre whales and shape-shifting thunderbirds. All have powerful, modern messages for the 'humans' of Mother Earth.

Acknowledgements

For Cliff, Beryl, Elaine and Joyce who walked beside me all the way.
You picked me up and dusted me off too many times to count.

Forward

You are about to travel a journey with a special lady of sacred words.

Our technological and scientific world has possibly become infinite with so much growth. The abilities to communicate in new ways and create medical cures are so promising and progressive. Never before has this been so profound.

However, there is a down side. We are slowly losing our human to human touch – those smiles as we pass each other on the street; the opening of a door for a stranger; the chats in line-ups; the cheery small-talk with a cashier; a laugh in the elevator; a 'real' phone call, letter, note, card or the simple ability to play, relax and enjoy.

As a child, I can remember walking in the woods in England and getting into the stinging nettles. But always close by were the dock leaves – nature's cure. I'd grab them, rub them on and there! A simple, easy, natural cure.

There must be a marriage between natural healing ways and modern medicine. But again, we are losing our way to our natural roots. Perhaps one of our greatest losses is the lost awareness of our own soul, our heart, and mostly, the trust in our intuition – the cardinal rule of life.

The author of this book was inspired from her heart and intuition - a truth, a trust, a learning in how one needs to love oneself. She weaves an incredible tapestry of experiences which take love, courage, strength, determination and true trust in self to succeed through natural and modern medicine. Her journey gives hope and healing to all who read her sacred words. Your world as you *see*, will change. Esther – you *are* the seer!

EZRA and Sue Roberts

Forward

I am honoured to be part of the team that journeyed with Esther as she experienced healing through not one but two bouts of breast cancer. Her determination to seek support outside conventional medicine to help her find wellness in her spirit and heart as well as body and mind, is a testament to the potential we all have for healing.

In my practice over the past twenty years, I have witnessed increasing interest in the use of alternative therapies and natural medicine. In just the last few generations much of the natural and traditional indigenous healing knowledge and personal health empowerment has been displaced by the medical/technical/pharmaceutical advances that have captured our attention and become the way of life. But now, as modern medicine fails to live up to its promise, as people search for empowerment and meaningful participation in their own health journey, they are once again looking to ancient knowledge and practices seeking out more natural options – ones that engage our whole beings and address the spiritual, emotional, mental as well as physical dimensions of who we are. The good news here is that natural medicine does work, especially when combined with Energy and Vibrational medicines. Rather than damage the human system, it in fact supports the innate healing and balancing mechanisms in the body.

I believe the renaissance of Spiritual and Energy healing with all the energetic helpers like Homeopathy, Essential oils and Vibrational medicine will continue and grow as the future medicine of the people. 21st Century medical care will inevitably continue to develop its high-tech aspect on investigating the physical plane but alongside this will be high natural medicine: the systematic and scientific use of natural and spiritual medicines that can effectively help prevent and treat ailments and disease. This integration of high-tech and high-natural medicine will be the next stage of medical care. Spiritual, ageless medicine will inevitably play an integral role in this medicine of the future. It is our hope this book will help bring the health care of the future to you and encourage you to make more natural health choices for yourself guided by the power within and your connection to the Divine – the Creator of all things.

I hope you find in these pages the en-courage-ment to carry you on your own journey to optimal health.

Dr. Anne Mageau, NMD, DNM, DHM, ROHP

Contents

1. The Healer Within 1
2. Soul Preparations 6
3. First Steps 13
4. Body Imbalances 19
5. Intuition 22
6. Messengers 27
7. My Psychic Gifts 33
8. Emotional Blocks 42
9. Guardians of Us All 46
10. Clearing Time 50
11. Stone Language 53
12. Facing the Bears 57
13. Red Heart Vision 61
14. Mountain of Tears 65
15. Surgery Shining 68
16. Healing Messages 73
17. "You Want Me to...What?!!!" 77
18. Get Well Message 85
19. There Be Dragons 92
20. The Sun's Reprieve 97
21. Terrible Choices 101
22. My Life, My Choice! 106
23. Uneasy Times 110
24. Final Bastion 114
25. Truths and Lies 117
26. Toxin Tales (From my Guides) 120
27. Healing is a Supplemental Journey 127
28. Dragons and Whales 134
29. Body Tour 137
30. Surrender unto Grace 140
31. To Go Boldly... 144
32. Listening for Truth 147

33. Meeting Marsha 150
34. Detoxing 153
35. What They Don't Tell You 159
36. Joyful Good Health...166
37. XI Returns 169
38. What About the Fear? 173
39. Healing Crises 186
40. My Body's New Renovations 191
41. Burying the Tumour and Celebrating 195
42. DNA Healing..202
43. Second Chance? Or Next Step? 207
44. What Women Need to Know...225
45. Our New Red Running Shoes 232
46. Turquoise in the Final Analysis 236

1.

The Healer Within

THIS BOOK IS FOR YOU IF YOU:

- Are not well
- Are worried about getting or already have diabetes, heart disease or other life-threatening illnesses
- Found a lump
- Have just been diagnosed with cancer
- Have cancer
- Are in the middle of treatments for cancer
- Are worried about a disease returning
- Need surgery
- Are overweight
- Have a loved one with one of the above

"There is within each person an Innate Intelligence that can direct the healing or correction of any body part if one will allow it to work unimpeded by obstruction."

Dr. L. Newman, (70:39)

I know it is hard to read or focus on anything if fear and worry are weighing you down. Yet the healing journey back to health is the same for every human being. The answers lie within us, within our inner spirit that always speaks the truth. Finding the cause of an illness is the first step on your journey back to health. Then, how do you get better? Do you want a therapy program individualized to your specific problems and way of looking at the world? Would you like to *know* ahead of time which therapies, foods and medicines are good for you and which are deadly, given your unique body's reactions? Instead of giving your power to someone else and expecting them to heal you, would you like to know how to heal yourself? Such wisdom dwells within you. Such mindful intelligence comes from every cell in your body, from your inner spirit, from deep in your soul. Would you like to know your soul's truth? Sense it? Feel it in your gut? Understand its symbolism in your dreams? Most of us have forgotten this inner wisdom we were born with. Nobody listens to it anymore. We don't know how. And we are dying because we don't! Science with its tunnel vision logic has seduced us away from our inner, much wiser, most powerful healer – our intuition. When I was diagnosed with breast cancer, I faced an ultimatum: Change or Die. This book is my journey: what I learned about healing a breast full of cancer, nurturing my body back to health – gently, carefully and wisely, without chemotherapy or radiation. Digging right to my soul, I **healed myself physically, mentally, emotionally and *spiritually* – simultaneously, wholistically, <u>on a daily basis.</u> The results surprised me and moved me into a new vision of myself. You can go where I went. I will teach you how.**

Cancer is so terrifying! The Big 'C' is so unknown. Every second person in Canada is now destined to get some form of cancer in their lives. *What is making us so sick?* How do we stop this nightmare? All we know as an ordinary person is cancer is bad! Deadly! Any disease brings a similar fear. Once diagnosed, a terrible aloneness overcomes us. Singled out, we feel abandoned, deprived of support and weak with fear. With no place to run, no place to hide, we have no choice but to turn and face the enemy bearing down on us.

Have you ever seen the latest movie version of King Kong? Remember how the girl eventually made friends with him? After her initial screaming and struggling to get away, numb with terror, horror and helplessness, she stood up to him! She did not cower, plead or whine. She faced him, tiny as she was and dared him to harm her. Every time he knocked her down and laughed at her, she crawled to her feet and glared into his beady red eyes. Finally, he became angry with her. He tried roaring in her face and still she faced him, unmoving. When he realized he could neither intimidate nor frighten her anymore, he walked away! He walked away, looking back at her with a frustrated yet reluctant respect for her courage. Just like this woman, your fear can not define you and who you are inside. This is what I want to teach you – how to stand up and face the King Kong of illness in your living room. By the time you finish my book you will be able to shrink him to a pet monkey and ship him off to the zoo (Kalamazoo?).

Whatever illness you have, read as much as you can about it. This is your first weapon. Then you make <u>informed</u> choices on how to deal with it. Take your time to learn the true cause of your illness. You didn't get it overnight and you won't cure it overnight. Real healing means addressing the problem from as many different angles as you can – so it never returns.

What weapons do you have in defence?

I will give you a book full of them!

I will back my intuitive inner wisdom with a wide range of information and solid research – years of it – from the best medical and scientific research along with a host of nutritionists, doctors, naturopaths, writers, poets, artists, philosophers, therapists, psychics, dreamers and down home, common sense, every day people. Married for over forty years, I am a mother of two, grandmother of five, a nurse, researcher and writer with a Bachelor's degree in psychology. I've written books and taught classes in personal healing and development, parenting, Canadian and Celtic history, Aboriginal philosophy, poetry, fiction and creative writing. I can decrease your reading by the hundreds of books I've read and quote in this one. Adding my sixty years of life experiences, intuition, dreams and knowledge, I offer many ways to help you get in touch with your own inner wisdom, along with some playful magic to both shock and entertain you.

In the back of my book is a bibliography of all the books and the latest available data I found for you. My reference notes: (70:236) means the book was published in 1970 and the "quote" is from page 236. This way you know how recent the research is and where you can find additional information.

Take what you want from this book and leave the rest. Actually, you don't have to believe me at all. Your reading this book, however, indicates it has a message for you. This is how the Universe works and I will explain such teachings to you. However, before you close this book forever, I urge you to read Chapter 35, *What They Don't Tell You.* If you are a woman, check out Chapter 44, *What Women Need to Know.* I found shocking information *everyone* on the planet ought to know about.

The spiritual philosophy of healing comes down through centuries of wise, intuitively gifted spiritual healers. Now, most people think 'religion' when they hear 'spirituality'. Well, I am talking about our **inner spirit, the 'I am'** that thinks, dreams, believes, laughs, creates, meditates and most of all, is aware of its own body and fragile mortality. It's our inner spirit who wonders how we fit into this vast universe and why we got sick.

I consider myself lucky to have both a Celtic (Irish/English) and Aboriginal American, (Ojibwa/Anishnabeg) heritage. As a writer this gives me access to both the fey world of fairies, dragons, druids and angels plus the world of Mother Earth with all her creatures and earthy wisdom. These two worlds are not separate realities but part of a much bigger whole. From this realm I bring you fascinating answers, truths so profound they will resonate deep within your soul, a place where science can neither enter nor understand.

I yearned to know: 'Who am I? What is my purpose for being here? Why did I get cancer? What do I have to offer the world? What do my dreams mean? Do guardian angels or totem animals truly exist? Where are mine? Who listens when I cry out for help? Who is that little voice inside? Who is the loud one? And how do I access truth on a daily basis? Does that inner voice always speak the truth? How can I tell?' Some answers are the same; some are specifically for each person. Seems we have to find our own. I will help you find your answers by sharing my experiences in finding mine.

Sitting in Aboriginal ceremonies; listening to Elder teachings; smudging to clear the energy around me; praying in sweats; taking my tobacco and creating a circle of silence in the quiet woods; meditating in my living room recliner; paying attention to my dreams and simply listening with a blank mind and open heart has given me spiritual answers so profound I am still in awe at the powerful energy surrounding us.

This universal connection and unity is fundamentally missing from science's perspective. It wants to isolate every issue, put blinders on and see only a tiny piece of the whole human being. Science wants a miniscule solution for a dynamic human with so many facets, not all can shine at once – nor can they be healed at once. Science refuses to step back and honour the complexity of each unique individual. Scientists dissect everything, the opposite of unity and wholeness. Consequently, their solutions are fragmentary, isolated and therefore, never long-term. Sure scientists can take a single cell and clone an animal but not an unprecedented original. Cloning is like buying a Prada purse copy, which fools nobody. Our Innate Intelligence, however, without any interference from science, or man, can put together four hundred billion cells, each in its proper place and produce a special, unparalleled baby in 280 days. This is the power of our inner spirit! Every person is part of an interconnected web as vast as this Universe, rather than a collection of parts. Real healing honours this web of interaction – far beyond scientific logic or fact.

Dr. Newman, in her book, *Make Your Juicer Your Drug Store*, believes if we put ourselves in harmony with the Laws of Nature, consume only what the body requires, think positive constructive thoughts and allow/trust the Innate (inner spirit) to direct the healing of the body, it will continue to operate for the good of each person. She wrote this in 1970! Today it is still a wonderful, wholesome way to heal: a mental, physical, emotional and spiritual process. Add this to more recent information and we can find a path to healing uniquely our own. We can walk it together because our desire moves us in the same direction – from illness back to joyful health.

I am not a doctor so I can neither diagnose nor heal you. That is *your* work. The choices, of how you do so, are *yours*. Your journey beside me is to find your own inner wisdom and learn how to listen to its truths. **Don't let anyone bully you into making hasty decisions**. Even if

4

you have just been diagnosed with some illness, you have time to learn about your disease and time to wisely, *intuitively* choose how to deal with it. Research shows it takes years to create any chronic illness so healing will not happen overnight either. I gathered this information and share it with you to brighten your path through these dark days. It is my gift to you.

2.

Soul Preparations

"You're the only kind of knowledge
They don't teach at any college
You're an education in yourself..."
Harry Warren and Al Dubin, *You're an Education*, (1938)

If you have just been diagnosed or you're afraid, begin with crying. I recommend screaming and wailing – lots of it – at least until the shock wears off. If you are very creative, you can set up a wailing wall and have at it until you can laugh at the insanity of it all. When my doctor said those horrible two words, "It's cancer", I remember folding in half like a car dealership wind doll when the air stops. I walked out of the clinic and drove home bawling my head off. I'm talking the wailing, bellowing, snot dripping howl of both fury and terror. I had no idea how to cope with cancer. Yet any competitive athlete will tell you the best way to defeat an enemy is to learn both his strengths and his weaknesses.

Suzanne Somers interviews Dr. Stephen Sinatra, a certified cardiologist and bioenergetic psychotherapist in her book, *Knockout*. He says anger is a good force when you have cancer. To survive, "Fight back! Get into your shadow side, your dark side and take it head on! (09:06-09). Feelings never lie. So honour them, experience them. He claims, "When you cry, you are healing the body." Deep sobbing releases the tension in your vocal cords, in your lungs, diaphragm and heart. Tears contain endorphins, healing chemicals. He found men who don't cry get heart disease (09:09).

So, are you ready to look your illness in its beady red eyes and discover how to stand up to it?

Thought so. Come along with me (you're allowed to sniffle). Know you are never alone. You have more help than you can ever imagine inside and around you. I will introduce you to it. I

6

will walk beside you as you begin your own healing journey. From now on, I am your Cancer Sister. I've been there and back. Besides, a burden shared is already halved.

When you are really sick, I know how the fear overwhelms you – makes your heart pound; your blood pressure soar; your stomach knot and your body ache with muscle tension and stress. This is your body's reaction to danger: the Flight or Fight Syndrome. Sadly, disease is not something you can run from. So, with gentle dignity, we gather as much information about it as possible and prepare ourselves for what lies ahead.

Every illness grows slowly. Did you know everybody has cancer cells? And they grow very slowly. Statistics show they have to multiply for up to eight or nine years before you or your doctor can even detect a lump. Your powerful body has already built a protein wall around them to stop their spreading. This is your body's wonderful line of first defence! It wants to be well. *You just need to learn how to help it.*

Right now, I want you to lift your head up and throw your shoulders back! Then, slowly breathe in through your nose to the count of four. Hold the breath for the count of four (slowly). Ease your breath out through your mouth to the count of four (slowly). Do this four times. As you do, imagine bringing in healthy bright oxygen and blowing out dark stress, pain, fear and worry.... Just imagine! You bring in the good stuff and release the bad. It's a win – win game! The yogi masters have used this relaxation technique for centuries. No, I am not saying you have to take up yoga – although it would be good for your body – just become more *aware* of your body and its need for oxygen, lots of it!

Now imagine four cancer cells in your body (we all have them) exploding. They hate oxygen! But your body loves it. Yet we are all notorious shallow breathers, depriving our bodies of one of its major life-giving forces. From this day forward, throughout the day, especially when you are stressed, do these slow deep breathing exercises. Imagine healthy oxygen moving into your body and surrounding the sick cells. Research shows oxygen is also the number one detoxifier! Carbon dioxide, what you breathe out helps you release toxins and dead, *unhealthy* cells from your body.

Better yet, go outside and breathe in fresh air. Now, face the sun. Don't look at it of course. Take off your glasses and let the cheerful light reflect into your eyes. Breathe in the sunshine. 11:00 a.m. has the best energy – part of a new day before its zenith. Did you know spending ten minutes per day in the sun's **natural vitamin D** can prevent almost 70% of all cancers? This comes from the World Health Organization (WHO). Latest research includes Multiple Sclerosis prevention too. Even Dr. Oz from the *Oprah Winnfrey* show says Vitamin D is toxic to cancer cells. Best of all, it's *free!*

Black people, because their beautiful dark skin repels the sun, need 20 minutes of sunshine per day to prevent cancer. Even breast cancer statistics show higher rates in lands with less sunshine and longer winters and lower rates in lands with more sunshine and shorter winters. From this day forward, resolve to go outside each day, whether the sun is out or not, face towards the sun, and breathe deeply. You just took your first step towards dealing with or preventing many illnesses, including cancer.

Let me share an Aboriginal teaching to help you understand how all this physical, mental, emotional and spiritual stuff works. Draw a circle and divide it into four equal parts. Make a dot in the very center of the circle where the axes meet. This is <u>you</u> and the four parts are your mental, emotional, physical and spiritual components. Native Elders teach that in order to become balanced, we must develop all four parts *equally and at the same time*. Mental of course, is about your brain, your thoughts and memories. You make it grow by learning, thinking and remembering so you can improve your daily life. Physical is about your body, you make it grow by moving, exercising, relaxing and eating good food. Emotions, of course, are about your feelings, being mad, sad, glad or bad. Nurturing ourselves means honouring all our feelings as real, truthful and necessary – every day! Our inner spirit of spirituality is something I will share throughout this book, because it is the least understood area in our society and its lack causes very unbalanced, unhealthy people.

First of all, I believe your spirit dwells under your rib cage, just below your diaphragm, in your solar plexus. Some call it a 'gut feeling'. It is the 'I am' and special because no two spirits are the same. It's an inner *knowing*. When we don't listen to it, we usually find ourselves in trouble, wishing we had. Then we pay the poor sad consequences of bad choices. We have this ability to know without knowing how we know what is right. We've just learned to ignore it because science tells us logic is better.

Elders caution about the two voices inside us. One is loud, negative and will always get you into trouble (ego) while the other inner voice is soft, kind, gentle, compassionate and forever truthful. Who you become depends on which voice you listen to the most. Elders give many teachings about humility. You must always listen quietly with respect. As soon as you demand, argue, criticise, ignore, you have stepped back into ego. Your inner spirit is about *who you are;* what *you* want, like, dislike, desire, dream about, think about, worry about and allow to hurt you. Your inner spirit gives you a sense of humour, honour, kindness, gentleness and love. What intrigues you, inspires you and delights you comes from your inner spirit. Throughout life, your spirit slowly reveals what is important to you and what makes you special, unique, a diamond in the making.

The four parts of yourself mental, emotional, physical and spiritual thus create your soul. In spiritual Judaism, Israeli rabbinical teacher Rabbi Eliyahu Ben Shlomo teaches how all forces of the spirit are activated by our inner self, which is independent of our mind and body. Something inside of us determines what is true and what is fraudulent, what is honourable and what is shameful, what is just, honest and ethical and what is wicked, iniquitous and base. This 'something' is the soul. When we do something wrong, there is a part of us that watches, *knows* it is wrong and cringes. Its reaction may be an internal shiver or shudder but it always *knows*. I believe this is our soul; I call it 'the Watcher'.

> "We don't realize that somewhere within us all, there does exist a Supreme Self who is eternally at peace. That Supreme Self is our true identity, universal and divine."
> Elizabeth Gilbert, *Eat Pray Love* (06:122)

In 1836, Ralph Waldo Emerson, poet, writer and philosopher, in his landmark work *Nature*, describes the soul as something through which the Universal Spirit speaks to an individual and strives to lead the individual back to it.

The Universal Spirit is really about a power or energy greater than us. I capitalize this 'Spirit' so you know the difference between it and your inner spirit (small case). Call it God, Mohammed, Buddha, Dios, Great Spirit, Higher Power or KitchiManitou (Cree word for Great Spirit or Great Mystery. Aboriginal people believe you can never know all, so it remains a mystery). The name you use doesn't matter; it is the same energy surrounding us, as vast as the Universe.

Our circular Aboriginal shields and the flags in sweat lodges represent the four colours of races: red, black, yellow and white. I believe the circle of the four parts of yourself and every human on Earth reveals a more profound truth. I believe Creator knew there was too much to learn about the four parts of a human soul. So Creator gave one part to each of the four races. Their job was to go away and develop the part to the best of their ability and then return and share it with the other three races. Together once again, all four races could develop the four parts *equally* thus creating balanced, harmonious souls and communities.

To the White race, Creator gave the physical component: the Gift of Motion. And indeed the white race has developed this magnificently! They created the wheel, engines, trains, planes, boats, automobiles, aircraft and spaceship. They travelled to the four corners of the earth and... the moon. The problem with the White Race is they have neither accepted nor fully integrated the other three parts of the soul to create a balance within themselves. They rush around too much, always in motion, creating stress and eventually illness in their incessant craving 'to go, go, go and do'.

To the Yellow race, Creator gave the Gift of the Mind. They too have developed it magnificently! Here are our world's greatest philosophers, thinkers, meditators, mathematicians (they gave us the abacus), technologists and wisdom teachers; the race of people who developed a form of martial arts and yoga that is truly mind over body. Their problem: they too have not fully developed the other three parts of the soul to create inner balance and harmony. They 'think' too much, suppressing their emotions and smothering their inner spirit with logic.

To the Black race, Creator gave the Gift of Emotions. This race had a harder time, because emotions have neither words nor thoughts, just energy. Yet the Black race, despite oppression, has found a beautiful, magnificent way to express emotions through music and dance. Nobody can dance or sing with such heart as the Black race! Emotions seem to be built right into their vocabulary and movement. Oprah Winnfrey is a class act of the Black race's gift, awakening her television listeners to their own emotions and hearts. Black people have given us rhythm and blues, jazz, tap, hip hop, rap and slam dancers. Historians finally admit our country music has bluesy undertones due to the Black cowboys who rode with the Western cattle drives after the Civil War freed them from slavery. Here too is the root of so much of our dancing and soul sound. They call this Soul music, and perhaps it is, but I believe it is more about emotions expressed from our soul. The problem with the Black race is they stay so much in their emotions; they ignore their honourable place in the greater circle of Soul.

And to the Red race, Creator perhaps gave the most difficult part, The Gift of the Spirit. Here is something that can not be touched or moved or thought or sang into being. It simply exists within us. The only way to find our spirit is through quiet humility, beyond the ego's loud dance. Perhaps that is why the Creator sent the Red nation to their knees in oppression and prejudice. Perhaps they needed to be humbled in order to find their true inner spirit, develop it by healing themselves first then sharing it with the rest of the world for its healing.

I would be remiss if I did not admit our Aboriginal weakness too. We are not planners, we live in the moment, not for tomorrow. We also dwell far too much on the past and the abuse we suffered. It is one thing to admit the dysfunction and family violence in our families and communities. It is another to *own* the responsibility of stopping it, dealing with our emotions, healing ourselves and our tormenters and moving into our real life purpose. Our biggest challenge is to realize the gift our tormentors gave us, forcing us to grow above and beyond the abuse to our greatest spiritual best. I can say this because I have written two books on family violence in our Aboriginal communities - its causes and its healing path (*A Family Affair and a Warrior's Heart*).

Canada, in the Cree language is *Canata*, meaning 'Clean Land'. Elders say our land was set aside by Creator as a place where *all* races of the world could come together, learn from each other and live in harmony with one another. Our warriors were not allowed to war against other races. No blood could be shed between the races in this clean land. Today, I watch people of all colours living, laughing and working side by side in Canada. Our schools contain a vast array of cultures and traditions, all sharing with one another and I rejoice.

Hopi Elders have talked for years about the prophecy of how the Red race would fall on its knees for a hundred years before it would stand up on its hind legs once again and teach the world about Spirit. From my book, *A Warrior's Heart*, a healing path through family violence for men and women, I give you the Hopi Prophecy:

> "Peace can only be brought about through spiritual ways, through kindness, understanding, gentleness and love. Only through these spiritual ways can we put aside the wrong actions of the past and repair the damage done to Mother Earth and the People of the Earth." (95:2)

The hundred years are over; Elders say *we* are the generation the prophecy has waited for. The blaming stops and responsibility for our own lives and actions begins. We are the people who must do the work, the cutting edge of healing, healing ourselves first, then projecting that healed inner harmony outwards. And we will do this one person at a time – wholistically, simultaneously – one day at a time. One Elder said Aboriginal people have one foot in the Spirit World and one foot in this World. So as Aboriginal people, we *will* teach the world how to heal and grow in balance and spiritual harmony. This is my cultural legacy, my purpose behind this Blue Diamond Journey of healing myself and then sharing it with you.

Yet down through the years of discovering my inner spirit, a part of me never fully believed or trusted in the Spiritual World I found beyond this physical world we call 'Reality'. My white ancestry questioned my dreams, meditations, gut feelings, pop up images and thoughts in my head as just an overactive imagination. I have a good one; I couldn't be a writer without it. Yet after my diagnosis, I soon learned I could never simultaneously dream up the synchronicity of things that happened to me and still feel such amazement and awe when they did! I'm just *not* that freaking good!

> "Synchronicity: a collision of possibles so incalculably improbable that it would appear to imply divine intervention."
>
> Karen Marie Moning, *Spell of the Highlander* (05:390).

After my diagnosis, the continuous signs and messages from this powerful, magical realm that I will call 'Spirit world' came in so many beautiful, wonderful, sometimes frustrating, sometimes challenging ways. Coincidence never happens so frequently. I kept a journal from my diagnosis onward. This book summarizes my walk through all my doubts, terrors, fury, grief, revelations and magical, mystical, spiritual answers. Then I found scientific research to back it up! It finally convinced me, beyond a single doubt, this incredible Spirit realm is as real as the world we live in today. **I tell my story so you may feel more at ease on this same pathway to truth, wisdom, magic and the joyful excitement of spiritual discovery and healing within yourself. True healing begins from the soul outward. We all have this ability. We just need to open ourselves to the possibilities. We just need to remember how!**

Dare the impossible! Dream big! At this desperate time in your life, what do you have to lose by trying everything possible to heal? Your sanity you say? In the wild dark days you live in, even you know how overrated that is! Perhaps one day, you will see your illness as a gift – but not yet!!!

3.

First Steps

"One can fight a danger only when one is armed with solid facts and spurred on by unwavering faith and determination."

Eleanor Roosevelt

So let's step into the physical quadrant of our Soul Circle. Did you know cancer is not a disease? Read Bill Henderson's book, *Cancer-Free, Your guide to gentle, non-toxic healing* (his website: www.Beating- Cancer-Gently.com). Having written a series of books about cancer, he states, "**cancer is a reaction**, to the lifestyle choices you have made over the past several years" He also believes the cause is about diet – a breakdown in cellular communication (07:45). I believe this lack of communication starts with our soul, with our Innate Intelligence. Every cell in our body has the ability to listen and respond to every thought we have. When we truly *want* to heal, we take back the responsibility for creating illness. When we learn the causes of our illness and address them, whether we have cancer or some other debilitating chronic disease, we begin our journey back to health and balanced wholeness – our way!

Cancer has many causes. Henderson says about 1/3 is caused by tobacco, the rest by food choices, obesity, excessive alcohol or occupational hazards like asbestos and formaldehyde – 5%. Only 3% of cancer is hereditary. He also addresses some emotional causes such as traumatic loss of a loved one, a bitter divorce or a root canal (07:44-45). Oddly enough, I did have a root canal three years before my diagnosis. Such traumatic issues suppress the immune system and give cancer cells the opportunity to grow.

Bill Henderson writes that if our immune system is healthy enough to fight off all the toxins it takes in or which reside in our body, we don't get the 'reaction' called cancer (07:46). Everyone has deformed cells called cancer. But remember these cells are still a part of us. We created them. To stop them, we need to know what caused them to grow. What caused us to get sick? If our immune system is functioning properly, then our body has the ability to kill unhealthy cells of any kind and kick them out of our bodies. (How disturbing that chemotherapy kills the immune system).

The Surgeon General, the National Cancer Institute and the world's top doctors and nutritionists agree eating fresh fruits and vegetables can boost your energy level, supercharge your immune system and maximize you body's healing power. Therefore, you need good nutrition: lots of potent vitamins, minerals and enzymes and you need them fast. I suggest you go out and buy yourself a juicer. This liquid nutrition is instantly accepted by your body and will begin its healing work within fifteen minutes! A good juicer works on centrifugal force, spinning the juice out one spout and the dry pulp into another container. The best ones have a stainless steel strainer that won't rust or disintegrate from the juices. Find one with only a few parts to wash. You can buy these juicers anywhere they sell appliances. They cost anywhere from $80.00 to $380.00. The cheaper juicers, however, have weaker motors which burn out all too soon.

You can buy juicing books or borrow them from your library or your friends. Many of the newer books have lots of reassuring information about what juicing can do to reverse almost any illness you have. Nutritionists can tell you exactly what fruits and vegetables are the best for the illness you have. Buy organic food if you can. Strawberries, one of my favourite fruits, are the most sprayed of all fruits with pesticides. Beware of the gigantic ones and know they have been fertilized to cancerous proportions.

Liquid nutrition has incredible healing properties. When you drink raw fruits and vegetables, your body doesn't use so many of its own digestive enzymes to break the food down, therefore, freeing the enzymes up for healing processes. Enzymes are like mini Pac-men, eating up the free radicals that can create cancer cells, while reducing inflammation and cleaning up your blood and tissues. I started with just 6 oz. of fruit juice in the morning and 6 oz. of vegetable juice in the afternoon to supplement my regular meals.

I guarantee you will love the incredible taste of fresh fruit juices. They will make your jaws ache with joyful delight! I usually try a combination of two or three different kinds. I add a carrot to every juice I make because its beta-carotene is a real cancer blaster. Peel the oranges, grapefruits, pineapple, passion fruit and kiwis. Apples, pears, peaches, lemons and limes are just fine with the skin and seeds. Mash bananas, softer berries and avocadoes in a blender, or hand blender and add to your juice, otherwise you lose the pulp and all its nutrients. If you can, blend in our Canadian raspberries, saskatoons, blueberries and high bush cranberries. They are powerful antioxidants (meaning they help remove toxins from our body) and anti-inflammatories. In addition, raspberries inhibit cancer cell growth, while strawberries protect cells from free radical damage of our cells.

Make only enough juice for one serving and drink it immediately. Vitamins quickly oxidize into the air, especially vitamin C. Swish the juice around in your mouth before swallowing. We have vital absorbers in our mouth, especially under our tongue, to give our body an instant 'hit' of nutrition. Bottled juices are usually made from the poorest, over ripened fruit that may already contain moulds and bacteria. Juices are pasteurized to kill these but boiling also destroys vital nutrients. Vitamin pills are made from this concentrated, boiled down, dried, pounded and over processed stuff – not too much of the good nutrients are left. Usually vitamins are added in a chemical form to 'enrich' the mix. You might consider this if you believe just any old vitamin pill will do instead of fresh juice.

As an aside about 'enriched' flour versus whole grain, Dr. Newman also mentions a little study done in the 1970's. They put a cockroach in a container with whole wheat flour and enriched flour. The smart bug ate the whole wheat flour but would not touch the 'enriched' (70:30). Enriched food is like someone stealing your car then returning your wheels and seats, saying how lucky you are to have them back!

Vegetable juices need a little 'tweaking' in the flavour department. Start with a simple combination of carrots and apples. I learned to add an apple, pear or grapes to sweeten the pot of any vegetable juice. You can also add a small slice of fresh ginger or parsley or bell pepper for flavouring – all have powerful healing abilities. Cucumbers are the next step then try some celery or radishes. Adding a slice of lemon or raw ginger would make any of the leafy greens like kale, endive, romaine, etc. go down with a wonderful zing. There are no tried and true rules here, let your taste buds be the judge. Any of the cabbage family like broccoli, cauliflower, swiss chard or bok choy, are awesome cancer fighters. For me, I preferred the cabbages cooked (except coleslaw). Yes, you do lose some nutritional value in cooking, but steaming it at a lower temperature, retains more vitamins and minerals. Amazingly, sweet potatoes, yams, parsnips and turnips (all with skins) can be juiced for full value flavour. By juicing, you only lose about 20% of the nutrition but you get instant, easily digestible minerals and vitamins for your healing body.

I recommend you try as many different vegetables and fruits as possible. Each has its own range of beneficial nutrients. Be brave, try a new one each week.

The American Cancer Institute admits 30% to 70% of cancer is caused by the food we eat. Actually, it is the incredible array of pesticides, fertilizers, additives, hormones and chemicals in the food. When you combine this with pollution and chemicals in our cleaners, body products, make-up, water and air, no wonder our bodies can not keep up with flushing these toxins from our system. The result: **a toxic build-up of chemicals in our body's lymphatic system and liver is one of the major causes of a weakened immune system**. Juicing helps on two levels.

Fruits and vegetables not only nourish our bodies; they also provide fast and easy natural detoxifiers to help the body gently flush toxins out on a daily basis.

Organic food ensures we are not adding to this toxic build-up. Fertilized plants have shallow roots because they are forced to grow fast and are harvested early. Organic plants, on the other hand, grow more slowly so they develop deeper roots and thus have more time and space to store nutrients. Researchers found we need to eat three apples and several slices of bread to acquire the same amount of iron and zinc found in one apple and one slice of bread available in the 1940's. (I wonder how they discovered this. Did they actually test preserved bread and apples from the 1940's?) Furthermore, organic foods, left on their own, develop their own immunity against pests and bugs. They don't *need* any chemical sprays. Because of natural crop rotation and nature's own fertilizers, **organic food has more nutrients than the soil-depleted, mineral deficient, fertilizer enhanced, herbicide raised, pesticide sprayed, genetically altered, hydrogen ripened 'normal' food in our grocery stores!**

Michael Pollan in his book, *In Defence of Food*, advises us to "shake the hand that feeds you." I explained this to the lady grower at my local Farmers Market. She stuck out her hand and we shook in laughter and delight. She said, "I will think of you when I'm only half way down the row and it is 37°C!" The further away food is produced, the more additives and preservatives it needs to reach you in edible condition. Any 'Food in a Box' has lost most of its nutrients by the time it reaches your table. Pollan says they already knew in the 1930's that processing food robs them of nutrients and vitamins. Also, calories are easier to transport (and preserve) especially refined grain and sugars (08:97).

In other words, if the food won't mould, spoil or rot in the very near future, don't eat it! It does *not* preserve your body. It won't rot due to the nitrates, plastics and gases it contains, which will clog up your liver ducts and store the junk in fat tissue cells. It is not a food, so it can not be digested or broken down. This is the frightening cause of our men's big bellies. Their livers are toxic from all the chemicals and unable to function normally.

On a recent trip to the Big Island of Hawaii, I visited the Kilauea Volcano. Signs everywhere instruct you to keep your car windows closed because of the toxic sulphuric dioxide spewing from the volcano. People with heart and lung problems were most at risk. Then I come home and find sulphur dioxide sprayed over our fruits and vegetables as a preservative! For whose benefit?!! Now you know why you cough after eating grapes.

I think I'll go out and invest stocks in organic produce. It is the wave of the future to a healthier lifestyle and a healthier planet. Yup, gotta go organic!

You will be surprised how fast your body responds to real nutrients. New research already links obesity with the lack of vital nutrients in the over processed 'white' food we eat. Our body's survival mechanism kicks in, causing constant cravings for 'more' because it is so malnourished.

Rickets, the ancient disease we thought long dead, has resurfaced in our North American children. Caused by a lack of Vitamin D (sunshine) and calcium, it results from a Western lifestyle of living behind glass and a diet of fast, over processed, nutritionally deficient foods instead of wholesome fruit and vegetables. Pollan calls them 'foodish' produce – made of fake stuff that trick our taste buds and nose into believing they are nutritious. Walk by any fast food restaurant and you'll know exactly what I mean!

Michelle Schoffro Cook, in her book, *The Ultimate pH Solution*, proves soda drinks block calcium absorption. It takes 32 glasses of pure water to neutralize one glass of soda, diet or otherwise. The phosphoric acid in soda actually leeches calcium and other minerals from bones, contributing to osteoporosis and rickets. Children now drink more soda and sweetened drinks than milk and water. Adults are no different:

> "1/4 suffer from metabolic syndrome, 2/3 are overweight or obese, and diet related diseases are killing the majority of us".
>
> Michael Pollan, *In Defence of Food*, (07:135)

A 2007 report entitled *Still No Free Lunch*, by Brian Halweil, a researcher for World Watch and published by the *Organic Centre*, states "30% of Americans have a diet deficiency in Vitamin C, E, A and Magnesium".

Pollan says we all eat at least 300 calories more per day than our parents and grandparents did – mostly in snacks – which are 90% fat, sugar and salt – the craving hook instilled in all processed foods. The more you eat, the more you want. If you watched the movie, *Super-size Me*, you know exactly what happened to the poor guy. He was so badly malnourished his body woke him up in the night craving more food!

Pollan believes any of our Western diseases like obesity, diabetes, cardio-vascular disease, hypertension and specific cancers can be reversed in <u>seven weeks</u> if we return to our traditional diet and stay away from white flour, sugar, rice, carbonated drinks, beer, powdered milk and cheap fatty foods like fries, onion rings and hamburgers (07:87). I'm not suggesting you give it all up. You can eat healthy stuff 80% of the time then indulge yourself with junk food once in a while. I do!

Kevin Trudeau, who calls himself the Whistle Blower for corruptive industries involved with cancer, food and pharmaceuticals has been jailed, threatened and sued for telling the truth in his research. He maintains people in other countries are slimmer than North Americans because they consume all the *real* foods they want such as pizza, pasta, ice cream, butter, beer, sausage and chocolate. They *don't* have diet sodas, artificial sweeteners, light beer, low fat junk food, sucrose, corn syrup or grains loaded with chemicals and preservatives. We are the only ones who eat animals filled with bovine growth hormones, antibiotics, ground up dead animals and genetically modified, chemically produced grain (07:37). If this garbage makes us fat, why wouldn't it make us sick?

Juicing every day gave me incredible results, probably because I nourished my body with food it needed. Even today, still juicing, I may occasionally crave a good piece of dark chocolate, but one small square satisfies me. Although some of it was stress-related from having cancer and surgery, I lost over twenty pounds. Then I worried about losing too much weight so I eventually gained some back. I give my husband, Cliff, his daily portion of juice too. Both of us have a lot more energy; people say we even look younger. My skin is soft, moist, glowing (also tanned from the sun) and my hair remains thick and shiny.

4.

Body Imbalances

"Wholistic experts see cancer as an effect of deep imbalances in the body, not a disease. These imbalances are caused by metabolic acids that build up in the blood and release into cells, tissues and organs."

Michelle Schoffro Cook, *The Ultimate pH Solution*

Calcium deposits, little white balls of it, showed up in my tumor on both the preliminary mammogram and ultrasound before my biopsy. I went looking for answers and found magnesium usually controls where calcium is deposited in the body. But when magnesium levels are too low, calcium can be deposited in odd places throughout the body, *including breast tissue*. Mineral deficiency was another clue to what caused the tumour.

We have hard water on our acreage with lots of iron. Fifteen years ago, we had a water distiller installed. I drank pure H2O water, with no minerals, for the same amount of time. My body obviously had serious mineral deficiencies that food alone could not balance. Mineral deficiency also weakens the immune system. Juicing, with its concentrated high mineral and vitamin clout, was exactly what I needed.

The next thing you should know is that <u>all</u> diseases thrive in an acidic environment. As soon as possible, get your hands on some good nutritional books on ph balance. All cancer tumours have an acidic environment around them. Some of it is caused by the toxins they secrete but most are caused by the foods we eat! Here is a whole new area of research that will blow your socks off. It's simple High School chemistry. Think of a ruler with one end acidic (vinegar) and one end alkaline (baking soda). What we want is a balance of neutral territory between the two. What foods are acidic? The biggest culprits are coffee, meat and all the whites: sugar, salt, flour, potatoes, rice, dairy products and sodas. This pretty much sums up our all Canadian diet – especially in our fast food restaurants! On the other hand, **all vegetables are alkaline**. Fruits, nuts, seeds and whole grains are only slightly acidic and just move you closer on the ruler to neutral – the healthy 'Home Free' place to be.

From my research, **no illness can survive an alkaline environment – not even cancer!** They all thrive in an acidic one. I will never be a vegetarian. Being a type 'O' blood type, I love my meat but I really cut back on the amounts. What do you want to feed your cells?

When you work towards feeding your body an alkaline diet, you are on your way to a healthier body, whether you are sick or not. John Hopkins Society, a major research institute and university out of Baltimore, recommends cancer patients build their diet to about 80% vegetables, eating the remaining 20% in this order: fruits, nuts, seeds, whole grains and <u>some</u> meat. They recommend fish (unfarmed) as the first choice, followed by chicken and turkey then pork, beef or lamb - all organic and therefore free of all the hormones and antibiotics. **They also recommend you cut out sugar, white flour and dairy products – completely!** Unpasteurized honey and maple syrup is fine in <u>very small</u> amounts. No artificial sweeteners of any kind, not even Splenda. Cancer cells love sugar. Dairy products produce a mucous cancer cells feed upon. Mucous also clogs our intestines, plugging up the biggest dumping ground for toxins flushing out of our body. Researchers have even linked dairy to sinus and ear infections – especially in our children. My lactose intolerant granddaughter suffered from ear infections all through her childhood. My husband, son and grandson have chronic sinus issues. I believe we can all benefit from this 80% vegetable diet.

Do I hear a whine? Remember our goal is to flush our body so it can heal itself and kick out the sick cells. Our body regenerates new cells every day. What kind are you creating? If you can stick to this diet 80% of the time, you still have some space to indulge your cravings.

I know this is not easy. I had to make these changes too. When death is staring you in the face, you change, or you die. But know this is the biggest adjustment you will have to make in your lifestyle. And no, you really don't have to give up that steak, just eat half of it and save the rest for tomorrow. Try one less piece of chicken or pork and add more vegetables. Make meat a side dish. When your plate is filled with ¾ vegetables and ¼ meat and bread, you <u>will</u> have an alkaline body. Also, be very careful with processed meats and sausages (I could not believe the nitrates and salt levels!! One serving of ham has over 2,000 mg. of salt). Read the ingredients and then consider whether to add all those chemicals to your body which is struggling so valiantly to flush them. If you can't pronounce it, you can't digest it. One man who lived a vibrant healthy life into his nineties had a motto: if it is man-made, don't eat it. Cancer, like any chronic illness, is serious.

Take back your life! Step up to the challenge of these changes. Stand up to your disease and stare it down! You can do this! You have the fighting spirit to win!

Now, while you sit and drink your juices, breathing deeply in the sunshine, let me tell you how I put this whole thing together, mixing the mental, emotional and spiritual parts and making them work for me. Most books offer only a few paragraphs about spiritual healing, muttering something about your belief system and praying. I think it is the missing part of all healing journeys. Best of all, it is *free*. You do not have to go out and join any religion. The answers to our healing, just like our Aboriginal Elders teach, are within each and every one of us. Elders believe what caused an illness will also help heal it. My friend, Sue, called it 'Active Reconstruction' – untangling the illness, gently, slowly and honestly.

5.

Intuition

"Intuitive ability is present in everyone because it is a survival skill, not a spiritual intention. Maintaining a reflective or meditative attitude, however, facilitates your reception of intuitions."

Caroline Myss, *Anatomy of the Spirit* (96: 38).

Though diagnosed with breast cancer, I grew very excited with answers I found. Oh, not all the time, believe me, but <u>many</u> times. Cancer frightens us with its potential to maim or kill in slow, lingering agony. Yet I chose not to live in fear. I spent no time wailing, "Why Me?" I already knew the answer. Why not me? I'm human and I'm a woman. Statistics say one out of two Canadians will get some form of cancer. One in four Canadians will die from it. Breast cancer comes to one of every three women. Why such high numbers? And what can we do as individuals to increase our odds? We have many answers within us; we just need to learn how to find them. Let me introduce you to your magical intuition and the powerful realm it connects with.

A few weeks after my surgery, my friend Teresa dragged me off to get my tea leaves read. The psychic, a retired nurse, looked at me and said, "Girl, you have a book to write! You are very good at it because you write very clearly and concisely in a way that is easy to understand." I had never seen this woman before. She had no way of knowing I had already written four books and edited two more. Yes, just another 'coincidence' on this new path I had begun. At the time, writing this book never crossed my mind!

She recommended a wonderful book of Canadian women writers called *Dropped Threads, What we aren't told,* edited by Carol Shields and Marjorie Anderson. Apparently there are several later editions of more Canadian writers. One of the authors talked about the Collective Unconsciousness, or a manifestation of spirit, which flows through the universe behind daily life and is available to all of us. In a study of women aged 52 to 65, **over 95% had mystical**

experiences. All of them felt a oneness, a harmony, light and joy and an intuitive certainty. 60% had a sense of 'felt' presence and 45% experienced voice and vision from this realm. Obviously, this intuitive gift in women is more common than the world wants us to know. In fact, the historical 'witch hunts' were caused by leaders who feared this unseen, uncontrollable (by men anyway) power women have. Instead of embracing and honouring this gift, like our Aboriginal people do, the European religious and political leaders called it evil and tried to destroy it.

Our Aboriginal women Elders were and still are respected for their spiritual gifts of vision, prophecy and inner wisdom. Traditionally, they not only taught the boys and girls, they sat on Council with their male counterparts as equal members, sharing their gifts and dreams for the benefit of the entire tribe. Women with strong intuitive, visionary gifts could talk the most headstrong warriors out of going to battle if they 'saw' an unfavourable outcome for the tribe's future. Jamie Sams shares the teachings of the Seneca, Aztec, Choctaw, Lakota, Mayan, Yaqui, Paiute, Cheyenne, Kiowa, Iroquois and Apache nations in her spiritually informative books, which include her *Sacred Path Cards*. She writes:

> "To sit on any Council as a representative of the People, a person had to have proven through example that he or she was worthy of the honour. Many years of being truthful, brave, compassionate, sharing, a good listener, a fair judge, a discreet counsellor and honoured Tribal member went into the making of the Council of Chiefs" (90:191).

Elders are still chosen under the same criteria in every Canadian First Nation or Métis community today. The words, Caucus and Senate comes to us from the Iroquois Confederacy and they mean a council of Elders – male *and* female – who sit in a ruling and advisory position in all the tribes and greater assemblies. When the Iroquois first met the Puritans and sat in council with them, they shocked the white men by asking where their women were and how any good decision could be made without their perspective and wisdom.

In her book, *Women Who Run With the Wolves*, Clarissa Pinkola Estés uses multicultural myths, fairy tales, folk tales and stories chosen from over twenty years of research to help women reconnect with their healthy, instinctual, visionary attributes of the Wild Woman archetype. I recommend this book to any woman who wants to find her intuition and understand how history stole it from her. This author offers another ideal of a Wise Woman who "symbolizes dignity, mentoring, wisdom, self-knowledge, tradition-bearing, well-defined boundaries and experience...with a good dose of crabby, long-toothed, straight-talking, flirtatious sass thrown in for good measure" (92:226). Maya Angelou, one of our twenty-first century Wise Women, fits this description perfectly. So do the many Aboriginal grandmothers and Wise Women I have sat beside, learned from and cracked up in laughter at their earthy wit.

At sixty years of age, I am proud to be in the middle of this ancient sisterhood of intuitive wisdom. It is a magical gift I try to use wisely, humbly and with great delight. Like my Celtic and Aboriginal ancestors, women intuitively make contact with universal consciousness by being as open as possible, stripping their thoughts of any kind of personal aggrandizement (big ego), or any desire for personal power, accumulated wealth or prestige. The wife of a past Premier of Alberta quietly involved in a great number of charitable groups, once told me, "We leave the recognition and accolades to the men. We just want to get the work done!"

To be available to such wisdom, one must learn to wait, hold the truth for the highest good, be open to the truth, be searching for the truth and be willing to accept the truth, no matter how hard or personally painful it may be. I have learned the Universe pulls no punches with the truth. It takes courage and often a dry sense of humor to humbly accept it.

My Celtic ancestors were often called the "In-Between People", because of their fascination with Things That Were and yet Were Not, things that fell betwixt and between reality's cracks. They studied ice that was water and yet was not; mist - neither air nor water; dusk and dawn - neither day nor night; noon – neither morning or afternoon; and Midnight - neither one day nor the next.

The Celts, like Aboriginal people, were also fascinated by the magical time in slumber, that short, quiet space betwixt waking and sleeping, when our ego is silent but our mind is open to profound spiritual messages. In this deeper state of consciousness, we are neither awake nor dreaming but somewhere betwixt and between these realms. Researchers at the Monroe Institute in Virginia study this phenomenon they call the Pedagogic state.

Some of my most powerful messages have flitted through my slowly wakening mind during this state. To be available to such wisdom, you must first pay attention to that quiet waking state – every morning. It may offer amazing messages from your intuition, your inner spirit. Think about the times you went to bed with a problem and awoke with the answer. Now, do it deliberately. Before you go to bed, ask your intuition some important question and see if you wake with an answer. Sometimes the answer may come within the next few days through a casual conversation, a book or magazine that opens on the answer, or a television show or radio discussion. Be aware, focus your attention, something greater than you is going on out there!

For men, intuition comes from their feminine side, should they choose to use it. This means being open to such messages and LISTENING to them. Aboriginal people believe every person has a male and female side, which again, they must develop simultaneously for inner balance. Women naturally approach a problem with flexibility. Anyone who raises children recognizes the need to be adaptable, flexible and a multi-tasker. Most men trust logic over their intuition. Still, some believe in their 'gut instincts' just like their female counterparts and have become quite successful as a result. Though I love our men and don't want to sound sexist, I believe women are more connected to feelings, especially their gut feelings, the root of all intuition. But we do need to teach our daughters, sons *and* men more about listening to their own inner truth.

When this happens, the border between myth and life is open and full of compelling interactions. The Merriam-Webster dictionary defines serendipity as the gift of finding valuable or agreeable things not sought for (74:631). I believe our intuition gifts us with valuable information we may not have sought but truly need. It provides wonderful, magical direction for future choices and actions.

Reflection, open-mindedness and generosity offer pleasure in *expecting* guidance. It's about faith versus the dreaded, passive, 'should do' that society dogs all women with. Aboriginal people also believe in this reflective, quiet meditation, a time set aside, on a regular basis, to sit in silence, clearing our minds of all thought, surrendering in sublime delight and prayer and listening for the messages. I truly believe this quiet meditative state is part of the inner balance we need to reduce our stress levels and raise our alkaline levels. When our spirit is calm, our body, mind and heart are also calm.

Albert Einstein also believed in this quiet time of reflection. To access true genius and create the theories that would change the way we see the universe, he said he "would close his eyes, relax and go into the still, dark place where God is." From Brandon Bay's book, *Freedom Is,* she writes, "Grace gives rise to all genius, all creativity, all answers" (06:14). Elizabeth Kubler-Ross, one of my favourite gurus, quotes a book called the *Quiet Mind,* published in England in 1972: "When human beings find a place of stillness and quiet at the highest level of which they are capable then the heavenly influences can pour into them, recreate them and use them for the salvation of humankind" (72:166). Our Aboriginal people called this 'Going into the Silence' and listening with quiet, joyful reverence. It truly soothes our soul.

We hear our inner spirit when we quiet our mind and just listen. I used to hear it only in meditation. But now, the messages come whether I'm awake, asleep or just plain old day dreaming. Suddenly some idea or image will blip across my consciousness faster than I can ever think. But if I hear a 'message' and feel my tongue wiggle, I *know* my ego just stepped in and I'm talking to myself instead of listening. Ah, beware the loud voiced ego; it always gets us in trouble!

From the book, *Dropped Threads,* I learned that when we think we have behaved badly or foolishly, others appreciate what they see as vulnerability and risk-taking. I am taking a risk here and feeling very vulnerable by sharing my intuitive healing journey through breast cancer. I found my own answers, in my own way and I stand by my right to follow them.

6.

Messengers

"Perhaps the day will come when our curiosity…will make us able to understand one another and to know what the Lord meant when He said, 'He that hath ears to hear, let him hear.' And we might well add, 'He that has eyes to see, let him see.'

Eleanor Roosevelt

Let me introduce you, gently, easily and with great logic, to my inner spirit world, this Universal Consciousness, which I call my Aboriginal 'Spirit World' or my Celtic 'Otherworld'. After my diagnosis, I fell back onto my Celtic/Aboriginal heritage for answers. My healing path led me into the amazing realm of guardian angels and totem animals whose assistance became as real as the cancer.

From my Aboriginal teachings come the gentle protocols of smudging, an energetically clearing of yourself and your surroundings before you pray. This is still done in many Aboriginal boardrooms, gatherings and powwows before any prayer or activities. It is a humble honouring of the Great Mystery of the Creator. Nobody can understand it all hence the mystery. Elders from various tribes follow their own practices and protocols. Please ask about them from others nearby before approaching an Elder for advice. There are also universal practices indigenous to all: for healing or advice, you must offer gifts and tobacco to an Elder and then humbly ask your questions, listening, LISTENING for their teachings. It could take some time while they think and connect with their spiritual helpers. Find the patience to wait in silence. I honour and thank all the Elders who have taught me so much about my culture and spiritual connections.

I also learned to 'Sit in the Silence', as the Elders taught me and wait for my own powerful messengers who with gentle humour and breathtaking wisdom, taught me hope, life purpose and healing - on a day to day basis. I wouldn't have missed this journey for anything! I tell my story so you can follow on your own path. **You are no different than me**. We all have the ability to walk this path to healing. In the process we walk through the fear of cancer and death, moving far beyond its clutches.

While researching and writing my fourth book but first fictional novel, *When We Still Laughed*, I discovered how similar the Celtic druid and Aboriginal beliefs were. For instance, both refer to God as "Great Spirit". Both believed we could access this Spirit World through prayer, meditation, dreams, drumming, singing and dancing. For the Celts, this 'Otherworld' was just around the corner of your house. For Aboriginal Americans, 'Spirit World' occupies the same space we do, we just have to believe in it to see it and communicate with the Beings who dwell there.

Contrary to popular belief, the Celts are not just Irish, Scottish and English people. Celts were the fair haired, fair skinned people who once populated *all* of Europe, much of Russia and Asia Minor. Their heartland was near the Danube River, named after their Goddess Danu, in what is now Germany. I spent ten years researching the Celtic way of life before I wrote *When We Still Laughed*. A vast number of Canadians have a Celtic heritage. This fascinating spiritual lifestyle and belief system deserves exploration to help us understand our inner spirit. It's your ticket to ride along with me!

The Celts and Aboriginal people believe Great Spirit sends us messages through His creatures. Both cultures learned a lot about their inner spirit by studying the animals around them, their characteristics and what their similar behaviour implied for humanity. This follows Dr. Newman's belief in putting ourselves (Innate Intelligence) in harmony with the laws of nature. The Celtic Druids believed we are all part of the same energy, whether we are human, animals, rocks, plants or water. Some Aboriginal Elders, like their ancestors, can still communicate with Earth Mother's creatures, plants and stones. In their prayers and ceremonies, Aboriginal people still pray for "All My Relations" honouring their planetary kinship with everything on and of this Earth.

I explain this so you will have some understanding about what happened to me after my diagnosis. You don't have to believe in what follows, I simply ask for an open mind. (Though if you are too open minded, your brains might fall out.)

I'll give you an example of Creator's powerful messengers. Years ago, our young teenage daughter and boyfriend came to me for help to get out of the drugs they had experimented in and got hooked on. I asked my friend, Vicki, an Aboriginal pipe carrier and spiritual teacher, to help us. She is also a drug counsellor. After we registered the two kids into a treatment program, we all went down to a river and prayed, placing an offering of tobacco in the water. As we walked away, Vicki said, "If our prayers are answered, the Creator will send us an animal messenger." Just then we entered a small clearing along the river bank.

Suddenly, right before my eyes, a chickadee appeared on a branch, then another and another! Soon the entire clearing was filled with over fifty of these tiny, shy little birds who *never* hang out in a flock! But there they were, singing their sweet little hearts out on a warm summer day. They even took turns dipping and diving over my daughter's head! Then just as suddenly, they were all gone and the clearing was silent once again.

While the rest of us stood in shock trying to process what had just happened, Vicki's eyes filled with tears. She looked at me and whispered, "You have to believe. You have to believe they will be okay."

And they were. Both have moved on to do good things with their lives – drug free. All of my family now keep pictures of chickadees. From that summer day forward, my husband and I resolved to feed the chickadees in our back yard - year round. For almost twenty years we have kept the pact. If we let the feeder go empty, the chickadees land near our unsuspecting heads and scold us with their little, "Dee dee dee!"

Ted Andrews is a well respected author who combines Celtic and Aboriginal American philosophies in his wonderful book about spirit totems called, *Animal Speak*, the Spiritual and Magical Powers of Creatures Great and Small. If you want to know more about your own spiritual totems, I highly recommend this book. Andrews writes:

> "Belief in the spiritual realms of life and all its varied manifestations is universal. The most common belief in many societies is that spiritual guides often use animals or animal imagery to communicate their purpose and roles to humans" (04:7).

Of course science scoffs at this intangible possibility. If you can't see it, taste it, touch it, feel it, smell it, cut it up and study it under a microscope, it's not real. Yet Andrews argues Spirit beings – whether in the form of saints, angels, ancestral contacts, fairies and elves, demons and even animal totems – fill our ancient myths and scriptures. He says when such beliefs are universal, they deserve some credibility. Quantum physics is slowly proving this realm truly exists! There are many dimensions to reality.

I believe Andrews who states Spirit Beings serve many functions on the planet. They help us to recognize our own innate abilities, they empower and protect us and they can help us *heal, inspire and grow*. Messages from these Spirit Beings link the physical reality we live in and the Spiritual dimension. These incredible messengers are part of the veil between the two worlds or realms. This is exactly how they worked with me throughout the long months of my tests, diagnosis, more tests, surgery and healing journey.

I am human so any human on this planet can go where I go. I don't consider myself unusual. This magical realm of Spirit Beings/Angels is not far away. More importantly, if you <u>don't</u> believe in them, they <u>can't</u> help you. Your free will blocks them from interfering in any way. I was in desperate straits, maybe like you are right now. I literally 'went for broke', seeking every bit of help I could find.

A totem is any natural object, animal, bird, insect or reptile whose energy you feel closely connected to. Cree People, cousins to my Anishnabeg ancestors, called these totem or guardian spirits, *Powakan,* meaning grandfathers or grandmothers, the real ancestral wisdom carriers. In Aboriginal beliefs, *Powakan* have the ability to show themselves in animal *or* human form. A snarling animal in your dream may instantly change to a smiling grandmother. You don't pick them, they choose you. Such animals will come into your dreams, meditations and visions (pay attention to the reoccurring ones). You will feel an unspoken bond, like an arrow through your heart, between them and you. I belong to the Buffalo Clan of my tribe. Every time I see a buffalo, my heart aches. Must be just another coincidence that my brother raises buffalo on our family farm. Animal totems may not be the animal you want, but they are what you *need*. Their habits and strengths will help you understand your own abilities, or a direction you can grow into. A mouse totem teaches as much as an eagle totem.

To find your totem, watch the animals approaching and looking directly at you. Watch for those who fly close to your head, want to touch you or lay on you. Andrews encourages you to think about which creatures fascinate you the most; which immediately draw your attention, fascinate you in a zoo? Which animal do you see most frequently in nature? Have pictures of in your home? Which animal frightens you? Those we fear the most often have a lesson, something we must come to terms with – like illness. (I'll tell you later about the animal that terrified me). Has some animal attacked or bitten you? Sometimes they will test your courage, strength, putting their mark upon you before sharing their power with you. Although you may be drawn to domestic animals, most animal totems are from the wild – from any land on the planet (or galaxy as I will explain later!). Dogs are really a connection to wolves, foxes, coyotes and bears, while cats are a connection to the wild panthers, lions, pumas and tigers.

As you begin to identify and recognize your animal totems, study them, look at their characteristics of strength, courage, attention to detail, ability to share, to fly high with great vision or crawl upon the ground, connected to Mother Earth's heartbeat. In his book, *Animal Speak,* Andrews gives you an overview of every animal, bird, insect and reptile, their characteristics and their possible messages and symbolism in your life. He explains every creature's spiritual kinship to us. Totems reflect not only who we are, but who we can be if we stretch, change and grow into our potential. In the process, you begin to understand your life more effectively. You will develop a more unique view of yourself along with a new look at reality. It can be an awesome revelation! It returns the magic you probably lost in your childhood. It teaches you how to play, once again. You may find yourself filled with new inspiration or discover new creative options in your life. **The more you understand your totems, the more you understand yourself.**

One final note, again from my Aboriginal side, about humility. Never brag about what spirit animals guide you. They are a *gift* from Spirit and they will leave as quickly as they come if you dishonour them by playing the 'I have bigger guides than you' game with anyone. Respect them and the totems will help you. Dishonour them and they'll leave, never to return! My advise, don't tell anyone who or what your totems are. If your totem animal tells you its name, don't pass it on. Note in this book, I offer a shortened version of their full names. You can share their messages. Hang their pictures on your wall, wear their amulets and thank them often for their help.

You can have many totems – some for life, some for a season and some simply for a single lesson – and then they are gone. So sit with ones you are drawn too, study them and invite them into your dreams for a visit. Think of it as playing - a joyful pleasure in trying something new. Open yourself to the possibilities. Also, the more totems coming to you, the greater the opportunities to help others. Still, you must always begin with yourself.

In these dark nights, isn't it a reprieve to think you can play and escape your harsh reality – for a time? At night, before you go to sleep, ask to be introduced to your own guides in your dreams and give thanks for their presence and their guidance. In the morning, pay attention to your waking mind, that pedagogic state. What messages, images or thoughts are drifting through? When you first wake up, don't move! Just quietly reflect upon your dreams and memories from the fleeing night. We have this ability! Our society and sometimes our religious leaders tell us we have no right to walk in this spiritual world but Aboriginal people have done it, safely, for centuries! This is part of God, the Creator's world. It is not dangerous or evil or devil made. In all the years I have worked in this realm, my loving guides have never steered me wrong. I know they have my best interests at heart. The final choice is mine. If I don't like their guidance, I can ignore it or just tell them to leave (and I have). Under Universal Law, they then must leave.

We have this ability, this built-in, Innate, Intelligent Intuition! We have a God-given right to use it for our own betterment. We truly *know*, deep down inside, what is best for us. *Where we go wrong is when we don't listen* to that quiet inner voice or gut feeling from our intuition. Science has pulled us too far from nature and her natural laws of survival, too far from our inner self, which speaks not from logic but from our soul. In this era of going green, honouring

Mother Earth, it is time to honour our inner nurturer. If our spirit dwells just above our belly button, then the message from our 'gut' is truly wiser than our over-thinking brain!

Caroline Myss, PH.D. in her book, *Anatomy of the Spirit*, The Seven Stages of Power and Healing states, "In developing your [intuitive] skill and trying it out on your own life, however, you must trust your gut responses – a fact I cannot emphasize enough" (96:39).

At this point, you are probably wondering, why spirituality? Why pursue these nebulous ideas, dreams, gut feelings and intuition? Why suffer the ridicule of those who ignore theirs and feel so righteous in believing money or religion or giving of one's self in service are all important. Why pin so much hope on something beyond our senses, beyond scientific fact?

I say there is *truth* in the messengers, dreams, gut feelings, even visions I experienced. Their truth played into my reality, over and over again, saving me, teaching me, healing me. It is a gift which improved my life, protected me and my loved ones and steered me in a good direction. Who is the bigger fool if I ignore it?!!

Science is slowly realizing the soul of humanity and nature are very powerful and its truth must fit into the world's awakening consciousness. Nobody can say what happened to me, or anyone in crisis, is unreal. It was my ultimate life lesson. Why would I deny its messages? Why would I not trust the powerful information coming to me in my darkest night? An Elder once prophesied science and magic would one day become one. I hope I am alive to see it. Then I will feel vindicated for sticking my neck out. Or rather, my gut!

For now, come and walk in my world.

7.

My Psychic Gifts

"The next time a coincidence occurs in your life, investigate it and dig a little deeper into what it might mean."

James Van Praagh, *Talking to Heaven*

After my diagnosis, I went immediately to my bird totem in a dream. I have been seeing, dreaming, meditating and talking with him and his mate for years. I leaned into his chest, wrapping myself in his wings. To my shock, he ripped the tumour on my breast wide open with his beak! He tore it into a funnel shape and pulled out a rectangular blue diamond, perfectly cut!

I asked him, "What is this about?"

And he calmly replied, "This is about you learning to love yourself like others love you. You must allow your friends and family to support you through this."

With that, he fashioned the diamond into a ring and placed it on my left pinkie finger.

The two birds showed me a vision, which still leaves me in awe. They told me the Elders' prophecy of a 100 year span of world peace is coming. Women the world over are donating their breasts, through cancer, to this cause. Cancer shocks all the family members into moving away from materialism and petty quarrels and back into the real priorities of loving and supporting one another. Furthermore, cancer gathers the community together once again, supporting their women through the trauma of cancer while raising money for a cure.

The human breast: is it not the ultimate symbol of love and nurturing????

I had already taught my family about love and support. I've also volunteered in community activities all my life. So I asked my guides if I could donate just a *little* piece of my breast. Like

I was in any position to bargain!! Not that it ever stopped me. The stunning answer came a month later.

I think I have always been a little psychic, I just chose to ignore it most of my life. I first 'heard' that inner voice in my mid twenties. We were living in Ottawa at the time, far from my western Canadian family and childhood friends. My husband, Cliff, travelled a lot with his job. I spent a lot of time alone with our young son and colicky baby daughter. Depressed and confused, I went for a walk one day while Cliff stayed with the children. I sat on a snow-covered fountain, alone in an empty schoolyard. I fretted about my life, feeling like I had no direction and questioning why I should continue living so unhappily.

Suddenly, I heard a cheerful masculine voice saying, "No, Esther, you have lots to do yet!" I spun around but the yard was empty. Somehow his laughing voice eased my melancholy. I got up, walked home and eventually signed up for nursing school, something I always wanted to do.

Eight years later, in my early thirties, I heard the voice again – at another crucial point in my life. Because Cliff still travelled a lot with his government position, I chose to work in doctors' offices, foregoing hospital shift work to be home with our children. Eventually, I grew bored, feeling like a glorified secretary, not using my nursing skills to the full extent. I started taking University classes in the evenings but with no real direction of what I wanted to be.

One winter night, on my way to class from our acreage, I stopped to throw a bag of fish bones into a country slough so our Irish setter would not eat them. As I threw the bag my wedding ring flew off too! I heard a faint, 'ping' as it landed somewhere in the dark.

Horrified, I jumped into the ditch and waded through thigh-high snowdrifts, frantically searching near fence posts and wire, looking for small holes in the snow or any possible sign of my ring. I climbed onto the road again but found nothing.

Finally, I stood in front of the left headlight of our truck, crying because I had lost the unique wedding band Cliff gave me when I graduated from nursing. It had specially designed holes to let my skin breathe and prevent an eczema allergy reaction. Of all my possessions my ring meant the most to me: a symbol of our marriage and continuing love for one another. I was afraid to leave, knowing I would never find the exact spot on this flat, dark prairie landscape. I literally cried out, "Help me! Please help me!"

And that same male voice answered, "Walk ten steps ahead and three to your right."

I never questioned, I never doubted, I just walked it. The final three steps to the right put me just past the *right* tire track in the snow. Sniffling and whimpering, I looked down but couldn't see anything.

I turned around. Just a few inches from the toe of my right boot, I saw a perfect circle of gold shining in the headlights! Crowing with delight, I grabbed my ring and stuck it back on my finger. I jumped into my truck and sped off to class.

Then the shock set in. What just happened? I vaguely remember driving the fifteen miles to class. I know I passed many vehicles but felt too dazed to dim my headlights. As I babbled to my classmates about the incident, they glared at me like I had truly lost my mind. For weeks after, I would stare at my ring, thinking it must be a fake, it could not possibly be my ring; what were the odds of ever finding it?!! Let alone being 'told' where it was. Too weird.

One day, as I prepared dinner for my family, I suddenly sensed our teenage son was in trouble. After school he drove away on his dirt-bike. I had no idea where he was. He could have gone in any direction from our acreage. Still, I got in the truck and drove, trusting my intuition. I found him immediately, about four miles from home, pushing his dead bike. He said he had been sending me mental messages to come and get him. I guess they worked.

Slowly I became intrigued by this inner voice, the vague feeling of warning and truth. How could I get in touch with it more often? Was it just coincidence I found an ad in our small town newspaper of a woman offering a class to introduce people to their guardian angels? I signed up. I met a gentle, soft spoken Earth Mother in long skirts and comfortable sweaters. She immediately singled me out of the class exercises and invited me for a private lunch the following day. In the quietness of her hotel room, she introduced me to my guides – all seven of them (one left after I graduated from University and others came in). She taught me to ask a question and stand very still. When I felt a gentle rock forward, it meant 'yes', sideways meant 'no'. With her peaceful confidence and quiet assurance, I 'heard' their names as they gently moved my body in introduction. One almost knocked me on my butt with her enthusiasm. She became my favourite muse, friend and mentor. I write about her messages and wisdom in my next book, *Wind Walker*.

My spiritual quest began in earnest. I found a quiet clearing out behind our home where I would sit and listen, asking yes or no questions and waiting for the rocking answers. With these answers came a quiet peacefulness I had never felt before. Eventually, I would just ask a question and sit with a blank mind until I 'heard' the message, like a thought popping into my head. Sometimes I scrambled to understand the actual answers, amazed at their truth and insights, ideas and words I had never considered before. They definitely weren't my thoughts.

I started taking psychology, historical, cultural and classical literature courses, hoping to find more intellectual, *logical* answers to this phenomenon I feared telling anyone about.

I never heard that one particular voice for several years until I lost my ring again. Playing volleyball with some friends in a neighbour's small field, I glanced down. My wedding ring was gone! I never felt it leave, had no idea when I lost it. Again, the odds were stacked against me. I had been running and jumping all over a meadow surrounded by a dense forest. Everyone searched on their hands and knees but we never found my ring. When darkness came, rather than spoil the evening party, I told my friends I would come back in the morning.

You may wonder why my wedding ring? It was the most valued thing I owned. My guides later told they were 'tests' to grab my attention. It worked.

That night, just before I fell asleep, I prayed for help and the same voice said, "It's by the boards." This time, I whispered a grateful, "Thank you."

The next morning, I returned to the field, walked to a pile of weathered boards at the back of the clearing. There, on the top board sat my ring, a perfect circle of gold. Who was I to question semantics of 'on' or 'by' the boards! Because I went immediately to it, my neighbours were furious, thinking I planted it there just to get attention. As a busy wife of an Assistant Deputy Minister and mother of two teenagers, juggling housework and university classes, yeah, I really needed *that* kind of attention!!

And so the messages continued through the years, coming stronger, clearer and more often. I asked more and more questions. Instead of 'hearing' answers I also began 'seeing' images or dreaming of future events. One morning while combing my hair in the mirror, I 'saw' a huge gash appear in my head with shards of glass protruding from it. Blood gushed from the wound and poured down my face. And the voice said, "You will get this today."

I blinked and blinked, trying to make the bizarre image fade. It was a nice, calm sunny day and I was in perfect health. What was this? The image took a long time to fade, the red slowly disappearing from my face. I shook my head and went about my daily chores, thoughtful but not too concerned. Sometimes I didn't fully understand the messages though this one seemed clear enough.

That evening, my seven year old granddaughter and I dressed to go the Nutcracker Ballet. I love ballet and she loves to dance it so the tickets were a special treat for us. Backing out of the garage we were immediately surrounded in a heavy snowfall – big fat fluffy flakes. My heart sank when I glanced at the car's thermometer: -2° C. Cliff had warned me this is a dangerous temperature, where snow and water turn to ice. The roads would not be good.

When we slid through the first intersection, my granddaughter asked, "Are we going to make it Grandma?" She's intuitive like me - one of my greatest teachers. Was it just a coincidence she had asked me earlier that day what it would be like to live in a wheelchair?

I remembered my early morning vision and knew the $200.00 tickets were not worth harming one hair on her precious head. We turned around at the next intersection. Suddenly I sensed both our lives moved in a new direction, like a fork in the road. We made it home safely, changed into pyjamas and consoled ourselves with hot chocolate and TV's *Toy Castle* ballet.

Bothered by the image in the mirror, I meditated several days later, asking my guides what would have happened that night. Their reply rocked me to my soul. They said, "You would have had both head and internal injuries from hitting the windshield and the steering wheel. But your granddaughter would have lost her legs. She would have been given a choice to stay or leave."

OH MY GOD!

I leapt from my recliner in horror, too upset to sit still, pacing in shock and agonizing grief from what almost happened. I could not have lived with it, could *not* have coped with the destruction of such a vital part of my soul, my precious, beautiful little sweetheart who *still* loves to dance. Even as I type this my eyes fill with tears. I could not have survived the grief and the guilt. I know it and I am so very, *very* grateful for the warning image from Spirit.

When I later told Cliff the story, he simply nodded his head, "I knew she would have some problem with her legs that night."

"Then why didn't you say something?!" I cried in horror.

"Because you had already returned." He replied calmly. What else can I say about men and their intuition?!!

After graduating from University in my forties and working for an Aboriginal counselling organization, I learned a deeper understanding of the visions, dreams and messages coming my way. In my workplace, I was surrounded by Aboriginal managers and co-workers who calmly incorporated spiritual beliefs into their lives on a daily basis. They easily accepted my stories and experiences as just part of my spiritual journey. They took me to sweat lodges and prayer ceremonies where I listened to Elders from many tribes who slowly and gently gave me many teachings about the Spirit World plus the inherent gift of spiritual messages and messengers. With them comes a responsibility to share them for the improvement of our families, community and nation.

I now paid vigilant attention to my premonition dreams of future accidents. When they played out in reality, I safely steered my way through them. I gratefully accepted their truth as a gift to protect me and teach me. I discovered I inherited this visionary gift from both my American Anishnabeg and my Irish Great-Grandmothers who also *knew* things long before they happened. My Irish Great-Grandmother read tea leaves. Is it just a coincidence her maiden name was Syer (seer) while her husband's name and my maiden name is Sewell? Perhaps my gift to 'see well' is *not* so far out there!

In the last twenty years, I have honed my skills somewhat and am willing to share how I did it. The biggest tip I offer you is to find a quiet place, either in the woods or in your home, a peaceful place you can return to often. I have a big old recliner that flattens out like a bed. I cover up with my warm fuzzy Indian blanket and I am 'gone' to my inner world in peaceful meditation. I enter my inner sanctuary, a stopping place, before travelling to the "Otherworld'. Your inner sanctuary can be a cave, a log cabin, Roman grotto, lofty perch on a mountain or inside a seashell. Add whatever comforts you want in your sanctuary: a soft chair, cushions, couch, throne etc. Make it yours; make it comfortable, a safe place deep within you. Then take the risk, journey in any direction from it. Discover a whole new realm waiting like your own movie unfolding. I always return to my sanctuary at the end of my meditation, like a train station, before I awake to this reality.

Close your eyes and meditate quietly. Pray and ask for guidance. Clear your mind of all thoughts. If they intrude, let them drift by like flotsam on a river. Then LISTEN! Wait and be patient in this silence. It may take several attempts but be patient and still your mind. I never bought into all the humming mantra stuff. It's too noisy and distracting. When you listen quietly, you'll know it is a message when something blips across your mind before you even think. Spiritual messages are faster than your thought processes and you will find yourself struggling to catch up and understand them, racing to find the logic. My hairdresser, Sandi, calls them 'Pop-up ideas' she's learned to listen to and follow. As soon as you think about an answer, be careful, you could be listening to your ego. Consider the messages, question them and test them against your logic and common sense. If you disagree, go back to the Silence and wait again. Wake up in the night when it is quiet and invite your guides to speak with you.

Honour what you see, hear, feel or sense. It is fun...really. I saw it as a game - especially when I was bored - long before I believed in what I saw and heard. I used to think it was just my imagination. Time and experiences taught me otherwise. The messages will give you new direction, new inspiration, a revitalized faith in a power much greater than you. These are gentle spirit messengers. Negative messages usually come from your loud ego. If you think the messages are coming from a negative spirit, tell it to leave. Under Universal law, Creator's decree, they *must* leave. You have the right of choice - your personal power. Somewhere along the way, I learned I could ask any new messengers the thrice question, "Are you part of God's Divine Path?" If they can not answer, "Yes" each of the three times I ask, then I tell them to leave. Often I saw them sucked away backwards, never to return. Your free choice ensures your own protection. You are in control of your destiny, your divine path – always.

You might ask why my psychic abilities didn't warn me of the cancer. Wait, it gets worse. That little lump showed up on all my mammograms for seven years! The cancer hospital had a file on me from twenty years ago when my doctor first sent me for tests! The doctors and technicians always assured me it was nothing but fibrous adenoma – a benign mix of fibre and fatty tissue. I am well endowed so who was I to question it. My advice to you or anyone you know: if there is a lump, deal with it! It is serious and definitely *not* normal!! In fact, start taking this book seriously and get on the detox wagon immediately. Tell your friends the same. It could save their life.

Even my psychic friends reassured me it wasn't cancer. It was 'blocked' in some way from us. Yet I continued to question, especially the last year before my diagnosis, when the lump grew bigger with odd little bumps of calcium on it. Psychics are here to help others but we usually don't receive a lot of answers or messages about *our* personal issues. Yet as I write this, I remember a reoccurring dream of wearing a white dress covered in ugly blue and green streaks of filth. I recorded this dream many times in the two years before my diagnosis without understanding the warning. Now I realize it was about the toxic chemical build-up in my body. I also dreamt about a pimple turning into a tumour on left my breast but I blanked it from my mind in denial, until now. I just did not LISTEN.

Seven is a powerful spiritual symbol in Aboriginal teachings. What it represented in my life, I just didn't know yet. Perhaps I would have simply fallen apart seven years ago. Perhaps because the research for cancer's healing options is more readily available today. And, perhaps I am now in a stronger place spiritually to deal with it and write about it. In any case, I finally went to my doctor and demanded a biopsy. Then they found it.

But I digress. On the day of my diagnosis, I knew absolutely nothing about blue diamonds; didn't know they existed. Yet somehow I 'knew' the diamond my totem gave me in my dream was a blue diamond. The very <u>next</u> day (this is how quickly spiritual synchronicity works) I picked up a book by my favourite author who wrote about three blue diamonds carried in a triangle by Mithra, an ancient Egyptian Sun god. The diamonds represented **love, knowledge and generosity.** I decided they were decent priorities to live one's life by. If this was about me loving me, perhaps I could start with these three. Eventually I would learn the famous Hope Diamond, one of the largest diamonds in the world, is also a blue diamond.

A few days later, Terry my pretty daughter in-law, gave me a book called *The Journey* by Brandon Bays, whose words literally leapt off the page and into my heart. Brandon had a tumor the size of a basketball in her stomach. She asked her doctor for a one month reprieve to try and heal herself in a holistic way before surgery. Brandon toured the world with the famous spiritual philosopher Deepak Chopra so she knew what she had to do. In one month, Brandon reduced her tumor to the size of a grapefruit. In three months it was gone completely – with no intervention from her doctor. One of Brandon's messages resonated with my own belief: 'Trust that what we need in life will come to us'. Everything happens for a reason. (Could be why you are reading my book!) Could I trust my guides? Would they give me what I needed? Would I like the truth?

Amazingly, Brandon described how we are all born as flawless 'diamonds'. But throughout life, we dump crap (negative thoughts, beliefs, guilt, shame, criticism) on top of the diamond and think we are the crap. If we are lucky, some workshop, book, illness or incident shocks us into digging for this flawless diamond, which is never marred, scratched or stained by life's dramas. The diamond is who we really are – our true inner spirit – the 'I am'. Brandon wrote, "Open yourself and let the diamond of your soul shine through." It felt like an echo of my guides' message!

The next day, I went for a massage. Anxiety and stress knotted my shoulders so tight I couldn't sleep at night. Waiting outside the therapist's door, I idly scanned the brass plated names of other businesses in the same building. I couldn't believe my eyes when I read, "Blue Diamond Jewellers". Another coincidence? Well, this made three, the magical number of messages the druids believed worthy of further study. In fact, they taught in triads, in threes, because they believed the human brain easily remembered three ideas at a time. Their philosophy still lingers in our jokes with their three parts. Repetitive messages in Aboriginal philosophy also meant, 'Pay Attention!'

I got excited. I didn't know where this was going, but I was onto something. I dug out an Aboriginal book with its ancient beliefs about each stone and its message and gift for humanity. Diamond represents, 'Fearlessness, fortitude and invincibility.' I needed all these qualities but a diamond's other symbolisms caught at my soul. Diamonds can help release negative old memories; increase creativity and inventiveness and help us find our life purpose. Was this a new direction for me?

In our Aboriginal traditions, if you have a problem, you always address it from a physical, mental, emotional and spiritual perspective. This meant I needed to dig deeper into the message from my totem guides. Their teachings always contain hidden meanings, making you think it through and find your own truth. They never interfere with your free will – a gift from Creator. But, if you ask, they will point you in a good direction.

8.

Emotional Blocks

"Let go of whatever doesn't feel good. Let go, forgive; let go and leave it upstream. Think downstream thoughts; go with the flow. Think of the emotion of 'relief'. Trust and believe that what you want, you get."

Abraham & Esther Hicks

Mentally, I drew a hard bead on my actions the year before my diagnosis. I certainly hadn't been very loving towards myself. I am the doer, the goer, the 'Get it done now, or, preferably yesterday!' in my family. Cliff retired and we immediately incorporated a Consulting business and later, a landscaping business. I ran with the bookwork, accounting, banking and endless legal documents. We also had so many family crises we practically lived on the road. We both come from big families and none of our siblings live near us. Our only break was the holiday from hell when our truck broke down on the second day. We spent three weeks waiting for our truck, dealing with a nasty Dealership's Service Department in Grande Prairie, Alberta. We ended up towing our truck to another dealership while our holiday trailer sat abandoned in a campground. We eventually rented a van and came home. I won't burden you with any more details. Suffice it to say, the last year before my diagnosis need never repeat itself! Stress is a major factor in cancer but my issues went deeper.

Emotionally, I forced myself to understand the message from my totem birds about learning how to love myself. I had blocked love from my heart and I believe the symbolic blockage became a tumor. I could give love with great sincerity and depth, but I was a *little too* uncomfortable letting people give it back. Old memories, old incidents left me afraid of being hurt at a level even I wasn't aware of, until now. I saw my purpose as being useful to others, obligated by duty to work and work and work. I didn't realize how much I resented the detours off my own path as a writer. I never wrote one word that last year.

"The refusal to honour and express our own emotions can sometimes reach pathological extremes."

Christiane Northup, M.D. *The Wisdom of Menopause* (01:412)

Dr. Northup writes of women who have a strong social support, whether it is family, friends or groups: "They are associated with increased longevity and decreased rates of tumor recurrence" (01:413). This validated my totem guides' message about me allowing my family and friends to support me. Instead of giving all the time, my journey became one of receiving.

I dug deeper. The cardiologist and bioenergetic psychotherapist, Dr. Sinatra in Suzann Somers' book, *Knockout,* believes emotions are the most powerful aspect of illness but they can also take it away. He says, "Whatever caused the illness was a powerful deep-seated emotion, but it can be taken away by reinvigorating that emotion into healing. Compassion, caring, attention and touch are the healing tools of nature (09:210). From my pioneer ancestry I have what people might politely call a sturdy build. My older brother called me, "Fats" when I was a child although family pictures show no such thing. He was just being obnoxious and I forgave him years ago. But on some level, I chose to carry that self-hatred throughout my life, always fighting with my weight. Seven years ago, when I turned fifty, I was so proud of all the weight I lost with TOPS. But as the years went by, I gained it back, along with a silent disgust for my heavier, aging body. Oh what this burning self-hatred did to my body!

When I read Dr. Sinatra's message, I put down the book and cried. I cried for all the times I hated my older body, no longer pretty or desirable or wanted – feeling invisible with my youth gone. I cried for the belief I was unloved, unworthy of love, never feeling that love, worst of all, never giving it to myself. I felt unnecessary just a work horse. I cried for all the memories where I felt unwanted, used, manipulated and abandoned. I cried the sadness from deep within my soul. I cried for a long time, as long as I had tears until my soul said it was enough.

From my psychology background and career, I *knew* thoughts create energy in our body and if we suppress them, they stay in our body. If we hang onto them long enough, they can literally make us sick. I *teach* this in seminars and Personal Development workshops. I once worked with prison inmates, the 'Lifers' who had murdered people, done their time in prison and were coming out, struggling through healing programs before they were released. These men, as they confronted the violence, horror and traumas of their youth, would break out in hives, rashes, shake uncontrollably or throw up. As they healed, their bodies and faces changed, realigning into a more upright, peaceful demeanour. They proved our bodily connection to emotions. When my parents died, the backs of my upper arms ached and ached. I rubbed them as I wept and grieved. One of my sisters had the same problem. Obviously she and I stored our emotional grief in our arms. Yet I never saw the bigger danger from my weight issues.

Recently, I read how our thoughts can become toxic chemicals to our body. **In fact, our thoughts, especially negative, angry, bitter, vengeful or self-hating ones, can turn our bodies from alkaline to acid! And acid is the perfect environment for disease, or, disease.**

Now I faced what years of self-hatred had done to my body. I don't believe it was a coincidence the tumour lay directly over my heart. It was a physical blockage over my heart's feelings. Still, I believe, like our Aboriginal Elders believe: What caused the tumour will also help heal it. I realized my upper arms still ached from seven years of suppressed anger about my weight gain. I *must* learn how to love myself, as I am. As I type this, I'm in shock; here is the key to the *seven* years of grief and self destruction before my diagnosis. Oh...My...God!

So I made a list of the qualities I like about myself. It was quite a modest list. But hey, I'm Canadian and we don't brag, especially about ourselves. I called it 'Extreme Self Care' and made the quality of my life top priority. Instead of giving, giving, giving, I vowed to say 'No,' to everyone unless it *felt* right to say 'Yes!' I chose to spend my time and energy on things I enjoyed. I chose what I wanted instead of what others wanted from me. I raised a fist to the sky and yelled, "I take back my life!"

> "I don't have to do what you say!"
> Mohammed Ali

This may appear extreme but I was in a desperate place, literally fighting for my life and I wasn't lying down to do so! Somehow, with death staring me in the face, how much I weighed seemed damned irrelevant, obsessively stupid.

I realized I was much more than a body. In fact I am not just *my* body; it is only a quarter of my soul and not the end all and be all of everything in my life. How did I reach this obsessive, narrow viewpoint of my self worth? I wish young girls and all women could realize this, get off the starvation wagon and see how beautiful and how important developing their soul is. I'm taking a crash course.

The truth: the tumour was a physical barrier I had created to block me from feeling love. I yearned for love and sought it in books and movies (a safe, vicarious love); in food (comforting memories of mom's wonderful cooking) and the 'sweetness' of life in chocolate. I truly looked for love in all the wrong places.

Now, I stopped and reviewed my relationship with family and friends. I searched for something I already had! Once the word got out about the cancer, our phone never stopped ringing. I was flooded with hugs, get well cards, prayers and flowers. I found it rather humbling to finally feel the wave of love enveloping Cliff and I. Our family and friends were there for us from the beginning and they never wavered through the long months following. They pulled us through so many hard days and dark nights. For the first time, I actually allowed myself to *feel* this depth of love, to let go of the fear and feel love *all the way to my heart* – beyond the tumour's barrier. I knew I was onto some deep truths when I felt the tumour physically vibrate many times during those first weeks. Emotion truly changes our physical body.

I dreamt of a beautiful, perfect rainbow going out from me to my loved ones and then coming back from them to me – a perfect circle of love – complete at last. My heart hurt from all the energy but it also calmed me in a world still uncertain.

In a beautiful Celtic book by John O'Donohue called *Anam Cara*, or Soul Friend, he believes we were sent here to learn how to love and receive love. Love's greatest gift is the awakening to the hidden love within. It makes you independent, freeing you to "come close to another, not out of need or with the wearying apparatus of projection, but out of genuine intimacy, affinity and belonging". Self love frees us from the hunger of always needing affirmation, respect and self significance from others. He summarizes it most beautifully when he writes, "To be holy is to be home, to be able to rest in the house of belonging that we call soul" (97:27-8). And here is the connection to all healing, right down to our soul.

Cliff and I met with the surgeon who offered me a choice of mastectomy or lumpectomy. I chose the latter and she told me it was a good choice. It was some time later when I remembered my 'bargaining' with my guides to donate only a piece of my breast. I smile as I type this. Who knew?

Then the nurse began all the information about chemo and radiation. I felt my face heating with fury. I wanted to stand up and shout, "No!" Putting all that poison in my body just seemed wrong. I have always tried to eat healthy and exercised by jogging, golfing, swimming, walking and yoga. I felt really disappointed that I had cancer. I thought I did everything right. My surgeon replied, "That's why you managed it for so long and why your recovery will be much quicker than most."

I didn't find this comforting at all. Then I dreamt of a white sign with tall red lettering, anchored by wooden posts into the grass and it said, "Hold on to Hope." Hell, I wanted to latch on with all my fingers and toenails.

9.

Guardians of Us All

"To accomplish this balance, we must live in harmony with All Our Relations, be rooted in this world through our Mother Earth, and allow our spirits to fly through the other worlds and be at one with those realities as well. Without being rooted in this world we cannot fully understand the purpose of our visions, dreams, potentials, or the Dreamtime reality."

Jamie Sams, *Sacred Path Cards*, (90:72)

My Celtic side believes in guardian angels right along with totem animals – same thing, different form. During the early years of 'listening', I realized my messages from angels or spirit guides came in a few sentences. Probably because they knew lengthy ones might send me screaming into the night! Now, their messages increased to incredible details mixed with a little Otherworldly humour.

Originally, I only heard their voices during crises so there were many years of total silence. Susan Smith (Smitten), who wrote the Western Canadian Ghost Story series of books, also wrote a book called *Guardian Angels*. She interviewed me and wrote about my experiences in her chapter called 'Guardian Voice' (04:195).

Why can't the general public believe angels *truly* exist? We decorate our clothes, cars, houses and gardens with angels. We put them on our Christmas trees and give them to our friends as gifts. Yet we are terrified to believe they are real and we can *talk* with them. I helped edit, *Heartbeat Angels*, a book of seventy-five stories from people who had personally encountered angels during crucial moments in their lives. They were just ordinary folks from our small country town. This was such a taboo subject some authors wanted to remain anonymous. Yet similarities in their stories, from people who had never met, added truth to their experiences. Their heart-warming stories make me wonder why people fear angels. People calmly accept the worst violence man can devise. Why can't they accept his best? Why can't he be made in God's image, gifted with God's messengers?

"Every visible thing in this world is put under the charge of an angel."

St. Augustine

Theresa Cheung, from England, wrote a wonderful book called, *An Angel Called My Name*. She believes, "Guardian angels can appear as: a bird, feather, child, a puff of air, a gentle touch, a song on the radio, a coincidence, a dream, a mysterious scent, a flash of insight or in other people who are consciously or unconsciously guided by those from a spiritual dimension" (08:ix). People have seen angels or departed loved ones in the shape of clouds, flowers that last longer or change colour or white feathers that appear in the most unlikely places (08:65). My gifted intuitive sister-in-law, Elaine, got up one morning and pulled tiny white feathers from under her eyelids! She has no feathers of any kind in her home and had no idea where they came from. After reading Theresa's book, she wished she had kept them! Our biggest challenge is to simply become more aware of these possibilities and the messages they hold for us. Cheung reminds us how our noisy fears, with their explanations clattering in our heads, are just our own self-doubts, anxiety and judgement, not messages from our angels (08:60).

Throughout this book, I will prove our Guardian angels *never* say negative stuff. Their messages are always consistent. You will learn the difference between their messages and our loud ego.

Angels do exist. When my daughter was very ill, I dreamt about tall angels clothed in dark blue robes standing outside my house. One day, my son, then in University, asked me why so many angels were around our house. His girlfriend actually *saw* one in the hallway of our house! Both described them as nine to twelve feet tall, dressed in deep blue robes. Then I shared my dreams of the same.

A mother's prayers are the most powerful prayers in the world. When she prays for her child, the angels come running. I asked everyone to pray for my daughter and I prayed often. One night, just as I fell asleep, my guardian angel voice said, 'You have been praying so long and so hard, it is time your prayers were answered.' And they were. Within a week, my daughter found the doctor who would walk her back to health because this doctor had suffered the same illness.

So with my own diagnosis, I pulled out all the stops and asked for as much spiritual help as I could. Before, Archangels seemed way too high in the angel hierarchy for little old me to communicate with. Oh the audacity to ask for an Archangel! Yet I always felt attracted to

Gabriel, perhaps because she was female. Some scriptures will hotly argue this, saying, at best, Gabriel was androgynous, though I doubt this word existed 2000 years ago.

That night, I dreamt of Gabriel before me. Two things made me literally drop my jaw in shock. First, she is not white but a beautiful creamy golden light, wings and all. Secondly, she *is* about fifteen feet high! And she said to me, "You aren't leaving. You have over thirty years of writing left to do." (Now inside, I'm silently squealing, 'Thirty years! I'll be in my nineties!' I always thought I'd shut it down around…oh… eighty-two. Seemed long enough to hang around this old world.) She continued unperturbed, "And don't be afraid of the abundance coming your way. Go and talk to the owner of the Blue Diamond Jewellers. While you are there, you might want to check out the tree sticks in the corner." She laughed and disappeared.

I woke up thinking, 'Tree sticks in a jewellery store? Maybe she meant the little metal trees displaying earrings?' But I hate earrings. My family have so many metal allergies I never bothered piercing my ears. But I love necklaces, bracelets and rings of real stones.

The next day I dutifully entered the Blue Diamond Jewellers. I checked out all the corners but found neither tree sticks nor earring trees. I asked the owner why he called his store the Blue Diamond and he replied, "Because it is the rarest, most precious gemstone in the world." Here was another dimension to what my totem guides told me, though I said nothing to him. He also explained he was a gemologist, buying the stones while his partner, a goldsmith, designed the jewellery.

It dawned on me why Gabriel sent me. I could have the pinkie ring made! My book sales would pay for it. We talked prices and design. I remembered the blue diamond of my dream was rectangular in a simple silver setting. The jeweller considered the cut unusual, saying most diamonds are round or square. He called the rectangular size an 'emerald cut'. He asked if I wanted white diamonds set beside the blue diamond but I knew it required no embellishments. Since the ring would be next to my gold wedding band, we compromised, setting the stone in silver and the ring in gold. He promised to phone other jewellers who might have this special cut of diamond. I left the store literally dancing with excitement. This was me loving me!

Forgetting all about tree sticks, I walked around the corner to a local farmer's market in the community hall. As I chatted to the vendors, I came across an old man selling his hand carved walking sticks. I decided to buy one for Cliff because we had recently bought telescopic walking sticks for our two grandchildren who love to hike in the mountains with us. It hit me when I paid the man. His booth was in the *corner* of the hall. I just bought a Tree stick in the corner! Not only that, it was a *Diamond* willow tree stick! I wanted to laugh out loud.

Gabriel's little bite of humour pushed my faith to a whole new level, where all the prayers, affirmations, testimonials, dreams or whatever, never truly convinced me. I couldn't have thought this one up! The synchronicity of diamond symbolism took my breath away. There was much more to this Spirit World than I imagined or believed possible. Gabriel's humour broadsided me. Here I was with breast cancer and I was laughing; so excited I could hardly stand it. I was 'in for the journey' and wide open for the next message! Bring it on!

That night, I slept like a baby. I dreamt I saw myself smiling and healthy in soft turquoise fleece pants, elastic waist and zippered, hooded jacket. I don't own such an outfit but I *felt* my happiness wearing it! Months later, my guides showed me exactly where to find it.

10.

Clearing Time

'Our organs weep the tears our eyes refuse to shed.'

Unknown author

Yes, it was clearing time, a gift of the diamond: removing old negative emotions, old hurts, old wounds, old, old stuff - washing the past away with forgiveness, understanding and my whole-hearted love. I needed to clear the crap from my blue diamond soul.

I went to work on the emotional quadrant of healing. I saw blood red and black in the energy around me – now releasing as I meditated the next morning. One of my psychic friends, Laura, once told me black energy is about illness in the body. I decided to sit with these colours and their corresponding emotions, trusting what I needed would come to me. Like Brandon Bays suggested, sometimes you simply have to sit in your emotions and <u>feel</u> them. I felt sadness, deep despair, anger and betrayal well up within me and I knew this was my body's deepest angst. I couldn't *feel* love for myself so I *ate* love with food, ignoring my body's pleas to stop then suffering the nausea and bloating consequences of overeating. I found myself apologizing to my sick body, feeling its sorrow and despair of being ignored, unloved and hated, especially as my weight increased. I vowed to treat my body with more respect. Was it a coincidence I pulled a card from a 'Life Cards' deck at my daughter-in-law's which said, 'I will treat my body with Love, Gratitude, Honour and Respect – forever more.' She gave it to me as a gift and I stuck it on my fridge. I made it my motto from then on.

For that particular moment in meditation, however, I simply sat in my emotions and let them release like smoke off my back and the top of my head. I envisioned the worst possible industrial polluted smoke boiling out of me and I focused on this image as long as I could. What I created with self-hate; I will heal with self-love. That night, I had a series of dreams all about clearing and cleaning:

1. A stack of cardboard boxes outside by our fire pit. They were full of junk I no longer needed. I booted them into the burning fire (waste garbage I no longer needed – spiritual cleaning).

2. My womb filled with plastic tags with a single word on each one: forgiveness, shame, guilt, cohesiveness, grief, mystique, please, self and more. I pulled them out, one at a time and threw them away (emotional clearing).

3. At my old office job, I cleared out the files and drawers before I quit my job and went home (past memories - mental).

4. Loads of dark, dirty laundry that needed washing and cleaning (physical).

If you suffer a dis-ease in *your* soul then it too must be healed from a physical, emotional, mental and spiritual perspective. This is the work you must do. There are no shortcuts to healing. You too must sit with your old memories (mentally) and negative thought patterns replaying like broken records in your head; sit with all your old emotions burning in your gut. Stop saying, "I'm fine!" Express your real feelings, honour their truth, release them and let them go. Then you move forward into healing and health. If you are still complaining about what someone did to you last month, last year, five years or even twenty years ago, you neither forgave nor healed from it. Your toxic thoughts create an acidic body. We *know* this; we *talk* about anger burning like acid! But nobody realizes the power of its opposite: healing emotions of love, forgiveness, peace, joy and hope change our body from acid to alkaline, neutralizing the dis-ease! Somewhere in your body, is a ball of guilt, shame, anger, hatred, revenge, or bitterness still waiting? It could be growing. Start digging!

I no longer needed to hang onto a past serving no purpose today. I cleared my acidic thoughts and worked daily to rebuild my body. I nourished my body with alkaline foods, thoughts and emotions. I said a quiet, "Thank You" in gratitude, joy and growing excitement. What next?

I dreamt the next night about staring through the steps of my basement at another pile of my stuff. I shone a flashlight through the steps and saw:

> A kaleidoscope, gift certificates, curing stones; testimonials; curing stones; glory light; a carousel, dream works weaving; stars and curing stones. (I 'heard' "curing stones" three times – time to pay attention to my stones!)

Such magical things I saw! Things I wanted to keep though I did not understand their full significance. So I called in my totem birds who arrived in strange silver cloaks (more about silver symbolism later). They told me they would help cure me; love me and not forsake me. I had work to do and things to write. They told me to dream big!

11.

Stone Language

"…crystals were valued for more than their beauty – they each had a sacred meaning. In ancient cultures their healing properties were as important as their ability to adorn."

Judy Hall, *The Crystal Bible*, (04:10)

Over ten years ago, during a sweat lodge ceremony, a 'spirit messenger' said I would be given the Language of the Stone People. I had no idea what it meant though I held a stone in my hand when I left the lodge. I regret to this day I never kept it. Today, my house is full of stones I gathered or purchased from all over the world. I also have a rock waterfall in my back yard, graced by a powerful 1,800 lb. sandstone rock shaped like a buffalo with an ancient grandmother's face on its belly. I call the rock, Shedoah. Soon, I shall write another book about her and the dreams we share. Since that sweat lodge ceremony, I have played with stones, held them in my left hand (it is closest to your heart) and listened in my dreams for vibrations or messages. Through years of experimenting, I am slowly learning the power of these Earth Mother messengers.

My little granddaughter is my greatest teacher. She hears the rocks 'sing'. One day she told me two of the rocks on my window ledge sang too loud, ignoring the other rocks' pleas to be quiet. When I asked her to pick up the noisy rocks, she chose two crystals, a smoky and a rose quartz. As she held them, I suddenly heard a high pitched 'innngggg!' like a tuning fork's vibration! When she laid them down the sound stopped. I have not heard it since.

Perhaps we don't normally hear stones because their vibration is too high. I wonder if animals hear them. When I watched the miracle stories after the tsunami wake of Indonesia, I was struck by the elephants who trumpeted their distress long before the waves hit. All of them broke their chains, including the isolated baby elephants, and ran away to the mountains, saving their passengers and their angry owners who could not stop them. There were no dead animals or fish in the flood. Did they 'hear' the rocks sing a warning? Was it possible? Apparently the residents of one nearby island noticed the animals fleeing the shores and followed them inland, saving all their lives. Yet nobody questions this! We know so little about the stones in our world. Our Aboriginal Elders call them The Stone People who hold the entire history of this world in their 'Stone Libraries.'

This is what my granddaughter, at the age of eight, wrote in one of my journals. I called out the spelling of the bigger words as she wrote:

"Rocks

Rocks are old grandparents. Rocks come from the ground. They come in all different sizes. Some people can talk to rocks. Rocks have feelings just like people. Rocks are very old. Some rocks feel sad so you should put it in the Sun because Sun helps the rocks feel happy. If you want to do something like crack it or put it outside, then you should ask it first and don't tap it because it's just like hitting. Some rocks are allergic to flowers and some are allergic to raspberries and saskatoons."

My beautiful granddaughter, the love of my life, also taught me how to look after my stones: important things like which side was 'up' and what they liked or didn't like. She very seriously explained how some stones like to be in or near water while others preferred trees or strawberries. She lectured me about not tapping stones, saying it was like tapping the glass of fish tanks. And, I was not to pick up a stone and take it without asking its permission first! I never taught her any of this; I didn't have to. In our Aboriginal traditions, our children are great teachers about Spirit World because they recently sat with Creator and their wisdom is really His.

When she was two, we asked her where God was. She looked up from her dolls and replied, "He's in the sky and in the ground. Sometimes I see him in the clouds. I miss him and want to go see him." With that, she casually returned to her dolls, leaving us reeling in silent awe.

From her I learned to pay more attention to the clouds, to meditate and simply watch them – just like I did as a child. Awareness, focusing our attention, is the first step in spiritual awakening.

The next day, I went to a stone store with my good friend, Joyce who also loves stones. I found a list of healing stones and as I read it, Boji Stones resonated with something deep inside me. It pinged, like an answering vibration to their name. I *knew* I needed them. I asked the owner but he had none.

So the quest began to find Boji Stones. My son and daughter-in-law phoned several cities and eventually found two in a nearby store. They had one pair left: one male, one female and they reserved them for me. Another coincidence? Two days later, when I picked them up, I immediately felt their powerful energetic vibration. I meditated with them, the smooth shaped female stone in my left hand (the feminine side, according to Aboriginal beliefs) and the angular shaped male stone in my right hand (the male side of our body). I felt different inside, like new, unusual energy flowed in and around me.

The only words that eventually popped into my head were, "Should have loved yourself sooner and better." (Ya think??!)

Boji stones have a strongly protective function and are very useful for overcoming blockages. This came from my favourite dictionary on stones called, *The Crystal Bible* by Judy Hall. She writes, "Boji stones clear blocked emotions and heal hurtful memories. They also reveal negative thought patterns and self-defeating behaviours for transformation. Going to the cause of psychosomatic disease (physical illnesses caused by thoughts and emotions), they dissolve blockages in the physical or subtle bodies. Holding a Boji stone will align you to your shadow self (the dark side of us all), bringing up its repressed qualities so you can gently release them and find the gift in them." (04:87). Now wasn't this exactly what I needed?!!

When you are in touch with your deepest self, you feel joy, delight and peace. Every time you are in touch, Spirit leaves you a clue, a little gift to ponder or intrigue. Remember moments in your life when you felt compassion, tenderness, clarity or a deep sense of well-being. Spirit is signalling you are in flow, right where you should be in that moment of time. I believe Boji Stones and the blue diamond were such gifts. I've unwittingly had others from the Stone People.

About fifteen years ago, not long after my prayers for my daughter were answered, I picked up a bible, which opened to Psalms. I seldom read the bible, preferring a more personal connection with Creator on a daily basis. The verse said for people who keep the covenant of prayer, even through the hardest of times, God will give them manna from heaven and a small white stone with a special word on it just for them. A month earlier, I had casually picked up a little stone from a ditch near our home (I hope I asked its permission). White and rounded like a cute little human butt, it attracted me with its 'shining' brightness. I stuck it in my pocket and left it beside my computer. After reading the bible passage I turned the stone over and went weak with shock. On the back in bold dark brown writing was the word, 'Legend'. A month later, I won a Grand Cherokee Laredo Jeep from a $5.00 shopping mall ticket. Talk about manna from heaven! Coincidence...again?

While in Australia a few years ago, I really wanted a black opal – another beautiful turquoise stone. I talked to jewellers everywhere we went learning about the opals but none called to me and the prices were astronomical. One day, in New Zealand, as I awoke, the spirit voice said, "You will get your stone today. Watch for it because it's in an unusual place."

Wondering down the streets of a little coastal town called Omaru, I passed an antique store. Something about the store's door appeared brighter, lighter. I shook my head and walked on by. When I later returned the door still looked unnaturally bright. I wandered in, gazed at beautiful antique dining room sets and wondered, 'What am I doing here? It's not like I can fold this stuff up and put it in my suitcase!'

Something drew me to the back of the store and a glass display case.

Inside, surrounded with other antique jewellery lay a beautifully cut opal stone. The owner said he was selling it for a friend who bought it in Australia years ago. From all the advice I gathered from previous jewellers, I knew this stone was top quality. I paid $50.00 Canadian, set it with a fire opal and still wear it.

The 'shine' of something is Spirit's way of getting our attention. My intuitive friend Teresa shops for groceries, buying only items with a brighter light or shine around them. She taught her husband, Bill, to do the same. I'm not so great at this although sometimes I hear, 'No' when I pick up a food item not good for me. Awareness of the possibilities lets us dream bigger than we ever imagined.

12.

Facing the Bears

"As reflected by our Ancestors, the victory of the Coup Feather is based upon the high ideals of Eagle. Those ideals are followed by action. Just as Eagle marks and kills its prey, so must we mark and attack the weaknesses that keep us from fulfilling our words."

Jamie Sams, *Sacred Path Cards*, (90:170)

I dreamt of a warbonnet; mine, with white feathers streaked with red and black. The feathers now hung well beyond my shoulders, longer than I had ever seen it before. Obviously, I am earning more feathers on this journey through courage and determination. Then I heard the words, 'You are honoured beneath your position.' What did this mean? I didn't have honour for where I currently stand? I didn't receive the recognition I deserve? All my old insecurities boiled to the surface. I sought clarity in my *Sacred Path Cards* from the powerful Seneca teacher and mystic, Jamie Sams. I randomly pulled a card called, 'Great Smoking Mirror'. She explained how the mirror, just beyond the smoke, is caught by a shaft of illuminating light or realization. Those willing to look will see the illusion of their personal myth. We must leave the myth behind and decide what we are – beyond the illusions. We need to stop cowering before our potential and live our trust" (90:291) Also, I must be a good reflection for others, encouraging their boldness by walking my talk. I was about to face a mirror chock full of shattering illusions.

Well, I stopped cowering. I'm *writing* this aren't I? Walk my talk – right. Then my friend, Bev from Moosejaw, Saskatchewan, mailed me an incredible bundle of information on Angels. Of course, I immediately looked up Gabriel. She is also the angel of communication *and* publishing; an intermediary between Heaven and Earth. Now I am getting a *little* freaked.

That night, I dreamt I was at our family farm in northern B.C. with a truckload of relatives. As we drove into the yard, a huge black bear stood by the driveway, unmoving, watching us. My nephew leaped out, yelling to my son, "Shoot him!

Then someone else yelled, "Look! There's more!" To my right, three more adult black bears appeared, their coats sparkling in the sunlight. Suddenly, all three rolled over, bellies up.

I woke up sweating in fear. Yesterday I went for a bone scan to determine how far the cancer had spread in the last seven years. Injected with purple dye and closing my eyes to fight the claustrophobic effect of a huge camera inches from my face and body was not easy. Now, unable to sleep, uptight from muscle spasms shooting through my neck and shoulders, I knew I had to face the fear.

Bears are one of my totem animals but in my dreams, I run from them, hide from them and even try to shoot them. It took me years to realize they were just *there* in my dreams, never threatening or attacking me. Now, I must stop cowering and face them. I realize the Bears mirror this cancer journey, my worst nightmare. From this dream, I knew I had to go out amongst the bears, while my family looked on in silent support. If I asked, I knew my son *would* shoot them too! I doubt it was a coincidence the dream took place in the middle of our family farm, the loving and secure roots of my childhood home.

I learned years ago to back into a dream and finish it the way I want. It may be a genetic gift because both my children can do this too. Scientists call it lucid dreaming: being in the dream, knowing you are, and manipulating it any way you choose. Artists who were extremely lucid dreamers envisioned alternate views of reality and painted/carved or wrote about them. Mystics and philosophers used this state for metaphysical exploration like Einstein did. Others might use it for clues in crime scenes, research problems, etc. (like the television series, *Medium*). Level one and two Lucid Dreaming is for people who have occasional lucid dreams. Levels three and four were for those whose dreams were more frequent with greater clarity. Level five was for the rare psychic lucid dreamers who were aware and in full control of the dream. I have no control over my initial dream. What I see is what I get. But if I wake up, I can often fall asleep, return to the same dream and control it any way I want.

The greatest problem with lucid dreaming is the dreaming mind offers metaphors, symbols or elements which can be difficult to interpret in the waking state. Luckily, my Aboriginal ancestors fully understood dream symbolism, especially the animal forms! The submissive pose of the three bears carried a strong message for me. Wolves do this to respect the hierarchy of the pack, from the Alpha male and female down to the lowest member. Even dogs will roll over, exposing their bellies to show they mean no harm. The bears' black 'shining' coats meant Spirit energy. So I went back into the dream, sat down beside the three of them and said, "Who are you? What do you want?"

They gave me their names. The first one, called Lot, represented my 'lot' in life right now – my struggle in dealing with the trauma of cancer and its possible spreading and uncertain outcome.

The second bear, called Angela mirrored my fear of death now staring me in the face – a possible slow, prolonged death, before I meet with the angels. This too could be my reality. I believe in heaven and know I have seen those pearly gates many times. It is my real home not this crap-filled hell! I have lots of loved ones waiting to greet me there because I visit them in my dreams and know how they live. My understanding of heaven and my dreams of it would fill another book. My biggest fear was the pain and suffering I might face *before* dying.

The third bear, called Helo, was the healing portion. Pain – I can only take it as it comes – one day at a time. I hate pain, am a real wimp. Here too is the aftermath of the surgery, the long healing journey of chemo and radiation plus the awkwardness of explaining the loss of my pretty breast. This will be my new reality. Whatever it looks like in the end, my life will be changed forever.

So many living, breathing, terrifying fears all portrayed in three black bears.

Finally, I walked up to the huge black bear still standing by the roadside and glared into his beady red eyes. I called him Gordon, such a stupid name for my tumour (no offence to your Gordons!). I snarled, "Here I am! Do your worst! I am here and damned if I'll sit on my pity pot, weep in fear or cower before you. Bring it on! You came into my life and I will not run from you any more! Here I stand. And if I fall down or you knock me down and eat me, *I will live on*! My spirit will live on, you Son of a @#*ﻑ‡! You can kill my body but not my soul! I am me! And I earned every f...... step that made me who I am in this moment. Let's get it on Buddy!" I was so furious energy poured through my fists and body. I wanted to pound his face in, totem or not.

None of them moved, they simply stared back at me and said, "You're a hero now."

Well, I didn't feel like one! And they could roll on the grass all day; I was *not* scratching their bellies! I literally stomped out of the dream.

Bear, when I looked it up, stands for courage, seasons of rest and growth; introspection and strength. Fine! Bring it on!

The next day, I sat in our wood shed and prayed amongst the dead 'tree sticks'. I prayed for a cleansing, clearing and balancing of the hospital ward and surgery rooms. And I asked God and all my guardians to be with me through the surgery.

Then I heard, "What about us. We'll pray for you too!" It was the Earth Mother creatures calling to me – all the ones I had encountered in my mediations for my unfinished book, *Wind Walker*. Be damned, I will finish that book too, even if I'm on my deathbed! I promised them so.

For the first time in ages, I felt a wonderful, peaceful sense of wellbeing spread through me.

From then on, I called my tumour Gordon. Cliff suggested we give him a second name, Recnac - cancer spelled backwards. Now who could be afraid of anything called Gordon Recnac! When I told my friends I was punting Gordon out of my life come next Tuesday, they howled with laughter.

13.

Red Heart Vision

"If at first an idea does not appear absurd it will never be successful".

Einstein

I have a confession to make. More happened than I wanted to tell you. It just seemed too far out there and I wondered if I *really* was losing it with all the stress I'm under. This is so hard to write about. I fear the criticism of people I know, including family and friends, as well as readers who will not believe; who will judge and condemn me because of their own beliefs, or lack of. Once it's out there, I can never take it back and I cringe in fear. Well, Gabriel called me on it. In no uncertain words, she told me to write the full story, raw, edgy with no sugar-coating. I can not squirm out of it.

So here is what I left out:

When I went to see the massage therapist, Gloria (next to the Blue Diamond Jewellers), she did some cranio-sacral massage. Since we didn't know how far the cancer had spread, she didn't recommend any deep muscle work. Cranio-sacral is more a gentle energy vibration through the therapist's hands from my head down to my feet. When she worked on my head, my toes tingled with energy. She gradually moved around to my left side and sat down at my shoulder. She told me to put my hand over the tumour. When I did, she placed her hand over mine and her other hand under my back, beneath the tumour. This gutsy lady didn't mind going all out for some truth and insight.

She said, "Now close your eyes and tell me what you see."

What happened next was like a movie unravelling. First I 'saw' a black patent leather purse, a woman's handbag, with a pink flap and a silver circle clasp. The purse suddenly deflated, remaining flat and unmoving.

61

When I described the purse, Gloria asked what was inside. I visualized opening the flap. Inside was a tiny red plastic valentine heart, about an inch thick. It flickered occasionally with a faint light. The heart was attached to a four inch silver stick connected to the bottom of the purse. I sensed yanking or forcing would not detach it from the purse.

Gloria asked, "Do you want to put anything else in the purse?"

I thought about it, "No,"

As I studied the circular base of the ornate silver stick, it slowly lifted away from the purse. I visualized picking up the stick with my right hand and turned it over. I flicked a tiny switch on the back side with my thumb, like a cigarette lighter.

Slowly, gently, the tiny red heart detached from the stick. I sensed it was more about timing than effort. The little plastic heart moved into my left hand and began to grow, softening and stretching into the shape of a larger, human heart. I set the purse and silver stick aside as the heart expanded and began pulsing with a brighter inner light. I peeled one, then two layers of clear plastic protection away from the heart. At first, I wondered if it might make the heart vulnerable, but I trusted it was strong enough to survive as it truly was. It started sprouting arteries and veins.

Gloria asked me if I wanted to keep the heart. I replied, "Oh yes! It is so warm and soft, I am quite proud of it!"

The light grew brighter and brighter, slipping out of the heart and surrounding it in a white golden glow. The heart literally slid up my left arm and into my chest, beneath the tumour. It seemed to fit itself into my chest with ease, adjusting to all my nooks and crannies. Its wonderful red glow spread throughout my chest, down my arms, body, legs and up into my head. It felt so warm, comforting and Mine! While the interior of my body radiated red, the white light drifted outside my body and swirled around and around, a soft golden mist that eventually bathed my whole body in joyful energy.

"It's a spiritual heart!" I exclaimed, "I want it, I love it and it's mine!" I felt the love and the ecstatic joy of it, like something missing and now returned to me.

Suddenly, the image changed and I saw the tumour, oval shaped with a dark purple/pink exterior pocked with little indentations in it (like the pits on a fruit stone). I saw its thick wall because it broke in two, like a cracked nut and inside...black emptiness. I didn't know what to do with these two pieces so I kept them with me. Months later, I would ask the Oncologist (cancer specialist) what colour a tumour is. He said it is injected with a purple dye before surgery so this *was* a good visual replica!

I remember going home from the massage in this joyful, euphoric haze. The image of that empty tumour casing calmed my fears while my new heart filled me with joyful anticipation. I slept like a baby that night, feeling my happiness deep within my heart, my *new real* heart.

When I awoke, early in the morning, still in that pedagogic state, I asked the angel Gabriel to come and take the tumour pieces away. I was desperate and had no idea what to do them. She came immediately; the empty shells disappearing in her hands. *Then* she told me about the writing I had to do, the years ahead of me, the abundance coming my way and the tree sticks in the corner.

My friend Jean and I analysed my vision. She is finishing her Masters thesis in Art Therapy. We discussed the symbolic images, social beliefs and values, playing word associations to draw out more meaning. You probably have puzzling dreams too so come and play with us:

First, Jean believed the deflating purse, a feminine article, meant a release. For me, the black purse symbolized the feminine mystique. A woman's purse is like her personal medicine bundle. It carries everything significant and necessary for what she needs throughout her day. Jean also felt the black meant mystery, the colour of the West direction on the Medicine Wheel, the same direction my totem birds come from. Pink is a feminine colour, always used in breast cancer articles and fundraising. The flap was my breast with the tumour inside, opening up, releasing whatever is inside. The silver circle clasp could mean the spiritual component of a circle with no end – immortality and eternity. Silver symbolizes purity and truth, reflecting an individual's self-esteem and my fear of expressing my feelings. Shamans and healers often talk of the silver thread linking our body to our soul. Silver is the catalyst releasing the potential of the soul, similar to a baby's umbilical cord. Could the switch I flicked symbolize the awakening of my soul's potential? That tiny light barely flickered in the plastic heart yet it grew to a brilliant light, filling and surrounding me. Was the 'timing' right now? Did the silver stick's easy detachment from the purse symbolize the tumour detaching just as easily from the breast protect or hide my potential?

The red valentine heart, like a greeting card heart, had layers of meaning for us. Valentines Day is the eternal day of love, of sweethearts giving, receiving and proclaiming their love. The hard plastic heart, small and stunted, represented my repressed my emotions, hidden out of fear and vulnerability. Now I risked all, pulling the protective coatings away, trusting my new heart was strong and beautiful enough to withstand anything. I literally had a change of heart: from false plasticity to warm, loving, human, soft, alive and mine.

The red heart's detachment from the silver stick, more about timing than brute force could represent the growth of my inner spiritual heart so I could <u>feel</u> the love within and around me, nurtured completely with Spirit light and energy. From John O'Donohue's book, *Anam Cara,* a Soul Friend of either sex, like a kindred spirit, comes a deeper meaning. "We do not need to go out and find love, rather, we need to be still and let love discover us" (97:11). More poignantly for me he continues, "Where before there was hard, bleak, unyielding, dead ground, now there is growth, color, enrichment and life flowing through the lovely wellspring of [inner] love" (97:27). This little treasure of information brings new validation and depth to the symbols in my vision.

The empty purple tumour symbolized a shell broken – like a spiritual death and rebirth into something better (my daring to ask Gabriel for help in removing it). I now believe it symbolizes my journey back to Spirit by discovering my true heart and allowing it to grow to full potential – true, real and free.

I had fun thinking this through. Jean laughed when I told her, "Here I am with breast cancer and I'm excited!"

I asked to *feel* Creator's and everyone's love for me, to open my new spiritual heart and *feel* it coming to me – full rainbow circle (full silver circle), perfect giving and receiving. I awoke the next day singing an old Don Williams song: "You're all I need; I love you so...these are the ties that bind." It made me cry.

The ties, the veins and arteries on my new heart, reconnect me to my body, mind, heart and spirit – to my very soul - and now, to others as well; warming me, loving me, nourishing me and healing me. For what made me sick, will also heal me. What I created in self-hate, I will heal with self-love.

So now you are up to speed on what really happened that day. Believe it if you want to. It's what I saw and what truly happened.

Another one of my psychic friends, Laura, who also does readings over the radio, had this to say: 'Silver is about spiritual healing. The red heart is love coming in for healing. It is healing now and will detach easily when it is time.' She says I will heal easily and well. She sees no death around me whatsoever and that I will be okay. I cling to the hope found in my dreams, visions and friends.

14.

Mountain of Tears

The next day after my encounter with the bears, I was still furious. In my journal I wrote:

> "So here I am, facing my own friggin' King Kong. He's called Gordon Recnac and damned if I will cower. Bring it on, you son of a #@*&%! Maybe one day we will be friends like that girl and Kong, but today I am too f........g angry! I can't see the good in this journey yet. I'm in the middle of it with no vision for the future! * %&@# (insert swear words of choice here)! But as one friend protested, "You can't help what you see!" No, I can't.

Cliff and I decided to take a trip to the mountains and get a load of wood for our little wood stove in the family room. I love the radiant heat of this stove and find comfort in its gentle warmth through these unsettled weeks waiting for surgery.

We stopped at a clear cut mountainside to collect some of the dried pine the loggers had left behind. While Cliff stayed near the truck sharpening his saw blade, I walked to the crest of the hill. I put out my tobacco in four directions to honour a twisted tree stump, its roots exposed and barren in the snow. It had not died easily, refusing to leave its summit view, a stubborn sentinel to the destruction around it. I climbed upon its roots and gazed at the panoramic view with its distant conifers and white topped mountains.

In the warm, quiet sunshine, I let the tears flow. I cried for the raw exposed hillside below me with a road viciously slashed across Mother Earth's breast. Just like mine would soon look – forever changed. I cried for the scarred and broken trees lying at my feet. I cried at the senseless violence around me, like cancer leaves in its wake. I cried for the people the shattered trees reminded me of: broken, mangled, dying and dead from cancer. So many lost.... And I cried for myself and the loss of my life as I had known it; the life I took for granted. Most of all, I cried for the sheer helplessness I felt in the wake of the massive destruction surrounding me: physically, emotionally, mentally and spiritually....

My arms burned with suppressed grief. I sat and released the sorrow pass from my body – where it lay stored far too long. Tears rolled down my cold cheeks, releasing the acid of self-hatred from my body. Oh how they burned! Destructive, unloving, sorrow-filled judgement and criticism, feelings I had swallowed so painfully through the years….

When my tears finally stopped, the land remained peaceful and silent in the sun's warmth. I drew in the cold air and breathed out a sigh. Earth Mother always had lessons for me. Why did the miniature spruce fingerlings look so cheerful, poking so merrily through the snow? Was there a bright hope in all this destruction? Everything seemed so pristine in the clean, shining snow. I watched the sunlight catch sparks off the snow crystals, tiny blue, red, yellow and orange lights, charming me with their rainbow lights.

Here was renewal after the destruction. Here I sat, surrounded by a wilderness stubbornly continuing to flourish despite the devastation. Here was continuation, a timeless peace. Life did go on, despite or perhaps in tandem with destruction. I liked that. Peaceful serenity filled my soul like the snow filled dark crannies and shadows on the hillside. I could have sat there forever trying to grasp it all.

Perhaps the white snow is about Creator's plan for us - his vision for cancer and women's part in the donation to a better world. Bigger still, was it ultimate nurturing, the traumatic righting of people and priorities beyond petty quarrels and materialistic rush? Out here, surrounded by God and Mother Earth's majestic mountains and forest, I felt at peace with my tiny piece of eternity.

Both my parents were abandoned by their parents, leaving me a legacy of never being 'good enough', never worthy, loved, cherished or wanted. Yet my parents were loving, cherishing, kind, generous and thoughtful people. It is like a DNA memory, deeper than I realized. From my parents, I learned to serve others, please them, love them and enjoy them; but not myself. I was far too critical of everything I said and did – never good enough, never worthy enough. I hid my true soul from everyone, including myself. Continuing this through the years became *my* choice. I forgave my parents their legacy years ago.

> "But if we both come from love, are part of this Greater love, why do I need your love and why do you need mine?"
>
> Unknown author

I never realized how deep those beliefs went. I believed my body must be slim, youthful and it was through my twenties, thirties and forties in order to be liked or loved. I believed it's all I had to offer. During those years I had a beautiful figure (37-26-36"). I'm vain enough to admit it but the price was too high. I believed I must *remain* perfect in size to be loved perfectly but I missed entirely the concept of being in love with myself, accepting my body as it aged, sitting with my emotions, nurturing my spirit and thus honouring my soul for who I really was inside. I grew through these years yet never recognized or acknowledged my maturing body.

How do we change such warped ideas about our bodies? Society, of course, bombards us with magazines and models who are slim and therefore worthy. I grew up in the era of Twiggy, the applauded skinny girl who appeared on every magazine in the country. Only later did we learn about her self-destructive anorexia. I have watched generations of young women copy her: no curves, no breasts and no hair. With dawning horror, I wondered if the gay designers of the fashion runways were subconsciously trying to turn our curvaceous young women into the harder, angular attractiveness of young men. Today I am comforted by the more realistic models gradually appearing in our media. I whole heartedly applaud the Dove commercials with their lush feminine bodies. Sensual, beautifully rounded, nourished and cherished, here are our Madonnas, our earthly women who know how to love and cherish themselves *and* others.

I wanted to feel that love inside myself, radiating outward from my soul, from my new spiritual heart, newly formed, newly emerging, and newly experiencing life. As I intend, so I will it to be. It's Creator's legacy of our free will.

I meditated in my comfortable recliner one morning and saw powerful dark red energy pulsing behind my eyes. I visualized white Mother Earth energy coming up through my feet, filling me, releasing the acid of black and old red blood anger from the past. I laid back and opened my hands and visualized long black and red water/acid energy, leaving from my arms, legs, body, fingers and toes. I released it, giving it back to the Creator – up, up and away. Without the shadow side of myself, how can I ever learn to love the light? I felt pressure points in my shoulder blades releasing, blowing out the agony and burning pain of such deep sorrow.... Surrendering the burning energy freed me, clearing my body for the next healing step on this journey.

Behind my closed eyes, I watched the colours slowly change, to grey fumes, then pink, to green, then white. The green was a vomit green of sickness and I saw it, loved it, and watched it fill with white light. I released it and turned it into diamond blue and then violet. And so it flowed, free and unfettered. I breathed in the light and expelled the darkness. I felt it, felt it, *felt it* all the way from my heart. A new green light finally came in, a healthy, vibrant emerald, from my heart chakra energy, gently filling my body with kindness, love and joy – mine! Healing means paying attention, *willing* change to enter. The pain in my body gradually eased, my cramping legs calmed; my hands rested palm up, my fingers relaxed, curling gently, my shoulders sinking into the chair beneath me. I felt exhausted and at peace.

15.

Surgery Shining

"We have often focused our attention anywhere and everywhere but where we should be looking: within ourselves. Our answers come from our experiences, our flashes of insight, our intuitive universal guidance, and our natural connectedness with everything and everyone that defies all barriers, even the perceived barrier of physical death."

Linda Georgian, *Communicating With the Dead*, (95:49)

The next day, the Blue Diamond jeweller called and I rushed down to see the diamond he had purchased. It was perfect. He kept saying, "This is a beautiful stone, easily worth twice what I paid for it. I can't believe I paid so little for it!" I only smiled at him and replied, "I can." Through the years, I have learned if Spirit wants me to have something, I get a bargain I can't refuse.

The jeweller told me his life story. He is the spokesperson for Stars Ambulance, the red emergency helicopters who saved his life. Badly injured in a car accident, he suffered brain damage, a broken neck and back, shattered ribs, collarbone, hips and legs. They eventually took him off life support. He struggled so hard to breathe they put him back on. After months of relearning how to talk and walk, he now moves easily with a slight limp, is happily married and has a daughter. He told me he experienced a Near Death Experience (NDE) but does not talk about it because people think he's crazy. I found this so tragic. We think nothing of watching murders, violence and death on T.V. yet we fear the good stuff like miracles and heaven!

That night I dreamt I drove our truck down a highway where rain had washed out the road, twisting the pavement into a mangled, muddy quagmire. People drove into it before they were aware of its danger, their vehicles slipping and sliding gently into one another, then bouncing off in slow motion, with no real damage to anyone or their vehicles.

I managed to drive our truck down into the ditch without hitting anyone but got stuck in the mud. Walking to the horse trailer hooked to our truck, I brought out my beautiful black Arabian stallion. I quickly rode him bareback through the chaos to dry ground on the other side.

Cliff yelled from the truck, "Where are you going?"

I replied, "I'm going home."

He pointed out home was back the way we had just come.

I told him, "Then I will just ride around it." And I did.

It's been years since I dreamed of this black stallion who comes to my rescue. I love horses, rode them since I was old enough to hang on. On our family farm, we raised part Arabians who raced the wind, their tails flying like flags. The glossy blacks were my favourites. But we never owned a horse like the black stallion in my dreams! A horse in Ted Andrew's *Animal Speak* represents travel, power and freedom (no kidding!). He is associated with both burial rites and birth. Having cancer is like death of one life and the beginning of another. A stallion and his taming represent the taming of dangerous emotions. I would say I tamed quite a few savage beasts lately! Horse also represents a new journey, a ride in new directions to awaken and discover new freedom and power. I can only hope this cancer is a mere short quagmire in the greater road of my life. Best of all, the stallion brought me safely home, to where I truly live. Oh how I love dream symbolism when it makes sense!

Four days before my surgery, I went shopping – and dancing. I bought myself a beautiful low-cut red top (last chance to show off the girls), matched it with a long black skirt that swirled around my ankles and stepped into my dancing pumps. Cliff and I went to a big band banquet and danced the night away. We took dancing lessons for years and love everything from the rumba, jive, country two-step and polka to the beautiful old-time waltzes....

During the last week before surgery, I ate lots of raw pineapple. Bromine in pineapple, provided you are not allergic to it, speeds the healing process after surgery.

Finally, it's surgery day. The tests and post-surgery instructions are done. I'm lying in the operating room; my arms stretched out and taped to a board like Jesus on the cross. I'm fully prepped with an inked "yes!" over the tumour area near the top of my left breast. (I wrote it myself, per staff instructions, adding the exclamation mark for flair). I shiver in the cold air and dull light from nearby windows. From where I lay, I notice soft indentations and aging wrinkles on the back of my left arm. Suddenly I feel a wave of compassion for my naked shoulder, so helpless and alone.

"Say goodnight" calls the cheerful anaesthetist. A tingling ripple arcs through my body as I whisper, "Goodnighhhhhh...."

I awake in the recovery room. My surgeon tells me they got the tumour and took out six lymph nodes because they found cancer traces in them. I growl, "Well that's not very good!" I want to close my eyes and wish her away. I can not deal with this right now.

She smiles tiredly and replies, "That's why we have medication."

I'm not contrite though I know six women went under the knife today for breast cancer. Three of us were hers. She really is a beautiful woman with her blonde curly hair and aquamarine eyes. She is the best surgeon in the hospital according to the staff. I never asked for her but I got her, another coincidence?

I would not truly appreciate her gift until I saw the clean neat incisions she gave me. My tumour was at the twelve o'clock position on my breast. The surgeon's wedge incision removed it without changing my breast shape at all – besides a minor lift. (So what if one nipple is on high beam and one on low!) My left breast used to be bigger than my right, now it's the same size. The second incision, under my arm, where they removed the lymph nodes, follows the natural lines of my armpit. I also had a temporary plastic tube inserted in my breast and attached to a small suction pump to drain the remaining blood and fluid. Thanks to this doctor, I can wear sleeveless, even strapless clothes without a scar in sight. How lucky I am in comparison to some women!

I realized my bargaining paid off with stunning results. I truly donated just a small portion of my breast to the Cause!

I remember the incredible sense of déjà vu I had throughout the day at the hospital, like I had done it all, seen it all before. For weeks before the surgery, I 'saw' the incision on my breast. At first, I thought it might be the biopsy scar but it just made a tiny needle hole. No, what I 'saw' was exactly the same size and position of the incision I received that day. In addition, I had asked for spiritual protection before I went in and I got it. I barely felt the needle pricks, IV lines and tests. I asked to be surrounded by good people and I was. All the staff were kind and gentle. It made the day so much easier and I am so grateful. It makes me believe in what you intend, is what you get.

Breast cancer is simple Day Surgery these days. Thank goodness for Cliff's brother, Malcolm and his saintly wife, Elaine. She is a spiritual healer in her own right and she worked long and hard with me through the previous months. She and Cliff took turns through that endless day on the ward sitting beside me while I threw up, drank water and threw up again. They don't tell you until afterwards but regardless the type of breast surgery: augmentation (enlarging), reduction or cancer, every woman is violently ill.

Eventually the nurse gave me a shot of Demerol in the hip and we were off home. She was so good to me, asking how many barf bags I wanted for the trip. I replied, 'Lots! It's a new car!' She laughed and gave me a fistful. I refused to complain and moan from the pain. I simply dealt with it all.

We joked together as we left the hospital: Malcolm pushing my wheelchair, Elaine carrying my stuff and Cliff bringing the car around. I so badly wanted to sleep but closing my eyes brought fresh waves of nausea. I made it halfway home and threw up once again.

Elaine later told me she received many messages from her own guides as she sat by my hospital bed. They told her surgery was necessary, much healing took place and everything would be alright.

The next day our son, Jay, arrived with a huge bouquet of flowers and lots of hugs from him, his wife and four children. He reiterated I had obviously written this into my life plan. If I'd been warned, I wouldn't have gotten the lessons! A descendant of Aboriginal medicine men through Cliff, Jay calmly accepts his special gifts and goes about developing them in his own quiet way.

I was up and about, feeling good and living cheerfully thanks to our friendly pharmaceutical codeine. My daughter, Lara, had already called to see how I was doing. After that, the phone never stopped ringing.

> Two days later, I woke up singing:
> "This little light of mine
> I'm gonna make it shine!
> This little light of mine,
> I'm gonna let it shine,
> Let it shine! Let it shine! Let it shine!

I had just dreamt of my totem bird picking me up and swirling me to the mountain tops. He said, "You are healing now. God is healing you and we send you loving energy too. Watch the colour around you change slowly." And I saw the ugly pea green of illness behind my eyes swirl and change into white energy of love and light – God's energy of love and light! Oh let it shine! Shine! Shine!

16.

Healing Messages

"Where before there was anonymity, now there is intimacy; where before there was fear, now there is courage; where before in your life there was awkwardness, now there is rhythm of grace and gracefulness; where before you used to be jagged, now you are elegant and in rhythm with your self."

John O'Donahue, *Anam Cara*, (97:5-6)

As I awoke, I 'heard' the word, "Reinstated". What I was before, I have returned to: a higher level of awareness. It was not Creator's judgement but my own which created the deep hurt within and fall from grace. When I forgave, released the pain and the guilt, I embraced the freedom to be myself, healthy and whole once again. If I learn nothing else on this journey, this is my healing epitaph: I *will* love me; I *will* love who I am and all I am. Slowly I shall find my rhythm and stride it out.

Four days after my surgery, still woozy and drugged, I picked up my blue diamond ring at the jeweller's. It looked exactly like the one from my dream. I immediately slipped it onto my left pinkie finger – a perfect fit. When the jeweller asked if I wanted a box for it, I grinned, "No, because I'll never take it off!"

The next day, I watched a blue dolphin shape in a cloud, swimming west to east across the morning sky. Amazingly, it kept its form across the entire skyline. 'Dolphin', according to Ted Andrews, is about the power of breath and sound. It can open new creations and dimensions. It reminds us to use our breath in healing the body, mind and spirit.

When the Home Care nurse came to change my bandages, she reminded me to breathe deeply and cough often so the fluid, which settled in my lungs during the surgery, could be released before it caused pneumonia. Another coincidence? You be the judge. It would be weeks of research before I learned the real healing power of breathing deeply. Oxygen helps kill any remaining cancer cells.

My wonderful, beautiful family and friends spoiled me rotten. They sent me prayers, cards, gifts, flowers, books and food. I still felt slightly nauseous but I ate anyway and basked in the love of those around me. My loving friend, Joyce, came with a full Ukrainian supper and cooked it for Cliff, our daughter and me. She refused any help with clean up afterwards. The next day, another good friend, Candise, brought a salad, appetizers and dessert to match the ham Cliff cooked. I was the princess and did nothing.

That night, the three of us watched the movie, "Celestine Prophecy". I had read the book twelve years ago but never realized how much I lived my life by its insights. It reminded me we have all the help we need to follow our path, to walk our journey to healing and health. This is the hope I held onto and the gift I remind you of.

That night my incisions hurt so badly, I asked for Spirit energy to come through my hands and ease the pain. Instantly I felt the energies change, shift – so powerful I quickly asked for gentleness and ease. I 'heard' my guardian spirit say, "Ten minutes, don't move your hand from the incision for ten minutes." So I held my palm gently over the incision and believed, awed by the power vibrating down through my head and out my palm. At one point, I lost focus and felt the energy darken like my thoughts. I struggled to re-focus, hold Creator's energy, love, light and healing. Again, it poured through me into the incisions. I felt it go deep and sure around the crackling foreign drain in my breast. I listened to the countdown as they guided me down through the minutes...nine...eight...to the final minute of energy flow. I never bothered looking at the clock; I just closed my eyes and listened. At the end, I actually felt the energy close and I heard, "Sleep now" and I did. My guides advised me to do this for ten minutes every night for the next week. And I will, joyfully, gratefully and holistically. Wow! Desperate times bring incredible results! I had never thought myself capable of such a thing!

The next day, the Home Care nurse checked me for a temperature or infection, but the incisions were clean and clear, healing nicely and quickly. We concluded I overdid the exercises to regain my arm's full range of motion back. Consequently, the incision under my arm retaliated with a powerful, painful muscle spasm. Ouch!

I need to emphasize the importance of doing your exercises as your body heals. This is the *only* way you will regain full use of your arm and body. Scar tissue is rigid and unforgiving. Once it forms, it *never* changes. Exercising and moving while the scar forms is the only way to make this tissue stretch to the full range of normal motion. Please do your exercises faithfully. Take the stretch as far as you can, to the edge of pain, hold it, breathe slowly, relax then push it a fraction further. Continue to breathe. Release the movement and start again. It's a trick I learned in Yoga. Do this and you will have full arm and shoulder motion when the healing is done. I had my arm over my head within the first few weeks after surgery.

That night, Gabriel's wings appeared in my dreams before she did. She said, "You want a miracle? Here it is. You wished for healing and it is yours."

I fell on my knees and bowed my head in gratitude.

She replied, "Oh stand up! We heal all kinds of people."

It cracked me up and dumped me right out of my egotistical drama queen attitude. Oh how I love her humour, which says so much without a single negative word - ever!

In my hands she placed glowing, vibrant green, joyful energy. It looked like sparkling emerald tinsel only it moved, alive with energy. I found I could spread it all around me with always more to spare! I dropped some at the feet of my guides and they laughed in delight. I sprinkled it in my houseplants, on my chairs, couch and bed until my home glowed with its happy light. It still makes me smile as I write this. What wonderful stuff!

I felt Gabriel's energy rise up around me, making me laugh out loud at the sustained energy working its magic around me. I took it further and envisioned spreading the green joy all over my son's and daughter's homes too. Then I slept.

One of my psychic friends, Teresa, told me Gabriel's energy is healing energy and I had just spread it all around me! Teresa also helped me do some ionized footbath de-toxes to remove all the radioactive dye, anaesthetic, antibiotics and pain killers from my body. Neither of us could believe the horrible psychedelic colours in the water. The footbaths got subsequently cleaner and clearer within the next three weeks. I know there are debunkers of this wonderful, easy detoxifier. Try a few and you will not believe the brown, horrible sludge it draws from your body – mostly from your lymphatic system. This is truly the stuff of nightmares and illness!

My son and his pretty wife, Terry, brought me a DVD about Esther and Jerry Hicks who have written many books about Abraham, a consortium of wise spirits from the Spirit world Esther channels. They say what we think is what we manifest. If our thoughts conflict, we manifest a conflicted something we <u>don't</u> want. Our talisman, for want of a better word, is to pay attention to how we *feel* as we consider what we desire. Depression, fear and anxiety manifest what we don't want. But if we can even move into anger, what a relief! From there, it is an easy step into Hope, Trust and Joy. Ah! From the feelings of joy, we can manifest what we truly want! This makes so much sense: to fight the fear of cancer, or any illness, we must sit with our emotions, honour and release them, then move beyond them into hope and joy, manifesting returning health and new wisdom.

I thought about the times I had been afraid, cried, got angry, faced my fears through the bears and moved into hope, riding my black horse, trusting what I needed would bring me home. Now the joyful, healing green energy Gabriel gave me made perfect sense. In the energy of joy, I could manifest exactly what I wanted. I immediately set the intention the results from my surgery would be all good news.

To sustain joy, I focused on good times like the unconditional love my little two-year old grandson brings me. He cuddled against me one day, suddenly sat up and declared, "You still have your Owee!" We had not told him anything, thinking he was too little to understand. Yet he's intuitive like his Daddy and Grandma. I nodded and pointed to the incision at the top of my breast. He placed his little hand on my shirt above it and gently rubbed in a soft circular motion. Now who wouldn't heal from that sweet love?

I decided to hang onto hope and joy and let things manifest. Did they ever! I called my Saskatchewan friend, Bev, who just 'happened' to be a block away, driving down the street! She had brought all her books on juicing and gave me lots of tips. She'd even checked out the local stores and found a juicer machine. When Cliff and I arrived, a clerk was working right next to the juicer models. (That alone defies coincidence.) She gave us the last floor model with $50.00 off and handed us a $40.00 rebate we could mail to the manufacturer. The synchronicity and good deals made me chuckle. I told Cliff, "Spirit definitely wanted me to have a juicer!"

The juicing really increased my energy levels. The Health Care Nurses who came to change my dressing said I literally flew through my healing.

17.

"You Want Me to...What?!!!"

"I am sure there is Magic in everything, only we have not sense enough to get hold of it and make it do things for us."

Francis Hodgson Burnett

Our bodies truly have an innate wisdom we can tap into at any time. Our biggest task is to believe in it and *listen* to it. This spiritual component addresses our *intentions*, our free will, our inner spirit's *determination and drive* to heal. The medical profession deals extremely well with the physical but it is not trained to address the spiritual. Neither are the volunteers and therapists. They help with some of the emotional and mental but still, not the whole person. Doctors know the slightest thing can make one patient die while another will fight on despite all odds. This is the inner spirit at work and it truly is powerful and magical. Still, I questioned it all...very loudly.

I learned a little technique called, **'The Muscle Test'**, from Kinesiology – the science of touch. If you remember nothing else from this book, remember this amazing technique. I place a vegetable against my body, just below my breastbone, where my diaphragm is (as close to my spirit as I can get it). Then I would relax and ask my body if this vegetable was good for me. I then let my mind go blank. If my body approved, it gently surged *towards* the vegetable, rocking me slightly forward. If my body didn't need it, was indifferent, it would not move. When I held a bag of brown sugar, I was shocked to feel my body rock backwards so hard I stepped back to catch my balance. Later, I would read how sugar feeds cancer. When I try this in the grocery stores, people just see a middle-aged woman holding something close – obviously too near-sighted to read the label! I played with apples, oranges, pears, cantaloupe, figs, raisins, dates, mangoes or grapes and got a satisfying yes! Grapefruits, celery, peanuts, all sweets and breads, except a good multigrain – nope! Soya milk is out; rice and almond milk is in – for me. This was me loving me and I listened and respected the messages. Soy milk produces estrogen, feeding hormone sensitive cancers like mine. You'll find more information in chapter 44: *What All Women Should Know.*

Of course, I'm human so I 'fudged' it once in a while. One night, I ate some homemade peanut brittle and got so bloated from gas I couldn't sleep. As I sat in the quiet night, I felt calmed and comforted by my warm, beautiful home and the wood stove beside me radiating a gentle heat. I am home. I am alive. And I'm okay. Soon I will sit and let the loving energy flow once again through my hand and into my incisions, my breast and arm....

In our Aboriginal teachings, every person has one 'Hour of Power' every day. It brings our highest energy, our greatest creativity and our clearest connection to our spirit, feelings, thoughts, body and Creator. This hour remains constant throughout our lifetime. You can find yours by looking at the twelfth hour opposite, when your energy is at its lowest point, when you usually get sick or simply run out of gas. My Hour of Power, unfortunately, is 4:30 in the morning. So, 4:30 in the afternoon is when I am most tired, when I will get sick or feel depressed or have brain fog. I can neither learn nor create anything at 4:30 in the afternoon. I'm only good for contemplating my navel or watching paint dry.

When I was in University, I often arose at 4:00 a.m. and studied for exams. I was rested, my mind clear and fresh and best of all, nobody interrupted me. Today, I often write at this hour for similar reasons. Cliff is used to me wandering around the house at night. He just rolls over and goes back to sleep.

So it was no surprise when my guides woke me at exactly 4:30 a.m. one morning. What they said, however, infuriated me. I heard these clinical, very precise words, "To heal, you will need to have sectional (sessional?) radiation and we strongly recommend you take it. If you do, you will heal precisely as we tell you to."

Half asleep, I asked, "Do I need chemo?"

They answered, "No, there are alternatives and we will help you with them. You will be okay. There will be other women soldiers you will meet during your treatments who will help you through it. You will heal and be okay."

I leapt out of bed and stalked into the bathroom. I took a long drink of water, slammed the glass down and fell back into bed, pushing my arm up until it hurt. Damn! I did not want to take that bloody radiation! I didn't care what they said!

Gabriel came back in saying, "You put this into your Plan. You must do it and then write about it for all the women who have no hope and no prayers for us to help them heal."

"What was I *thinking*?!!" I snarled.

I turned back to her, "Will you help me through this?" She nodded.

"Will you help me heal, cleanly, clearly and pain free as possible?" I felt so relieved when she nodded. I am such a wimp about pain.

"Can I have a hug?"

She immediately bent and wrapped me in her arms. That's not easy for a fifteen foot angel but she did it so gracefully.

"You can do this," she said. "Thousands of women undergo it every day. You are not alone in this massive problem."

I climbed out of bed and wrote this down in my journal. I also asked her, "Can I go to Ireland in June? Can you help me make it happen when all this is over?" She smiled and nodded once again.

Now you may be shocked at my audacity. First, I am Irish and we'll bargain with the devil if it gets us what we want. Secondly, I needed an incentive, a bright goal beyond the treatments. It would be some time before I learned I meant June of the *same* year. She didn't! As I write this, I'm still waiting for my trip to manifest.

This reminds me of a funny but true story worth repeating here. A woman wanted proof of the Spirit world. So every time she prayed or meditated she would cry out, "Give me a sign! Show me a sign!"

One day, three signs fell on her car.

One fell from a service station as she gassed up; one flew off a trailer she followed down the highway and the third fell on her car from a parking lot meter. She was not amused.

You might want to be a *little* more specific about what you ask for or choose to manifest.

At this point of my conversation with Gabriel I was still upset with my guides so I told her, "Okay you can go now."

She laughed at me. "I have more to tell you!"

I quickly apologized for my rudeness. Angel protocol is still new stuff to me.

Here is what she told me, word for word as I wrote it down:

> "In the beginning, there was plenty of time for words of freedom, hope and praise to God. But times of healing are upon us and each must make a choice to heal, change their ways or die. You have no different choices and still you make the choice to live, to do what you have to do to survive. That is commendable and precisely what we want you to do.
>
> "Open yourself girl! Open to all the possibilities that come your way! You didn't have to do this but you chose it as one more soldier in the fight for a cure for cancer. We honour you in your goals and determination to walk through this to a greater cause. Get the community to back you. Use your resources in family and friends. It is a good cause, a good fight that needs worthy recognition such as yours.
>
> "Then write! Write your heart out and tell the world about us all, so we may come into the homes of all women who fight this good fight to a better world of peace, harmony and health. We say to you, 'Go with the flow and be healthy forever more.'"

After she left, I thought about her words. It dawned on me the respect given to each of us to choose. Even the angels can *not* enter our homes or help us if we do not believe they exist. Our lack of faith blocks their path. The way I see it, what do we have to lose in *believing* they can help us? They are part of the good stuff! Never have I experienced anything bad, negative or dangerous in their communications with me. Why is it so hard for humanity to believe in them? Surely by now, you can see their consistent humour, kindness and gentle wisdom. The choice is ours.

Now I faced a bigger dilemma. They want me to *write* about them? Dear God! Who will believe me? Not my family and many of my friends! Most have never seen this side of me – for good reason! They will laugh, call me crazy, shun me forever! I get defensive and angry just thinking about it. Sure I like Eleanor Roosevelt's famous saying, "What you think of me is none of my business". But saying it and *believing* it are two separate realities. Just like my life. Yes, I come from good farm stock. You work hard, live a good honest life and help others. Now I'm supposed to share what I see in my dreams, visions and experiences? Damn! But lying is not an option either. I'm supposed to tell it like it is, like Gabriel said. Maybe, just maybe, some people need to read this for their own journey. So I will write my story for them and the consequences be damned.

Of course my guides remind me my credibility lies in my forty year marriage, raising two children and loving five grandchildren. Being a nurse and graduating from University with a major in psychology degree, a minor in English gives me the knowledge to interpret and write the medical research data. My past five published books prove I'm not a slacker and of course, my own journey as a breast cancer survivor makes me walk my truth. So shall it be. (Damn!)

I know I can't move a river; I can only go with the flow. I understand the bigger purpose, I just don't like it. Yet I must do this, just like all the women before me. How can I be a coward in the face of their courage? *I can not and I will not*!

But I can cry and I did – for the courage I need to write my story and for the helpless despair overwhelming me in the endless night....

Still, tears end, faces dry and we all go on, calmer, more determined and yes, more accepting of tomorrow.

I went back to bed and cuddled with Cliff. He just opens his arms and holds me – no questions asked, no explanation necessary. He's just there – always.

I awoke to bright, golden dawn lighting up the sky in soft pinks, yellows, blue and mauve. I felt like I reached a turning point in this war. I can do this – heal my body lovingly, gently and wisely and I can write my story too.

In the morning when I meditated, Gabriel still sat there, loving and supporting me in the early sunlight. She said, "You'll win this fight. You are wisdom incarnate right now. And we need your words." She pulled no punches when she added if I 'crossed over' (died), I would never manifest anything on this physical plain – where it is needed now.

My wonderfully intuitive friend, Joyce, laughed when I whined about having to write this story. I admitted how Gabriel called me on my honesty when I tried to squirm out of writing some of it. Joyce said, "Well, you Shit! Had I known you tried that I would have come and kicked your ass too."

She later called me back and said her angels had a message for me: This work I do, I must not underestimate the gift I have been given. I have been through a lot to reach this point in my life.

"Damn straight!" I growled and we laughed together. She told me she loved me and I was finally able to say it back, right from my heart.

Back at the surgeon's office, all my tests and surgery results were in. The doctor came in smiling. "Your perimeters are clear and we found cancer in only one of the lymph nodes!" The wall around the tumour stopped it from spreading until the biopsy needle punctured it, thus leaking some of the cancer cells out into the nearby lymph node. The surgeon said, "If you have to have cancer, this is the one to have." Mine was called 'Muccinae Colloidal' a rare, slow growing cancer, which does not spread. She told me, "The Cancer Institute will be calling you to set up your treatments of chemo and radiation."

Those blasted words made me argue, "Well I accept the radiation but do I really need the chemo? I just don't believe in that poison."

She shrugs, "Take it up with them," and leaves.

I cry on the way home, so damned frustrated and helpless. Cliff's eyes are full too. My life seems totally out of my control, no matter what my guides tell me.

That evening, my sister-in-law Elaine put it in perspective. "The outcome could have been so much worse. I was so afraid the cancer had spread after all those years." She used to volunteer for the Cancer Society for years and knew its devastation. "This is good news, they got it all and the radiation will guarantee it won't come back."

My sister Beryl reassured me, "Radiation is really part of God's energy too. Instead of fighting it with fear and anger, why not see it as loving, healing energy?"

I decided I could do that. I always preferred the optimistic, positive outlook anyway. And just like that, my peaceful sense of healing returned. Not bad work for a single day on the emotional rollercoaster called *Cancer: to Hell and Back'* – 46 times.

I dreamt of a tropical island retreat, a place to live out the rest of my days. It felt like a place to dream, live, love, laugh and write. My guides showed me an island called St. Francis and they tell me this is where my home will be. And I dream of writing thirty books and loving it! I dream of Cliff beside me, carving his Soapstones (his artistic gift) and enjoying this life with me. And best of all I dream of having full health for the rest of this life. I asked my guides where this island is and I thought I heard '*Aleutian*'.

When I awoke, I frowned. The Alaskan Aleutian Islands are too cold for the tropical island I saw. After months of dreaming about this island I realized it was a place for me to dream, rest and meditate *only!* What my guides really said was, 'Illusion', a meditative place only. Of course, I can travel there any time, regardless of where my body is - for the rest of my life. Just goes to show I still need to LISTEN a little better! Connection to Spirit World is not always as clear as we would like. But practice does improve it.

May I suggest you question every message you get? It's how I learned. I asked for clarification on everything I heard, saw or dreamed. I wanted the 't's crossed and the 'i's dotted before I believed anything. One of my old friends, Nadine, used to say I questioned so much my guides probably moaned, 'Oh no! Here comes Esther again! Quick! Grab the Angel Valium!'

Sometimes you just have to lighten up and be silly. Sacred and silly are part of the balance in Aboriginal spirituality. We believe irreverence is the perfect balance for reverence. We are human, we do silly things, we make mistakes and laughing about it kicks us out of ego drama and back into true spirit form. The angels are masters at irreverence. My guides gifted me with the blue diamond ring info then Gabriel broadsided me back to reality with the tree sticks stuff. If we have a sense of humour, you can bet Creator does too! So get over yourself and laugh out loud at the drama you surround yourself with. Your mind makes life too serious and fearful. I hope you've learned by now your silly mind is not in control anyway. Your soul, the watcher, is.

I played the next day; the first in a long, long time. I've had this dry cotton mouth since before surgery. Pain killers made it worse. My surgeon recommended sucking on candies and chewing gum to stimulate the saliva glands. I hate candy and gum. At this point, I had not read the research on cancer and sugar, but intuitively, I didn't want to try it.

I awoke in the night realizing my dry mouth was caused by stress! A mechanism activated by our old flight or fight drama! I massaged my throat and jaw with gentle fingers, working pressure points along my throat, jaw, cheeks and around the ears. When I hit sore spots, and I found plenty, I massaged in gentle tiny circles to relax and sooth stressed nerve endings. I began to understand this throat issue needed gentle reactivation if I am to write and express my truth. My dry mouth needed both physical and emotional healing.

Then I remembered the Seneca teachings of a little girl who survived starvation by putting a rock in her mouth and sucking on it to make rock soup. Since I had 'heard' the crystal stones singing recently in my dreams, I decided to try one of them for the first time. I found a long crystal wand someone gave me years ago. I washed it with antibacterial soap and stuck it in my mouth. Suddenly, my jaw ached, stabbing pains shot across my cheeks. I imagined eating a tart apple, a juicy orange and bitter lemon to awaken the glands some more. I switched ends of the wand to balance the stone's polarities. I rubbed it up and down my face and throat. And the glands awakened! Slowly, achingly slowly, I felt saliva pooling in my mouth. I played with the crystal on my tongue, rolling it around like a child with an all-day sucker. It had been too long since I played at anything!

My guides also told me to drink lots of water with a squirt of lemon and honey. Months later, I would read lemon is alkaline, honey acidic, thus creating the perfect neutral blend to stimulate the saliva glands. Also, unpasteurized honey has natural minerals and bacteria which aide our digestive system. The anaesthesia and pills had cleaned out the normal bacteria from my intestines like an antiseptic wash. How perfect was this little homily of advice!

Two weeks later, I wrote in my journal my saliva now functioned at about 75% capacity. Talk to anyone who has had surgery and they will tell you the same. Sometimes you just have to play and experiment – a *little (?)* outside the box of conventionality. A dry mouth, however, would plague me for almost two years, while my body continued to flush the toxins.

18.

Get Well Message

"Spirit uses each event in our lives to draw closer to us."
Sarah Ban Breathnach, *Romancing the Ordinary*

Spirit Magic surrounds us. A wild rabbit bounded in front of my car one night so for fun, I looked it up in *Animal Speak*. Rabbit can inadvertently lead one into the faerie realm (like Alice in Wonderland). Like their leaps and hops, they remind us life is not a step-by-step movement, but moments of freezing (for safety) and great speed when the time is right. Spirit messages come the same way: when the timing is right, not every day. It means paying attention to Creator's signs around us - creatures suddenly popping into our lives; songs and poems which reverberate through our soul; clouds with specific images; books, which fall off shelves or just seem too bright to walk past; foods that shine with white light; dreams with symbolic meaning and waking thought messages. Such are the true magic from Spirit's realm. Then I began receiving new kinds of messages!

I dreamt the Universe sent Cliff and me greeting cards in rich, cream coloured envelopes with our names scrolled on them in elegant writing. Inside Cliff's moss green card, the caption read: "Me and you, we will surrender to the cause and fight for a cure." At first Cliff worried I was making the wrong choice in not taking the chemotherapy but my sister-in-law Elaine stopped him cold when she said, "Whatever Esther chooses will be the right choice for her." It calmed Cliff, allowing him to once again believe in me and the choices I made.

My greeting card had a soft turquoise cover in a thick, woven-type of paper. On the outside it said: "Get Well Again. Your happiness depends upon you." Inside, at the top right hand side of the creamy paper was a pale golden satin bow, like angel wings, centered by a grey pearl and tiny ribbons draping down. Beneath it were these gracefully written words:

Peace and Light be with you always.
The gift we give you of love and Joy
Will be with you for
the rest of your days.
We hold you to the honour
of writing your story.
May it be an offering to all who
Follow in your footsteps.
Blessed be the caring ways of
The Lord, our God.

- The Angels of Light and Mercy

p.s. We Love You

I wrote in my journal how I walked around smiling all the next morning. But now, as I type it into my computer for you, I cry and cry and cry. It is so beautiful and so humbling, the simplicity and power of the words. *Imagine!* I received a get well card from God and his messengers! I now believe anyone can!

In *A Dictionary of Angels* by Gustav Davidson claims there are 301,655,722 angels. Some say this is a modest number. According to his research, the **Angels of Light** (67:33) include:

Isaac, Jesus and Gabriel!

The **Angels of Mercy** (67:36) include:

Rahmiel, Rachmiel, Michael, Zadkiel and…Gabriel!

Also, I recently learned pearls turn grey from aging a long, long time. The process not only makes them rare, but priceless. Isn't this amazing?!! I laugh in joy and…reverence.

Phyllis Curott's words, from Sarah Ban Breathnach's book, seem so fitting here:

"Magic is what happens when you have encountered the Divine.
It is the life-altering experience of connecting to the divinity that
dwells within yourself and the world" (02:167).

Curott, author of two books on the spiritual practice of magic, reminds us how the world is full of magic when we fall in love. What we don't realize is that when we discover the universe is full of magic, we fall in love with the world (02:167). The greeting cards gave me magic to fall in love with. I hope you *feel* the power of these elegant words – just as they were given to me. Luckily I wrote them in my daily journal as soon as I woke up. I could still 'see' them on the page, word for word.

That night I dreamt of a round, flat turquoise jar with a light blue lid with the words, Blue *Tibetan Sea Salt.* It looked like bath salts. I heard my guides say, 'Korena has some in her 'Spa' collection of cosmetics.' So I visited this pretty young lady, the daughter of my good friend, Rose. Indeed she did have bath salts but thought they were from the Dead Sea in Europe, not the Himalayas. She is an independent representative of the *Beauty Control Cosmetics,* which sells these Hydrotherapy Mineral Bath salts. She had little paper samples but not the actual container, nor had I ever seen one. Yet when we looked it up in her catalogue, it <u>was</u> a round, flat turquoise glass jar with a light *silver* lid and turquoise words on the lid: *Luxuries of the Sea.* I body tested the sample and my body joyfully surged towards it. That was close enough for me! I fell in love with other salts she had in beautiful red containers but when I body tested them nothing happened. When I climbed into a warm bath of the turquoise salts, an incredible sense of well being flowed through me. These salts became part of my healing program: a loving, hot bath every week. Turquoise *again,* the healing colour of my totem birds.

Just as I drifted into sleep, in the magical pedagogic state before deep sleep, I saw a tiny bear cub, pure white! Now in the Aboriginal beliefs, any white animals appearing in our dreams or visions are very sacred messengers from the Spirit world. So, I looked up bear in *Animal Speak* again. The message was about going within and awakening the power, bringing it out into the open so the 'honey' of life is tasted. To awaken the power of the unconscious, we go inside to our spirit so our choices come from our position of power. Now, as I write this, I understand the full significance of this fledgling white symbol. In the weeks following this dream, I would face life altering choices. And I truly made them from within, from a position of power in my very soul.

Reoccurring bouts of nausea still worried me. I asked my guides for answers after staying up half one night with antacids and gas. We had joined some friends for a wonderful evening at our favourite Greek Restaurant. The food was excellent, just too rich and spicy for my oversensitive stomach. My guides scanned my body, saying my ingestion of food was good but my digestion needed stronger food enzymes because the anaesthetic and pain killers had destroyed them. Luckily I had acidophilus enzymes in my fridge. They restore any missing digestive enzymes, even neutralizing yeast infections brought on by antibiotics. My guides told me to take two tablets before breakfast for three days.

That night, I dreamt of sitting in a circle with a host of singing angels. They are so tall! Many wore the deep, dark indigo blue gowns of a hot summer sky. I invited them to enter the Cancer hospital and aid each and every one who suffered there. I believe all the angels need is our human *intention* of aid and they are free to help. Let it be so....

In retrospect, I see this host as the awakening of my awareness that such beautiful angels exist and are here to help us. *We just have to ask!*

In my dream, they showed me one of Mother Earth's natural hot spring pools. Beside it, wrapped in moss was a small cache of morel mushrooms. In the pool floated steamed/boiled (not fried) pink fleshed trout and salmon for me. I heard the word, 'steelhead'. Fish is one of the best sources of protein for a healing body.

Cliff and I once picked morel mushrooms with his brother, Malcolm, in northern British Columbia. They grow in areas burned out by forest fires the year before. Morels have ugly little brown and white rippled ribs running up the outside of their domed tops. Few Canadians know about them yet Europeans consider them a high priced delicacy. Unfortunately, most of our morels go overseas.

I had no idea where to get these rare mushrooms in the dead of winter but trusted Spirit would show me. Malcolm gave me the distributor he worked with in the city near me. I had the morels within two days! When the distributor asked me how much I wanted, I quickly asked my guides and heard, '50'. I panicked, fifty pounds? I'd *look* like a bloody morel! Then the distributor explained they came in 50 or 100 *gram* bags.

When I picked the morels up, I absently held them against me while I chatted with the distributor. Suddenly I noticed my body surging so hard towards the mushrooms it rocked me onto my toes! Obviously it craved the ugly little things.

Later, I asked my guides if I needed to buy more of the morels and heard, 'No, this is about settling your stomach and digestion right now.' Okaaay, I'll do this natural stuff. It certainly won't harm me in any way.

When I told the distributor about the cancer, he gave me a bag of Shiitake mushrooms for free, saying they had helped his friend who had a brain tumor.

My research into mushrooms revealed their curative powers date back to the Chinese Chow Dynasty, 3,000 years ago. North America is slowly getting on board. For example, the Lentinan extract in Shiitake mushroom stems is a known cure for cancer but not approved in North

America. Lentinan is a phytochemical, which boosts immunity and increases potassium levels. Potassium is "essential for the proper functioning of all the body's cells and nervous tissues" according to Michael Van Straten's book, *The Healthy Food Directory* (99:219). Portobello mushrooms are very high in Selenium which helps with immunity, heart disease, skin problems and cancer (99:218). Reishi mushrooms not only promote longevity, they also treat liver diseases, high blood pressure and asthma (99:95).

Yet the instructions on a bag of dry Shiitake mushrooms I bought at a grocery store say to throw away the *stems*. When I took a course in Asian cooking some twenty-five years ago, we cooked the *entire* dried mushroom after soaking it in water. *Why are we now being told to throw out the good stuff?* I always chopped the stems up and ate them with no ill affects. They are slightly woody but cooking softens them.

Ironically, buying the morels made me late for the Breast Cancer Support group. Somehow I had 'missed' the other two sessions too. My guides told me, 'You don't need to go'. I felt like a kid playing hooky and I loved the freedom to spend the day as I chose.

My guides told me to eat one meal a day with the morels. Using only four morels a day, I mixed them with garlic, lemon juice, honey and cream to make an incredible sauce for pasta. Other days, I made delicious omelettes. I decided to keep the Shiitake and eat them during the radiation treatments. I found Susan Weed's book, *Breast Cancer? Breast Health! The Wise Woman Way.* She outlined a nourishing soup with Shiitake to help the healing process during radiation. I decided I could do this. Oddly enough, I never found that bag of Shiitakes though I do remember bringing them home - another message from Spirit I never understood until I realized I *never* needed them!

Though I never mentioned steelhead, that's what Cliff brought me. A coincidence? Of course! I poured melted butter over a big slab of salmon, sprinkled it with a natural herb mix and scattered lemon slices over top. I baked it at 450 °F until it flaked. It was so delicious I hummed while I ate though fish is *not* my favourite meat.

That night I heard 'your iron is low, eat more dates, prunes and raisins'. So I ate bran and raisins for breakfast. I find this so exciting! My guides are telling me precisely how to heal, just as they promised! I thanked Creator for all his magical, wonderful messengers.

At 2:20 a.m. the next morning, Gabriel came back. She told me to write my book and not worry about condensing it, only to take a copy to my sister, Beryl, in Palm Springs. I wanted a break from the stress before I faced the upcoming chemo and radiation treatments so I booked a flight to California.

Gabriel also said, word for word as I wrote it:

'Don't be too affected by the vagaries of daily life right now. You are cleansing and clearing your pores, skin, heart and soul. Let it be so. Wishing for healing does not help. Let it be so for now. Go with your friends to the music of the bowls and simply feel the joy vibrate through you. It is healing, healthy and joyful. Stay in that state as much as possible. We are with you always and will wrap you in the 'Healing Blanket' day and night if you choose. The rest will come to you as needed.

"The gift you give to the world will be apparent soon, in its own time. Do not fret it is not worthy – it is. Care for yourself right now and walk in joy of all that you are and who you are. We love you so."

She kissed my forehead and left.

She always brings new lessons. I looked up 'vagaries' in a dictionary. I thought I knew what it meant but wanted it clarified. It means an 'unpredictable, capricious, erratic action or occurrence; whimsical or wild'. That certainly describes my life right now. I had asked Gabriel to wrap me in a Healing blanket at night almost from the first time I saw her. I wanted to be able to sleep at night without the stress, fear and worry keeping me awake. I must admit I have slept like a baby every night since – still do. Of course I still wake up later in the night or my early morning, 4:30 a.m. but always feel well rested. I never considered I could have the Healing blanket during the day too, never used it either. I do, however, ask for extra protection whenever I go out in public. I still feel vulnerable somehow.

My friends invited me to an Alchemic Bowl playing evening. We took a yoga mat and blankets, lying down as the player tapped each bowl, metal or crystal, with a wooden mallet, then rubbed around its rim, creating a beautiful, mystical humming vibration. It felt very healing and soothing. Just ask my friends who shook me awake whenever my snoring got too loud.

Just for fun, I later dug out Jamie Sam's *Sacred Path Cards*, which always bring special messages for me. I pulled the 'Shawl' card, about coming home and remembering what I once believed in and opening to my potential. Again, this seemed a puzzling reference to something I was missing. Now I see it as another portent of the coming weeks.

I also pulled the 'Shaman's Death' card, about gracefully letting go of old habits/thoughts/ cells and letting them die with dignity, replacing them, rebirthing them into healthy potential, creative ideas and new ways. I prayed for the death of any old cancer cells still hanging out in my body and for the birth of new, healthy, joyful, creative cells. As I will it, as I intend it, so mote it be.

I also remember a dream about death, about males in my life dying – one was my Dad, who passed away seven years ago. In my dream, he left and was replaced by my beautiful little grandson. Hand in hand we walked up a hillside together. I wonder if this dream symbolized the changes in my life: the death of my old life before cancer and this new one after cancer with its uphill travel. It seems to fit right now, especially with my earlier black stallion dream.

Gabriel came back and told me to stop fudging (my word) my story but to continue writing it as raw as it is. I told her I was still afraid of the criticism but she told me the world is more ready to hear it than even five years ago. She also told me to send a Query letter off to Readers Digest to see of they would be interested in my story. I did so but never received a reply.

I also told her of my fears of radiation, the more I read about it. She replied, "The lessons you needed to learn were minimal and you have done so. We will reduce the radiation, pain and suffering as well." It calmed me – again. The fear of this disease is so hard to face on a daily, hourly, minute by minute basis. I asked her if I needed chemotherapy. Shaking her head, she left.

Later in the day, I realized the morel mushrooms had worked. My nausea and indigestion were gone.

19.

There Be Dragons

"Throughout human history, different cultures have met with dragons but they have never learned to live with them."

Ciruelo, *The Book of the Dragons* (00:138)

So now, following Gabriel's edict, I must tell you about another dimension of my spiritual life. Set yourself down for this one!

Through the years, different psychics have told me they saw dragons around me all the time. I would nod, smile politely and think they were full of it. One day, one of the most powerful psychics I've ever met told me he saw an entire world of people in my womb, a birthing process he had never seen before and didn't know how to interpret. (Now I think it is about the healing books I write because I 'see' my books as 'babies' in my dreams). Suddenly he leaned forward and stared into my eyes, "You are a Dragon Master! Dragons will always be part of your life whether you want it or not. It's your destiny. And it will play out!" He walked away chuckling to himself.

I considered him certifiable.

Then I started dreaming of dragons: black ones, red ones, blue and green. Unlike the bears, the dragons never terrified me. Instead, they fascinated me; their silly antics making me laugh out loud in my sleep. The real crazy part is they call me, Dragon Master. They said in one life I was a Dragon Slayer but I have returned to assist them in this life (told you my life is weird!); my atonement to them. Ciruelo, an Argentinean artist draws dragons for many prominent publishers in the United States and Europe. His beautiful renditions of dragons in his *Book of Dragons* are the closest to those I see in my dreams. I treasure his colourful visionary masterpieces.

My highly intuitive friend, Teresa, informed me I have had many past lives as an Asian person. In one of them, I was also a writer and my books and scrolls still exist (I have no idea what my name was). She said some of my best lifetimes were in the high and peaceful mountains of Japan. This resonates with me on some level and explains some of the vivid mountain dreams I have. In Tom Cruise's movie, *The Last Samurai,* I felt drawn to the misty scenery and peaceful lifestyle depicted in those spacious mountain homes. I still crave the mountains whenever I am upset. What a wonderful 'coincidence' we recently added a beautiful Japanese daughter-in-law and her sons to our family. All descend from Samurai warriors.

Ten years ago, I met an Aboriginal woman who opened up another shocking piece of my life. I kept 'seeing' a bizarre image of a beautiful Chinese princess, dressed in imperial emerald silk and golden headdress, superimposed over the Aboriginal woman's face and body. I heard my guardian voice say, 'You killed for her'. That night I dreamt I was a powerful, well-trained samurai warrior, full of youthful confidence in my abilities. My fame spread to the Emperor who hired me as captain of his daughter's Imperial Guard. I took an oath to protect this beautiful princess I was half in love with at first. Spoiled and pampered, she demanded I commit terrible atrocities, torturing or murdering anyone who angered her. Finally, I could not stand the breach to my personal honour. Having sworn fealty to her father to protect her always, I had no recourse but to kill myself upon my sword. In my dream, I watched myself die, dressed in full ceremonial uniform.

I inwardly cringed when the Aboriginal woman later told me she loved everything about the Chinese; emerald green her favourite colour. If this was a past life for both of us then perhaps the woman paid karmic atonement in this life. Her experiences of abusive relationships, alcoholism and racial prejudice have etched deep lines in her thin face. Yet she rose above it and became a social worker, quietly helping others. When she lost one of her clients to suicide, I took her to a peaceful lake and let her heal, surrounded by the silence and eternal beauty of Mother Earth. I have not seen her since.

When I was thirty-two I suffered a debilitating, agonizing illness. I lived and breathed pain throughout my body for four years. It felt like someone beating me with a stick. I often looked for bruises but never found any. Medical tests revealed nothing. The doctors finally concluded it was a virus which would eventually go away. All through those years, one word kept popping into my head, "Atonement." I finally went to an Aboriginal shaman who healed me.

Who knows what it all means. I give you this background to help you follow my story.

A few years ago, I dreamt of a beautiful egg placed in my hands. Bigger than an ostrich egg, the shell swirled in living colours of blue and green against a white background (turquoise again).

In the dream, I nurtured the egg until it hatched a tiny, sweet ruby red dragon. I called her Elia (not her full name). We travelled together, me carrying her through several of my dreams as she quickly grew bigger.

One time, I asked her if she could fly. She replied, "Yes." So I threw her into the air.

She fell hard, 'Splat!' on the ground! Like a sack of flour exploding in every direction as she lost some skin and scales.

Appalled, I ran to her, gathering her gently in my arms as I cried, "Are you okay?"

Her reply was reedy and weak, "*Yeah…*"

Yes, she could fly but not just *yet*! Well, what did I know about dragon babies? Still, we stumbled along together until she grew so huge she carried me on her back, like in the best of dragon movies.

Elia taught me dragons fly by elevating themselves. They use their wings only to move energy around. Sometimes they play with balls of energy, swatting them to each other like a gigantic basketball game. These dragons have a wonderful, wacky sense of humor, always cracking me up.

I write about Elia and the dragons in my upcoming book, *Wind Walker*. She introduced me to a whole world of them, another dimension in my dreams which still fascinates me. They are so huge! I stand about the height of their eye, yet I am not afraid, I'm just too excited!

Anyway, I dreamt of Elia around this time of my healing. She is now so massive she literally explodes all arms, legs and wings, into my dreams. Lifting me to her back, she shot through powerful red and orange energy, straight up a massive cliff wall. The steep climb had her grunting in focused exertion, powerful flyer though she is. At the top stood her mate, a formidable black and rust dragon called Xi the Dragon General.

He, like Elia, can take human form, which he did before he hugged me. He too has become a good friend. Several years ago, while shopping for a comfortable yet dressy walking shoe, I found a perfect pair in black and rust leather. Worth over $100.00, they were on sale for $30.00, the last pair in that style. Only a few days later, I met Xi for the first time in my dreams. He smiled and pointed to my new shoes, "You wear my colours!" And I still do. My shoes still look like new, outlasting any pair I ever owned. Through the years, Xi, Elia and I have shared wonderful conversations as we sat upon immense cliffs and mystical mountains where dragons love to perch.

Xi asks me to write about them too – these dragons who waft pure, loving energy around the world out of sheer love of mankind. Theirs is red *heart energy*, returning now. And I wonder about my own red heart growing bigger. Dragons call themselves 'the Honour Guard' of which Xi is their leader. In my dreams, I have seen platoons of them amassing like fighter jets, row upon row on the ground. They protect humans against injustice, lies, destruction, violence, pain and suffering. They are powerful to behold; determined yet just; strong yet gentle; kind yet fierce. They are guardians of the spiritual spaces and energy fields surrounding planet Earth. They levitate, using their wings to direct energy flow, easing the load of the Lightworkers on Earth. They watch the war in the Middle East with great attention, saying good will prevail.

But I pout. I do *not* want to write about them in this book! At least in *Wind Walker*, they seem more fantasy than fact. I put myself far enough out on a spiritual limb with my blue diamond story. Who will believe this?!! Dragons are my best kept secret. Nobody knows about them except a handful of my closest friends and one of my sisters, who has a cheerful orange dragon. She keeps him so busy she often 'sees' him lying on the ground panting.

Then I met a grandfatherly massage therapist who happily admitted, out of the 'blue', he has dragons guarding him every time he drives his vehicles. Apparently, each vehicle has a different dragon guardian. When I asked him what their names were, he confessed he had never asked them. He just wondered why the heck they even *liked* humans!

When I taught several classes of grade fives about their totem animal or angel guides, I asked how many of them dreamt of dragons. At least five or six in every class put their hands up, grinning ear to ear. In every class, at least eighteen said they dreamt of flying. I cried, "Oh...I hope you never lose the magic!"

So, if we *are* crazy, at least we have company! Besides, my life is *never* boring! Instead, its guides to meet, places to fly, dragons to play with and dreams to dream....One of my friends exclaimed, "I bet you can hardly wait to go to sleep at night!"

She's right.

Xi tells me he and Elia will be there throughout the radiation treatments. I ask for his protection for my heart, lungs and bones since I read how the rays damage them. I am especially afraid because the rays on my incision will be right over my heart. He gives his word then tells me the hard, leathery skin from the radiation will be like a piece of their dragon skin over my heart. I climb into his lap and cry. This is so hard, facing the fear, the burn, the pain, the disfigurement and the long healing time. I feel so overwhelmed by it all.

I watched Oprah and her series of Ekart Tolle's *A New Planet* and I understood more fully the ego and its control over us all. I see the changes on this planet, the gifting and giving; the forgiving and service to others and I smile in delight. We are getting there, just as the dragons said we would.

I promised to write about them, knowing Gabriel will hold me to my word. And I have.

Later I considered the breast cancer survivors who created the Dragon Boat paddling teams. Perhaps they can have a new name, "the Dragon Skins".

20.

The Sun's Reprieve

"You..., who are on the road
...must have a code...that you can live by."
Teach Your Children Well, a song by Crosby, Stills & Nash

I flew to Palm Springs for a break and to visit my sister, Beryl. My sister-in-law Elaine told me that I would have very vivid dreams while I was there and that I would heal some more.

The second night there, I dreamt I was a male buffalo; four legged, woolly headed and amused with the odd sensation of walking on four legs. I am Ojibwa or Chippewa and I belong to the Buffalo Clan. Another bull kept challenging me, pushing me around, chasing me and generally irritating the hell out of me. The only way I could avoid him was to change back to human form and climb into the back of a truck box.

Then I awoke, disgusted with my cowardly actions. I dove into the dream again, changed back to a buffalo and butted him in the rear. I heard him bellow about his 'Johnson', crying, "Oh, don't hurt me!"

What?

Johnson is a male password for penis, for masculinity. He challenged me, forcing me – again – to stand up for myself. Yet when I did, he wimped out. Instead of hurting anyone, maybe I should use my male energy right now. In Aboriginal teachings, we have both a female and a male side and we must work to develop the two – simultaneously - creating an inner balance of masculine and feminine energy. I need to stop my oh-so-feminine pouting, crying, whining or wimping and climb into my masculine side, stand up for myself, face the bloody treatments and write the damn story!

Only in hindsight do I see the greater significance of this dream. I would meet this irritating buffalo bull with his Johnson issues, in real life – and soon.

My spirit name is White Buffalo Woman, given to me first in a dream and then in an Ojibwa naming ceremony. I wear a white buffalo necklace I seldom remove. The year before my diagnosis, I lost the pendant for over six months and was devastated. Imagine my surprise when just before my surgery, it showed up on the lip of my new washing machine door! I have no idea where it came from. I wore it to the hospital, pinned to my clothes since I couldn't wear jewellery in surgery. I spilled water on the shirt so when I came home, still half drugged, I threw it, buffalo and all, into the dryer. Imagine my surprise when I opened the *dryer* and there, again, was my buffalo on the lip of the door. I fashioned a new chain for it and still wear it today – my talisman, my symbol of strength, wisdom, determination and gratitude.

Then I got another message from my guides, "Olive Oil is the best healing oil in the world. Drink lots of it."

I asked how much per day, surprised at the word 'drink' not 'take'.

They replied, "1/4 cup per day, especially during treatments and for one week thereafter."

I asked if I could add it to my morning juicing and they agreed. I thanked them gratefully.

Magically, in Palm Springs, I found my turquoise terry cloth leisure suit! One night, I dreamt it was in a store with jeans hung high on one wall to my right. The suits were several rows to my left, near the middle of the store. The very next morning, I walked into a store, noted the jeans high on the wall and went immediately to the suits exactly where they were in my dream - same colour and texture with 60% off. In addition, I bought the top in XL but a smaller size pants fit me perfectly even with my long legs and 5'9" height. I still wear this suit as I sit and type my story. It feels soft, warm and joyful to wear.

At another store, to my surprise, I found myself pulling out business suits. I haven't worked in an office for years. Yet here I was, checking out an elegant grey, tiny-checked suit jacket with pretty black and white trim. To my amazement, I immediately dug into the black suit pants. I own six pairs of dress pants: I don't need anymore! Then my fingers latched onto a pair of size 12 pants – something I have not worn in years. Then I 'heard', 'You will need this.' In disgust, I tried to put the pants back but I swear they *stuck* to my hand. I felt like a comedy act: me trying to hang the pants up and my hand refusing to let them go! Finally in a huff, I threw them over my arm and stomped off to the dressing room, determined to prove the stupidity of this exercise. When I put them on, the pants and jacket fit like they were made for me. Total price:

$29.00. Another bargain Spirit knew I couldn't refuse. Back home, I wore this classy outfit to a banquet, graduation ceremony and award celebrations - a wonderful investment indeed.

In Palm Springs, I healed some more. I sat in the sun and breathed deeply. At this point, I had not found the research about sunlight or oxygen therapies. Yet somehow I knew I needed this, letting go and letting God help me, searching for a bigger purpose. I spent so much time in my brain, analyzing options, scenarios, outcomes, work, duty and responsibility, I forgot to play, to believe what I needed would come at the right time. The shopping spree proved this! This whole trip became a lesson in trust and faith. So Beryl and I shopped, walked, swam, read, talked and laughed together, like the close sisters we are.

On my last day in Palm Springs, I lay in the sun idly watching a tiny rose finch sing his heart out on the bird feeder over my head. He stayed for a long time, watching me watching him. When I looked him up in *Animal Speak* back home, it said he reflects an increased variety of potentials that are likely to unfold within my life. Anytime a finch arrives, life is going to become more active (04:141). And did it ever!

My sister Beryl, a wonderful intuitive healer and humanitarian suddenly turns to me, "Teach the children well."

I stare at her in wonder, "Why did you say that?"

I had just awakened with the old 70's song playing through my head!

> "Teach the children well, beyond yourself, of how you go by.
> You, who are on the road, must have a code that you can live by.
> Don't you ever ask them why, if you did then you would cry, for they love you."

She frowns, "You told me you wanted to teach and heal people with your writing."

Yes, but why did she bring it up now, on the heels of my dream? After reading my unfinished Blue Diamond manuscript, she urged me to complete it as soon as possible. She volunteers in hospital emergency wards in USA and Victim Services in Canada, using her marvellous gift for gently helping others in crisis.

In Palm Springs, I had the time to read, *Dropped Threads*, the anthology of Canadian writers I mentioned at the beginning of the book. One paragraph near the end of the book hit me hard. The woman (can't remember her name and no longer have the book) wrote:

> "Unless you pen the book, you will never see your soul written out. Unless you barge in, uninvited, you will never be part of how decisions are made; they will be made without your knowledge and without considering you at all."

As I stared at my sister, I realized I wanted to be heard, counted and involved in the decision making for cancer research and treatment along with healing through natural, logical, intuitive cures. I'll write this book and nobody can stop me! I'm on the road and I have a code I *will* live by!

21.

Terrible Choices

"Believe nothing, no matter where you read it
Or who has said it, not even if I have said it,
Unless it agrees with your own reason and
your own common sense."

Buddha

Choices are hard and take long soul searching. Chemo looms now, my choices are here. I read and read and read books, online information, plus pamphlets and brochures from the breast cancer support group. I read about the terrible side effects of chemotherapy, Tamoxifen, radiation and I weep, crushed by the weight of my harsh reality. Every time I even think the word, 'chemo' I hear a loud, 'No!' I have heard that voice too many times in my life, during crises when I needed help. It never steered me wrong. I sense if I take chemo, the consequences will be horrendous – far outweighing the good. Time becomes the enemy as I struggle to find my way.

I know the cancer has not spread. Finding it in one of the lymph nodes is not tantamount for concern, especially when they found it in only one and removed six. The real issue was the size of the tumour: 3.3 centimetres. But it was contained; the perimeters were all clear, according to my surgeon. So now I move into treatment and prevention, addressing it on many fronts. My guides tell me to make Tamoxifen my friend. I need to take it for a short while before a new drug appears of greater benefit to me. It sounded like lentinan the extract found in Shiitake mushrooms. I am to take 4 servings per day of Shitakes throughout my treatments and afterwards too. They are so good for protecting my liver as I heal.

I also hear, 'No Selenium' which surprises me because it is recommended in many of the books on healing from cancer. I body tested a bottle of Selenium and my body quickly backed away. Later research revealed selenium is found in nuts, which I love and eat almost daily.

I called Elia last night and she took me back to Xi. He held me for a long time then flew me to some peaceful waterfalls to help me relax from these stressful decisions. I 'see' his dragon face, heavy with scales and gleaming yellow eyes. Yet I am unafraid. We have been friends for a long time and his presence comforts me. This Dragon energy makes me who I really am. He will be there to protect me and my body from all harm and I feel his radiance shoot through my fingers and toes.

After I cried, my guides told me the Gamma rays of radiation are needed and healthy for me. They are the Dragon energy I write about and work with.

I see my crown chakra opening like a lotus flower, letting the energy flow easily and with great healing power through me. If I block it, it can harm me. If I love it, it heals me – forever. And I know I will be okay, the cancer will never return.

That night I dreamt of a heavy, metal coated sock for my heart. I must use a visualization technique to spiritually put it on before each radiation treatment and remove it immediately afterwards. Its little rectangular remote control lets me activate and de-activate it accordingly. So awesome this spiritual protection!

Later I dreamt I rested, finally, on the tropical shore of my 'Illusion' island, watching the sunrise at dawn. I felt emotionally, mentally, spiritually and physically exhausted. My arms ached from the stress of 'swimming' through this long journey. Finally, I am on shore and I am alive.

Yesterday, Jana, my friend and yoga teacher brought me a DVD on cancer and some oil from her friend Don who cured his lymphoma with it. I 'hear' I should not use his mix because it is not compatible with my body type. Jana also has some Aloe Vera plants. Their juice is recommended for the radiation burn site – one of the few things you can apply safely between treatments. Blessed be my friends!

Joyce called and I talked about how hard these days have been. I thanked her for her friendship, for being a sounding board as I talked and dreamed and cried and worked my way through this. She is such a dear friend.

Cliff remains supportive, saying he agrees totally with my decisions. He makes me laugh and cuddles me close when I need it most. I love him so much, my lifetime friend and partner.

My totem guides came back and took me in their arms. They tell me to go easy on myself, I am still convalescing; the six weeks from surgery are barely up. Doctors told me not to lift anything over ten pounds during this time. Already, I am swimming, hauling wood for my little stove and packing my two year old grandson. My guides also told me to limit my juice to only 6 oz. If I have some left over, to just sip it throughout the day. I struggle with occasional bouts of indigestion, stress related I'm sure.

We go to the cancer hospital and get processed through with a number, plastic I.D. card and endless, endless, frightening information. They take us, thirty at a time, on a tour through the wards, the chemo and radiation units then to an auditorium with falsely bright pep talks from survivors well into their eighties. It is not reassuring to any of us. I can see the fear, confusion and overwhelming terror on all our faces. In the hallways, I watch patients, blank faced and ghastly in colour, many in wheelchairs, as they await elevators to convalescent wards upstairs. A pretty blonde teenager with spiked hair leans on her crutches, half her leg missing. She searches nearby faces for their reaction to her plight. The gas chambers must have created a similar reaction.

Then we meet the oncologist, a bright, handsome young man who seems very sympathetic. Yet something about him disturbs me. I don't care that he's gay: I accept anyone's sexual orientation and simply look for the soul beneath the face. Yet I sense a deep hatred radiating from him and directed at me. I have never seen him before so I can not take it personally. He says I have the ordinary, 'run of the mill' breast cancer, not rare or exotic at all and he shrugs it off with a sneer. (Why didn't the surgeon tell me? She had all the reports before he did). Though the cancer has not spread, the oncologist group of doctors want me to take the requisite chemo, radiation and five years of drugs.

When the oncologist examined me, I felt his satisfaction that I had a lot of fluid swelling around the incision – another thing for me to worry about. As a nurse, I know it is caused by the missing lymph nodes. By lying on my back for about fifteen minutes in the middle of the day, it allows the 46 remaining lymph nodes throughout my body to pick up the excess fluid and flush it away, thus reducing the pain and swelling. He tells me none of this, offering no solution at all.

He goes through the side effects of chemo, which I must take first, then radiation and then tamoxifen citrate tablets. On his little chalk board, he writes eight to ten horrendous, staggering side effects for each. *All* these treatments together increase my odds by 20% of the cancer not reoccurring. He carefully adds this 20% to the top of the 50/50 chance of it coming back or not. He brushes off the radiation, saying the worst is hair loss. Cliff and I listen quietly. I feel my face getting redder and redder with fury and stress. Inside me, something is screaming, 'No! No! NO!'

When the oncologist is done, I ask, "Where are the alternatives? Are there any natural health options to these therapies?"

He immediately goes on the defensive; I can see it in his stillness and closed face. "I just gave it to you."

I frown, "I'm talking about other cures. Where is the world-wide research on nutritional alternatives? You pride yourselves on being the top research hospital in Canada. Where is the research for healthier, natural alternatives?" Radiation started in the 1940's; chemo in the 1960's, with very little change that I know of.

His nose comes up, "They are too sporadic and poorly done."

It literally takes my breath away. In the past seventy years people have raised billions, no trillions of dollars for cancer research and it is '*sporadic and poorly done?*' On behalf of all researchers I don't get it. I know how much work and care and thought go into the methodology and testing in any research project.

I stall, "Well, I don't like the thought of chemotherapy. I need some time to think about this."

He nods looking serious and thoughtful, "I will call you in a week and we will talk more then."

Grateful for the reprieve, I leave as quickly as possible.

Again, I cry all the way home. Something inside of me is screaming, "No!" every time I even think the word, 'chemo' and I don't know what to do. It is so overwhelming and stressful. Every time I go to the doctors they steal my individuality and my choices. To them, there is one choice and it infuriates me! Then I hear the messages from my guides and I am truly caught between a rock and hard place.

For years now, I have lived on my intuition. I have heard this 'No!' before. I know it comes from my inner wisdom, that Innate, Intelligent self. In the past, when I heeded it, everything turned out well. If I ignored it, I paid the sad consequences of a bad choice. I wondered if it was just my ego refusing, out of fear, out of distrust but I sense it goes deeper, I *know* it does, deeper to my soul and it is shouting, louder and louder 'No! NO! **NO!**'

That night, exhausted and feeling beat up by the medical profession, I fell asleep watching TV. When I awoke, a little boy sang Karaoke. Words flashing at the bottom of the screen from Whitney Houston's song spoke directly to my heart:

'If I fail, or I succeed,
I will have lived as I believe.'

Oh how those perfect words resonated inside me, comforted me. This was exactly how I felt! I realized the only way I fail is if I do *not* believe in myself and what is right for *me*. Here was the deeper message from my earlier dreams about going deep within myself and making a choice from my place of power.

That night, Gabriel came in and I knelt in front of her once again. We went over my diet:

1. Juicing is good, focus on vegetables and fruit as the major part of my diet.
2. Bread is okay but minimize it to 1- 2 slices per day.
3. Milk is okay in coffee, some cheese for protein but not lots.
4. Sugar – have only one small portion per day for the next year, and then it will be okay.
5. Soy is out. My research later revealed Canadians now eat more soy than Asian people who truly eat it in moderation. (Ever noticed how many products now contain soy lethicin? Yet the verdict is still out whether it is good for us or just cheap filler.)
6. Nuts are okay except peanuts. (I would later discover peanuts have a carcinogenic mould found in both raw nuts and peanut butter).
7. Some meat is okay but never a major portion of my meal.
8. I'll start with 1 tablespoon of olive oil in each cup of fresh juice, but gradually move it up to ¼ cup once my radiation begins.
9. Shitake mushrooms will also help me through.
10. Remove all parabens from my make-up and deodorant, etc.
11. Detoxify regularly.
12. Use my Muscle Testing ability constantly with new foods. (It had already backed me away from sugar and soy products).

In the coming months, as I healed, we would 'tweak' this diet several times. Gabriel also told me to go and play and to say, like a mantra:

'I AM HEALING NICELY. I am okay and will be fine. I am filled with joy' (she reminded me of the green joyful energy still around me).

Later in the night, my beloved bird spirit guides came in and we hugged. I laid my head in their lap and rested. I felt their love and they showed me how the healing power of love boosts my survival to 100%!

22.

My Life, My Choice!

"How can it be that our breasts, these beautiful centers of nurturing, fullness and pleasure, are looked upon by so many as inadequate at best, or breeding grounds for cancer, pain and fear at worst? In what kind of culture can this happen?"

Christianne Northup, M.D.

The stress from yesterday at the hospital made my upper arms ache with sorrow, worry and fear. I needed an outlet. My surgeon gave me permission to return to my regular swimming exercises. That afternoon I went swimming and hummed happily to myself the whole time. The pool was not busy, allowing lots of peaceful space around me. Later, I sat in the steam room and let the sweat pour off me, taking some of the toxins, I hoped, from my body as well. Afterwards, I felt weakened, overdoing it obviously. I have not yet found the balance of exercise, rest and healing. Now I must choose which path I take to healing.

I realized I play the odds just like everyone else. I have a relative with an enlarged heart who is supposed to lose weight. Instead, she chooses to cook and eat with great enjoyment, one of her gifts to her family and friends. She enjoys her life (literally fills it with joy) and lives with her odds. To her, quality is more important than quantity. We can *not* live in fear. We must stay in the joy of each day; it's all we have anyway. Tomorrow, we could be hit by a bus. So be it.

So, I'll say 'Yes' to Tamoxifen, it stops the cancer cells from digesting estrogens which starves them and they die, anywhere in my body. It strengthens my bones and I pray for its healing powers.

I say 'Yes' to radiation only because my guides recommend I take it. They told me they will tell me precisely how to heal and I believe them. They have given me so many healthy alternatives to eat and heal with, why would I not believe and trust them?

And I say, "No!' in a loud, powerful, determined shout to the poisons of chemotherapy. This is *not* me loving me! No. And it *feels* clear and concise. I trust my intuition. Hell, I'm betting my life on it!

Then the oncologist calls me, only *two* days after I saw him, on a Saturday no less. Now I'm feeling 'pushed around' and bullied unnecessarily. He told me he would give me a week. And he's angry. I hear it in his voice. Why?

I tell him I intuitively refuse the chemo. I ask him if I take it later does it change anything. I tell him my surgeon told me with a lumpectomy, the cancer might come back in the breast tissue; with a mastectomy, it might come back in the wall of the chest. He says that is false. It will come back in some vital organ and be terminal. Who do I believe?

Luckily, I had just read Susan Weeds book, *Breast Cancer? Breast Health, the Wise Woman Way.* I recommend this book to any woman facing breast cancer. The forward is written by Dr. Christiane Northup, the woman who writes exclusively about women's issues and women's bodies. She talks about healing the Wise Woman inside and the lessons in breast wisdom. Dr. Northup says we can not nurture others fully or well unless we also nurture ourselves. Our breasts know this and will not be silenced in the attempt to bring this to our attention. (This was my lesson from the start).

Dr. Northup states a need for balance, for heeding inner wisdom, a need for pleasure and for passion. As women, we've been taught to ignore this so we lose touch with the wisdom and power of our breasts. Aboriginal women laugh about what they 'see' through their breasts – an intuitive, sensual wisdom which men can't understand.

Susan Weeds says the Wise Healer Within has been silenced, ignored and ridiculed both outside ourselves and within each of us for the last several millennia. We live in a culture out of touch with Women's Wisdom. She summed up my dilemma in *writing* about my inner wisdom.

Dr. Northup writes:

> 'But what if each one of us were to remember her woman's wisdom? What if we remembered that every cell of our breasts could be nurtured, rejuvenated and healed by the energy of touch, pleasure, love, whole food and green healing plants? What if we collectively discovered that our healer within has never gone away, that she has simply waited, biding her time until it was safe to come out and speak her truth?

> ….She is the balance bringing healing back to medical care.

....She is the voice saying, 'I am going to be all right,' (despite what the doctors tell her).

....She is the voice of the heart, the same voice whose energy heals our breasts, regardless their current state of health. Let her wrap you in her warmth and challenge you when you need it.' (95: xi)....

Her words echo through the long months of this, my blue diamond journey! It's time for me to come out and speak my truth. The imagery I experienced at the massage therapists so many months ago, the dreams of death and nurturing make more sense now. I just found my Wise Woman Heart. It fills me now, wrapping me in its warmth. I WILL BE OKAY! Even if I die, I WILL BE OKAY!

And, no, I will <u>not</u> take chemo! I hugged Susan Weed's book to my chest in a wave of relief and gratitude.

Susan writes about the ancient grandmothers who say:

"We insist that you trust your inner sense of rightness and be willing to act on your own convictions. Walk with truth and beauty Granddaughter. There are no wrong paths. Each woman is unique and we support you no matter what confronts you. And to remind you that you can leave a trail of wisdom, a trail of beauty, no matter what path you choose. That is the Wise Woman Way of the world 'round."

In my Ojibwa teachings, the grandmothers, those old spirits of feminine wisdom often speak like this. The above words were not breaking news to me, but simply a reminder for me to return to my traditional beliefs (just like in my earlier dream). I needed to see the perfection in every problem. Every illness is a gift. I needed to allow breast cancer to have its own beauty, its own truth and its own way of offering health, wholeness and holiness, as a vision of completeness with things *just as they are.*

Susan Weeds goes on to say breast cancer is an initiation where one's former self dies and a new self emerges - another reference to death and rebirth. She believes breast cancer must be a larger story, a mega-story with an archetypal resonance, a story revealing the power of breast cancer. For her, breast cancer brings us all together in a chant vibrating with respect for women, for our breasts and the Earth's sweet breast. Breast cancer can thus be an ally of wholeness helping us nurture health, wholeness and holiness inside and out, healing the Earth as we heal ourselves. This is exactly what my totem spirit guides had revealed to me the very night of my diagnosis. What an awesome validation!!!

I was still furious at the way the oncologist, the woolly, pushy buffalo with his Johnson issues, tried to bully me. (Remember my earlier dream?) Luckily, my son and his wife were visiting so I vented on them after I hung up the phone. I had never heard, in any of my research, the stuff the oncologist talked to me about. Does he really hate women that much? His deep anger is his issue; I refuse to make it mine.

Then Spirit sent me a phone call from my wonderful friend, Joanne, who had breast cancer over ten years ago. We discussed the whole issue of choice. She got the same run around and chose for herself as well, using her inner wisdom to guide her, despite what the doctors said. She encouraged me to stand by my own convictions. Each woman is an individual and each woman has the right to choose her life.

I cried, 'Thank you, my friend! Thank you for all your support.'

She suggested I go online and look up some of the latest research. I have and I will continue to do so. On the internet, more and more doctors are speaking out about the horrible side effects of cancer's medical treatments, the ancient 'slash, poison and burn' mentality. There *are* alternative healthier treatments available. In the following months I asked my guides to bring them to me and I found lots of them. The more informed I am the better choices I can make. And I will *not* be bullied!

That night, I read through my journal and assessed all the Spirit messages and guidance I had received through these past months. They were so beautiful, amazing, inspiring, truthful, wonderful and joyful. I believe I am walking *my* path. The blue diamond on my finger reminds me so every day. And I walk it with purpose and truth. It's all I wanted right from the beginning.

23.

Uneasy Times

"Those who have developed 'psychic powers' have simply let some of their limitations they laid upon their minds be lifted."

A Course in Miracles

Gabriel came in as I knelt and prayed. She took my hand and we flew to my tropical island in the Pacific. We sat on a mountain, staring at the sea and golden orange sky of a new dawn breaking. She told me I needed to rest and relax for the hardest part is choosing and sticking to it.

She told me, "Under no circumstances are you to take chemo! You are a 'Sensitive' and we do not allow them to be poisoned in such manner – ever! The radiation is a guarantee. It will weaken your heart for a time, so you'll be tired but you will recover. The dragon skin you acquire is a tough skin over your heart for protection but it allows you to grow."

She went on, "In the beginning, there was more time to heal and grow but now time is of the essence. Mother Earth has given humanity a reprieve but we must change our ways. She could have swallowed the people who did not believe. Instead, she has given humanity more time to discover and honour her gift of life." I saw an image of continental coastlines sliding into the waters. But it did *not* happen. This reprieve I felt in my bones because of the parallel in my life.

Gabriel continued, "You have thirty more years of work to do. You will heal and grow beyond this to write and write again. You will help so many, many people. This is your work, your plan when you came here. You never fit in because you truly are one of us and we will help you." Now I am in shock and wonder if this is, again, just my ego talking! I mean…really…how far can this go before I truly am insane?

She also told me I would come to this St. Francis Island many times in this life to rest and write, but not to live there – like I did in another life.

I asked her, holding her hand, what her life was like. Had she ever lived on Earth?

She replied, "Not on this vessel, for the Earth is a vessel in the sky." She divides her time – not days like ours – between her work at God's side and talking 'simultaneously' to the four hundred and some people like me. (I would later read Gabriel is one of the most powerful archangels of all. She sits to the left of God's throne.)

I told her it's a whole new way of multi-tasking! We laughed. I kissed her hand and thanked her for her presence in my life from Creator.

She indicated she understood my need to cling right now because of my worry and fear, but I am stronger than I think, strong as my belief and faith. So I sat upright once again.

When I awoke, I immediately wrote our conversation down in my journal. I felt calmer and more in touch with the Wise Woman within. I have moved to another level of understanding and it has not been an easy journey. Yet, I am here, I exist, I will write it all down for those who follow behind me – my gift to all who need strength to deal with their problems. Always, we have options and choices.

I picked up Doreen Virtue's book, *The Lightworker's Way*, Awakening your spiritual power to know and heal. I read of her struggle with religious philosophies in relation to her spiritual gifts. I can relate though mine are medical. She attended a workshop at the Learning Light Foundation in Anaheim. Her instructor, Lucretia Scott described the four different psychic gifts available to all mankind (97:112):

> Clairaudient – clear hearing of messages
> Clairvoyant – clear seeing of pictures, images and dreams
> Clairsentient – clear emotions, hunches, smells or physical sensations,
> Claircognizant – clear thinking, receiving information as complete ideas; knowing without knowing how we know.

According to Dr. Virtue, we have one or two of these channels in which we are naturally gifted. In my Aboriginal teachings, we must develop our spiritual gifts to the best of our ability and use them wisely to help others. Virtue writes, "The more you accept psychic abilities as a natural part of life, the more frequently they occur….Additionally, trust your psychic impressions, and you will feel increasingly guided by your higher self and your angels." (97:120).

Okay! Years ago, I 'heard' (clairaudient) messages. In the past fifteen years, I began 'seeing' (clairvoyant) images behind my closed eyes during meditations and in my dreams. Both gifts are growing and changing, becoming stronger and clearer all the time. Still, I need the support of my research, books and others' experiences, like Doreen's, to really believe in these gifts (and my own sanity). It comforts me to know I am not alone.

I decide to visit a Chinese herbalist I have known and trusted for years. Victor Shim of the Tao Dao Acupuncture Clinic has kindly allowed me to use his name in my book. He is well respected in his field, world renowned actually, and has written books on both his healing practices and the herbs he grows and processes meticulously in his lab. His phone number is 780 425-1754.

He tells me breast cancer is the easiest cancer to cure because it is in a fluid environment, easy for his herbs to reach and flush from the body. He has been curing women for over twenty-five years with herbs from two flowers: lobelia and saffleur. According to him, they will flush any cancer cells I have left in my body, within two weeks. I walk out in shock, struggling to process this in comparison to the eighteen months of chemo and radiation at the cancer hospital. That night as I swallowed his pills I 'heard' the words, 'These are your chemo'. I almost choked on them!

I feel like I could sink through my chair as I sit and meditate. My mind reels with choices, stress, fear, confusion, prayers and endless panicky thoughts. It is so hard to go against the medical system, like another gigantic King Kong sitting and waiting outside my door. So I sink deeper and deeper into Mother Earth until I find the cavern from which I wrote my book, *Wind Walker*. I lie down against a stone wall, totally spent. A full figured woman in a long silvery green dress appears beside me.

"About time you got here," she grins. "You think you can just laze about?" She gently kicks my leg.

Without lifting my head, I lazily kick her back saying, "Have a seat."

She laughs and sits beside me. She tells me she is an Earth Mother Spirit.

"As in Gaia?" I ask and she nods but her challenging attitude rubs me wrong. "Are you part of God's Divine Plan?" I ask the thrice timed question.

"No! I am part of Earth Mother's."

So for the first time, I ask three times, "Are you part of Earth Mother's Divine Path?" And she replies readily and easily, "Yes!"

She tells me she has watched me for a long time, coming and going from this cavern but knew I wasn't ready until now to see her. "About time too," she adds. "This is Earth energy to tap, but you never have. You have simply looked at it and played with it. Now it is time to engage the energy, even the Earth Cancer Energy that I am."

Now I'm really uneasy. Something about her doesn't ring true; I feel it deep within me. But I listen as she continues, "There are five ways you can heal yourself and go on:"

1. Take the Chinese herbalist's medicine, all of it for twelve days.
2. By then you will be into the radiation treatments – take them all and feel the Dragon Energy flow through you
3. Love yourself daily. When you wake up, tell yourself you love you. And just before you go to sleep, tell yourself you love you. This is the most powerful healing method in the world.
4. Tamoxifen and the others will ensure the cancer never returns. Make friends with it and use it wisely and well.
5. The final chapter of the Dragon Women's club you will soon be joining – the Honour Guard of the Dragon Skins will love you and support you forever more.

I fell asleep and thought no more....

24.

Final Bastion

"If cancer is caused by a deficiency, it is not caused by a lack of chemo and radiation!"

Dr. Lorraine Day, *Cancer Doesn't Scare Me Anymore (DVD)*

Cliff and I drove to a mountain retreat for a break before the radiation treatments start. It was so beautiful and I breathed in sunshine and fresh mountain air. We laid in the hot tub at the motel and vegged out, too emotionally exhausted to even talk about the coming months of treatment. Little did I know my life was about to take another direction.

When we came home the next day, we watched the DVD by Dr. Lorraine Day, called, *Cancer Doesn't Scare Me Anymore*. She had breast cancer and refused all treatments, choosing to heal herself the natural way. She laid it all out, the whole history of cancer, the powerful companies controlling the Health Industry and the lack of research being done to cure cancer. Tamoxifen is handed out like candy. Cancer is big business and they still use the archaic, bizarre remedies from the 1940's and 60's, ignoring all the new biochemical and nutritional research. The horrendous side effects, over <u>sixty</u> of them, from chemo, radiation and the drugs are not explained to the unsuspecting patients. The side-effects keep patients on drugs and therapies for the rest of their life.

Dr. Day (could even be a relative, since my Native American great-grandmother was a Day) from Berkeley California, a doctor who taught other doctors, outlined the ten step health plan she healed herself with. All of it, besides the food, which she says you have to buy anyway, *is free*. Her advice parallels John Hopkins Society and my philosophy of healing physically, mentally, emotionally and spiritually. Here is a conglomerate of their advice and mine:

10 Steps to Health from Cancer

1. **Proper Nutrition**: plenty of fruits, grains, vegetables and nuts in their natural form, unprocessed; raw or fresh juiced. Vegetables, raw or cooked should make up 80% of your diet; the rest should be fruits, whole grains, nuts, seeds and some chicken, pork or fish. No lamb or beef unless it is organic. Make meat your side dish, one serving only per day. Become a Flexitarian: you are as healthy as a vegetarian and have your meat too! No sugar, no dairy. You can use natural, unpasteurized honey or maple syrup in small amounts. Stevia, an herbal plant extract can also be used for sweetening.

2. **Exercise**: four hours per week – make it part of your life, something you love to do. Walk, do yoga, swim or whatever makes your body sing.

3. **Drink 8 – 10 glasses of water daily** – filtered, not tap. You may add some squeezed lemon juice per glass to increase your alkaline levels.

4. **Sunlight** – boosts your immune system; keeps your body functioning normally. This natural Vitamin D can prevent most cancers. Be in the sun for at least 10 minutes per day (11:00 a.m. is the ideal summit time) – face it but don't look at it!! Expose as much skin as possible – weather permitting and truly have a sun bath.

5. **No Chemicals** – no drugs (if possible), no sugar, caffeine, additives, preservatives, sodas, alcohol (no more than one glass/day of wine) or processed foods.

6. **Fresh Air** – outdoor air and breath it in deeply. Oxygen is a natural deoxidizer in our bodies. Cancer dies in a well oxygenated environment. Breathe in to count of four, hold to count of four, breathe out to count of four.

7. **Proper rest at night** – be in bed by 9:30 p.m. when the healing hormones are produced.

8. **Stress relief** – learn to trust in God and that you will get well. Laugh lots and do things you love to do, with people you love to be with. Avoid negative thinkers and news.

9. **Attitude of Gratitude** – be thankful for what you have, no blaming, whining or judging. Commit yourself to doing everything possible to heal.

10. **Spirit of Benevolence** – care about others, pray for them; don't focus just on yourself.

After watching the DVD, I cried and cried while Cliff held me. I can not put my body through the radiation! I can *not*! Not for anything or anybody. It is bizarre, cruel and potentially deadly! According to Dr. Day, it *causes* secondary cancers. Well why wouldn't it? It is from *Uranium*! If my cancer is about me loving myself, then radiation is *not* about me loving me! I can not and will not put such poison in my healing body! But it is so hard to buck such a powerful medical system and I feel so alone. The stress is astronomical. Cliff just tells me he agrees totally with me and will back me whatever I choose. He's as shocked by the video as I am.

I knew where I stood when I phoned my sister Beryl and cried out, "I will die before I let them put that crap in my body!"

That night, I went back to my guides in fury. I snarled, "I'm *not* doing any of this! No chemo, no radiation and no drugs! I don't care what you say. I'm choosing for myself. It's *my body and my life*!" Damned if anyone would tell me what to do! As tough as the choice was, it felt right for me. I can't speak for anyone else but this *feels* right for me, Yes! Damn straight!

They did handstands, and danced around in joy.

What the hell?!!!

They cried, "This is the decision we wanted you to make! This is the true, gentle, Wise Woman Way. Yes, if you had chosen radiation, we would have helped you through it, including the tamoxifen – but it does have nasty side effects."

"Then why all the hype and information about taking the blasted stuff?" I yelled at them. It made no sense at all. I wanted none of it or them. I was so bloody furious I yanked myself from their presence.

It took me several days to realize the incredible gift Spirit World offers us all. It is *our* life, *our* choice about how we live it and they will support us, *no matter what we choose*. Susan Weeds was right; there is no wrong path, only choices. What we believe, from our soul, is the truth for each one of us. I realized my guides and angels would have supported me through all the treatments, should I choose that path. In fact, they recommended some options but when I chose differently, this delighted them because this was the choice they *hoped* I would make. *Yet they would not interfere with my free will.* They are truly not allowed to.

25.

Truths and Lies

"From time immemorial healthy people have held sick people hostage. I believe hostage holding of the sick is immoral, fundamentally unethical and needs to be stopped."
Dr. Hulda Regehr Clark, Ph.D., N.D. *The Cure for All Cancers*.

Now the real work begins – learning how to heal – gently, slowly and wisely. I fully understand my position: Change or Die. But I have TIME. The tumour is gone. I have time to heal, as I learned to do in the past months, with help from my guides, totems and angels, all messengers of God. And I will continue with research to back up what they tell me. I accept nothing without constant research and thinking it through *before* I choose.

Instead of going for my first radiation treatment the next morning, Cliff and I went and visited the man who had sent me the DVD. He had two stomach tumors and was sent home to die. That was seventeen years ago. He inspired us with his cheerful good humour and realistic practices for healing. Since he knew her and her family personally, he recommended Dr. Hulda Regehr Clarke's book, *The Cure for All Cancers*. On the back of her book cover, Dr. Clarke writes "Give me three weeks and your Oncologist will cancel your surgery". Inside she writes about the cure she found for any cancer, saying, **'please read my book before you have any pieces of your anatomy removed that you will need when you are well."**

She has been curing cancer patients, terminally ill ones too, for over twenty years. A Saskatchewan born biochemist (Magna Cum Laude) with credentials in Canada and the USA, she isolated the parasites she claims cause cancer. Walnut hulls from the Black Walnut tree and Wormwood from the Artemisia shrub kills the adults and developmental stages of at least 100 parasites. Cloves, taken together with the other two ingredients, kill the eggs. I discovered Black Walnut oil is also a powerful detoxifier.

Did the world praise her for her work? Nope. The American FDA jailed her twice, saying her black walnut oil is too toxic. So what do they say about toxic chemotherapy? She is forced to live in Mexico to avoid further persecution from the United States. But she continues her research and her findings are constantly being published in a series of books. Most naturopathic practitioners carry her books. Yet the public has never heard of her. I hate conspiracy theories but this whole concept makes my hair stand on end.

According to Dr. Regehr Clark there are three things you must do to heal your cancer: (93:26):

1. Kill the parasites and all its stages.
2. Stop letting isopropyl, propylene glycol or cetyl alcohol into your body.
3. Flush out the metals, common toxins and bacteria from your body so you can get well.

Dr. Regehr Clark also advises cleaning up your environment, throwing out any health care or cleaning products, solvents or *foods* with isopropyl alcohol, propanol, isopropynol or cetyl alcohol, the main causes of cancer. **She found that 100% of all cancer patients have the solvent isopropyl alcohol accumulated in the liver and their cancerous tissue**. To her list I add parabens and Sodium Lauryl Sulfate (LSL) – both known carcinogens although you hear nothing about them in Canada.

Ever wonder where the giant piles of yellow sulphur at oil refineries went? Well, they made it into a new food group, called sulphites, another preservative. Most soap has sulphur (sulphites and sulphates), so do dried fruits (one of my favourite 'candies'). Now I know scientist say the minute amounts used are within healthy limits. But who monitors the cumulative effect when it is in practically everything we eat?

Read labels and gasp in horror. These chemicals are in your cosmetics, shampoo, conditioners, hair spray, toothpaste, mouthwash, mousse, body lotions, shaving supplies, nail polish removers, sunscreens, perfumes, glues and of course, rubbing alcohol. I found propylene glycol in my favourite vodka coolers and a delicious looking pecan pie!! Another big culprit is the aluminum in deodorant, baking soda and crackers of all things. Women, the household caregivers and cleaners, plus the biggest users of body lotions, soaps, shampoo and makeup are exposed daily to a dangerous number of these toxins. Why are we convinced splashing hundreds of deadly chemicals all over ourselves, our family and our environment will make us clean? They're killing us!

If you have children, read their skin product labels too. Baby lotions and sunscreens contain a horrifying blend of toxic preservatives and binders to extend shelf life, not us. This garbage is everywhere and we are unknowingly slathering it all over our babies!

Be careful in Health Food Stores too. I accidently bought a health store hair conditioner with methlyparaben *and* cocamidopropyl. If you think these toxins aren't dangerous, check out the latest organic products which quietly advertise "No parabens, No propyl, No LSL!" What you don't know can kill you.

I changed every product touching my skin, buying only organic, natural and essential oil products. I use rubber gloves whenever I clean or paint. Every abrasive, dangerous product contacting your skin, eyes, nose or mouth invariably ends up in your liver. I use a salt crystal ball called a Deo Ball for deodorant and it works just fine. I changed to organic baking soda and powder, crackers, toothpaste, soaps and hair products. I make my own mouthwash from a cup of boiled water and 1 teaspoon pure salt crystals. For my face I use Vitamin E oil. I accidently discovered this oil is a natural sun screen too! Although you still need to be careful of too much sun, Vitamin E oil washes off in warm water so no other skin products are needed. People tell me I look younger every time they see me.

As consumers we do have power. If we stop buying the garbage, they'll stop making it.

The biggest healing journey is slowly removing the cause of cancer from the body. Dr. Regehr Clark writes about oxygen therapies, mineral supplements, detoxifying and cleansing the organs, especially the liver. She cautions about detoxing too fast because it dumps a large load of toxins back into the blood stream and intestines. If the system is already weak it can almost kill the person. I read somewhere how all cancer patients have thick blood. I wonder if toxins are the cause. So again, slowly, and gently is the course of action. I still believe juicing daily is the most gentle, nurturing way to detoxify. I'll go into further detail in chapter 34.

As I said earlier, this is a healing journey for everyone! We are all inflicted with toxins and parasites. Our bodies will manifest illness in many different ways besides cancer. Healing our sick bodies means removing the cause! The journey back to health is the same for everyone.

26.

Toxin Tales
(From my Guides)

"Love opens the door of ancient recognition."

John O'Donohue, Anam Cara

Wendy Mesley from the television show, *W-5,* made a documentary, called *The Answer to Cancer,* after her breast cancer diagnosis. Her private testing found over 40 toxins in her body. Apparently she embarrassed the Canadian Cancer Society because they had not done any research on such a possibility. Folks, THIS IS NOT BREAKING NEWS! Nutritionists and biochemists have studied toxic build-up for the past forty years! Look at my bibliography and the dates their books were published. The latest research has found **Cancer is not even a disease. It is a reaction, a result** of a clogged lymphatic system and a congested liver due to a build up of toxins. I wanted to know how many were in my body.

When I asked my guides, I heard, 'Over thirty." The worst were parabens from the moisturizer I had slathered all over my face, neck and upper chest for the last twenty years. My Mom had used it so I considered it safe. It probably was in her lifetime, before they added the 'junk'. Now I understand why the tumour started in a blocked lymph duct at the top of my breast. The second toxin, believe it or not, was chicken nuggets. I hate hamburgers, so I always ordered chicken at fast food restaurants. My guides told me these little nuggets – the 'garbage' dumps for chicken scraps, fat and skin chunks also have many hidden ingredients including MSG. I read somewhere oils used for deep frying, if rancid, become toxic too. The third toxin was soda pop. This surprised me because I don't like sweet drinks but I do buy them occasionally. My guides said an accumulative effect apparently happens from something in the aluminum cans. A year later, they were vindicated when the media warned about toxins called PSB in the plastic lining the cans. As I mentioned earlier, soda pop also causes rickets.

Over the next month or so, my guides slowly gave me the full list of toxins in my body. I would think about a product and 'hear' "Number 26!' Number 15!" I learned to quickly write them down until I had my entire list. Was there any duplication of numbers? Yes, two, but I simply moved them up or down one space to an empty line. My guides reminded me cancer is a disease of the soul and it must be healed from the soul outward. Not all toxins in my list were physical. I'll talk about them individually later. Check out this list and have a look at your own life and home.

30 Toxins in My Body From My Guides

1. My face and body moisturizer – had Methylparaben (a known breast cancer carcinogen in the US) plus Isopropyl and Iodopropynyl
2a. Frustration (Stress related to having cancer)
2. Chicken nuggets
3. Soda pop
4. Wheat – "wheat is no friend of yours and never will be"
5. Chemicals, sprays and pesticides (a worker at the Mayo Clinic said every tumour is laced with these toxins).
6. Cheese – especially orange (dye)
7. **Ignoring your roots – ancestral waste products (DNA cellular memory)**
8. **Dilemma – feeding yourself versus others (they won)**
9. **Currying favours where none was needed**
10. Body lotions and sprays (I had sprayed my chest for years with a perfumed one)
11. Hand lotions
12. Butyl alcohol – found in soaps and deodorants
13. Fabric softener
14. Self-disgust (for my body and some of my behaviour – over critical)
15. Yellow-green household cleaner
16. Bleach
17. Ethers – thoughts provoking despair, fear, sadness, disgust and anger
18. **Mask of Deception – (not seeing other's and hiding myself too)**
19. **Gatherings – your self not included**
20. **Carrying the weight of others**
21. **Sharing of self when none was needed (energy drain)**
22. **Garnering faith in the circle of non-believers**
23. **Halving of self to please others (a sacrifice unwanted)**
24. Pharmaceuticals: antibiotics, pain-killers, decongestants (accumulative effect)

25. Toothpaste and mouthwash
26. Milk and butter (unless organic)   Not Toxic
27. Hair spray   wine
28. Shampoo and conditioner   beef & pork (in our area)
29. Soaps for cleaning   Dish soap (Palmolive)
30. Clothes soap   dental fillings

36. 36. Carpets
39. 39. Sugar – not an issue unless paired with wheat, dairy or hydrogenated oils

52. Honouring Thyself.

This last one made me laugh out loud. Yes, toxic by its very absence! (Just a little bite of Spirit humour!)

Most of the above are self-explanatory. Our bodies absorb anything we breathe, walk through (electromagnetic energy) or put on our skin.

I started addressing the emotional and mental toxins:

Toxin #17, Ethers – thoughts provoking despair, fear, sadness, disgust and anger were about my negative self talk. This one shocked me when I started paying attention to which thoughts dogged me, upset me, depressed me and ruined my day. Yet they were only *thoughts* with no grounding in reality, no logic or truth. I learned they came from my ego and past memories of criticism playing like a broken record, useless and cruel. I never realized how mean I was to myself. I concentrated on catching these thoughts, stopping them cold then turning them into realistic, peaceful ones. I changed my acid thoughts to alkaline – every day.

The bolded numbers on the Toxin list came in last, a long litany of lament. Ancestral roots were DNA *memories* of poverty, oppression, prejudice and resulting grief, which affects us subconsciously. They are coded into ideas like 'you must work hard for everything you get; you don't deserve anything special and must feel guilty for having what others don't. No matter how much money you have, why do you fear abandonment, poverty and living alone on the streets? These are ancient ancestral memories, generations of them, built into every cell of our body. We must honour them, accept them then move beyond them into who *we* really are today. We all deserve abundance! And it is readily available to us if we *believe* so.

Coincidentally, around this time, I began writing my family's history for an upcoming family reunion. As I researched and read my parents' family tree notes, I saw it all: the horrendous poverty; alcoholism and violence, the war years; the anger, abuse, prejudice and the defensive bluster dating back to my great-grandparents – on both sides.

Then I dreamt of my Irish Great Grandmother, Margaret Emmaline Syer, who died in 1885. I have never seen a picture of her. I doubt any exists. In my dream, she looked a lot like my sister Beryl in body shape and size – just shorter. Her curly hair appeared more faded red than Beryl's bright strawberry blonde curls. Emma had sparkling green eyes like three of my other siblings (Beryl's are brown). Later, while reading through Dad's memoires, he mentioned she had red hair but nothing about her eyes. He had the grey-blue eyes and dark hair of the Black Irish while his father's were brown. Amongst my seven siblings, we have a blonde, two strawberry blondes, one redhead and three brunettes. Three of us have green eyes, one hazel and three with brown. Mine are actually brown with green flecks. Who knows for sure where the colors came from? At least it gives some validation to my dream.

Great Grandmother Emma showed me why my right hip never stayed in balance with my left. It was always higher, making my left leg longer, cranking my spine out of alignment and causing no end of hip and back problems. She said it came from generations of prejudice the Irish faced. "When we cocked our fist, we cocked our whole right side in challenge and defence. It is now time to release it." I woke up remembering how my Irish father, his brother and one sister all suffered with unbalanced hips. My Chinese herbalist confirmed this, telling me my right hip has poor circulation and I need to massage it regularly.

Emma told me, "Heal the liver and the hips will too." Would you be surprised Louise Hay, in her book, *Heal Your Body*, explains how the liver is the seat of anger and primitive emotions (98:64). Her accompanying affirmation is: "Love and peace and joy are what I know." Whenever I say this to myself, something inside shifts and eases. **My guides tell me the liver is the heart of the soul.** No wonder we must begin our healing journey with the liver's angst. And also why congestion of the liver *causes* cancer!!

Great-Gramma Emma told me her Irish husband from Dublin also carried the grief of prejudice – he more than she because she "just had too much to do". According to Dad's notes, she *was* a very hard worker. Her husband, on the other hand, often took to his bed in a state of deep melancholia. People considered him lazy. I think he suffered a debilitating depression from every cell in his body. The Irish oppression by the English dates back hundreds of years.

Here are my ancestral roots requiring healing from the soul outward. This is about anger too, the hatred the Irish had for the English and vice versa. It serves no purpose to cling to such emotional toxins. I must also reach forward and heal my family, children and grandchildren. I notice my son has similar hip issues. The DNA memories can not continue.

Emma also carried the angst of being judged, criticized and condemned in Ireland as a witch who saw the past and the future (remember her maiden name was Syer as in Seer). In Canada, she was more cautious, only reading the tea leaves of close friends and family though she 'saw' much more. She admitted it hurt her – shining her light under a rock – afraid of condemnation. Here is my DNA's deep seated fear of revealing my psychic gifts to the world.

Through the centuries, I reached back and she forward. I thanked her for the gift she gave me of 'seeing and hearing things'. I honour her by writing about it for the entire world to know.

Toxin # 8: The dilemma of feeding others came from my mother who never let anyone leave our home hungry - a generous quality from her pioneer upbringing. Yet if one piece of chicken was left, she gave it to one of her children regardless of how hungry *she* was. I took it a step further and put *everyone* before me. I treated family, friends and strangers better than myself. This journey, as my guides said on the very first day, is about learning how to love myself, to make myself the priority.

Toxin # 9: Currying favours when none was needed. All my life I bent over backwards to help others, do for others, please others while ignoring the cost to myself, my body, mind, heart and spirit. Though not requested, I went out of my way to do nice things for others. I never realized its cost to myself in resentment, exhaustion and lack of self-esteem when it was neither acknowledged nor reciprocated. I also realize the favours represent my desire to be loved.

Toxin # 18: Masks of Deception was a deeper blow. I trusted people far too much; believing they were all good (better than me). It took me years to look behind their masks and realize some of them weren't! Meanwhile, they had dumped their crap on me, manipulated me, lied to me and used me. I have several people at the top of this list who I must now forgive and stay away from. I felt so poorly about myself; I thought everyone was better than I. How sad. Here is the trap of looking outward for validation and personal value instead of inward where the real truth waited. I need stronger personal boundaries about what I will or will not accept from others. It is also about trusting my inner intuition when I meet people.

Furthermore, I wore my own Mask of Deception, not showing the world who I *really* was either. I have been pushed, shoved and drug, kicking and squealing into 'outing' myself with my spiritual connections and guidance by writing this book. You are full witness to this carnage!

Toxin # 20: Carrying the weight of others is something too many people do. And others will let them! It relieves their burden and responsibility. Worrying about others, trying to help them solve their problems are powerful energy drains. Only as we age do we see the bigger picture of how society duped women into this role, with no thought or care to its long term effects on us. I can not and I *will not* do this anymore. I honour my own needs and allow other people to honour theirs. Part of it is trust; part is faith: trusting people have their own spiritual guides to help them, their own lessons to learn and having faith in their intelligence to make their own choices. They can solve their own problems. In our Aboriginal teachings, we are *not* our brothers' keeper. We can walk beside people, listen, encourage them and tell them stories about how others solved the problem but the choices are theirs, and only theirs, to make. We don't walk in their moccasins; we don't know their hearts so we don't have the right to tell them how to walk their path.

I used to hold Women's Gatherings at my house. We had a smudging ceremony, talking circle, drumming, singing and a feast afterwards, once a month. Women came, talked, vented, cried, laughed and shared their lives in a circle of sisterhood and support. Some stayed, so happy to have found a safe place to share and learn from one another. Others came once and never returned, their faces blank in criticism and judgement of the whole silly idea of Aboriginal teachings.

Now I faced the toxic toll these Gatherings imposed upon me. My psychic friend Sue scolded me, saying I thought I had to help all these women, offering my support and advice too freely. She says they never used my good advice anyway. My home and I were just their sounding board and dumping ground. They drained my energy and left happy, relieved of their burdens. I realize I gave away too much of myself and my energy - something people didn't know how to use anyway. They sensed my spiritual strength and wanted it, instead of garnering their own.

Sue explained how all that negative energy became 'stuck' to my walls like dark energetic glue and it literally made me sick. My home, my beautiful sanctuary, was now loaded with other people's 'stuff', not mine. She recommended I cleanse, clear and balance it with smudges and prayers every day for the next month or more. Talk about a toxic build-up! I never realized such a thing could happen! Yet I have learned our physical environment often mirrors what is happening inside of us.

In and outside the circle, I spent too much time talking to people, trying to convince them of our Aboriginal beliefs, trying to teach them its values, the non-believers especially. Now my guides called me on it – splitting myself in half to please others – a sacrifice unwanted. People have their own beliefs, their own faith. I need to just LET IT BE!

It's time to get real, create relationships from true partnerships, side by side companionships, with people who love me for who I really am.

Never again will I risk my health to please or help anyone. If I sense a potential energy drain on my body or spirit, I quietly and firmly refuse. **What a long hard lesson to realize I don't *need* anyone's approval**. I don't *need* to please anyone. I can say 'No' without guilt, relaxing into deep relief because I choose what is best for me. Now I ask myself, "If I do this for.......will I resent it later?" If so, my answer is "No thanks"! I hold my energy just for me. My beautiful red glowing heart is just for me. The Blue Diamond on my finger is just for me. I share only what I choose and keep the rest, just for me. I give by simply being who I am and the energy just flows down through me and out upon the world, taking nothing from me.

These were tough lessons to build healthy borders. I struggled in the following months, catching myself repeatedly when I fell back into old habits. I learned to not answer every phone call, every doorbell ring, trusting my intuition to tell me whether the caller was sincere in their purpose or just another energy drainer, looking to me to solve their problems, despite my own healing issues.

Honouring myself? How the bell tolled.

27.

Healing is a Supplemental Journey

"Take back into your own hands the responsibility for your health. Regain the power that our Creator fully intended for you – and your loved ones – to have and to live a healthier life."

Dr. David S. Dyer, Cellfood.

My friend, Rose, took me to see Lanette, who channels a group of spirit healers she calls Noah. She opened a health spa after they woke her one morning at 3:00 a.m., insisting the community needed one. She was the first of many soldiers offering alternative therapies I encountered. When I told her I had refused the chemo and radiation, she responded, 'Good for you!' Her mother had healed herself from cancer and spends her life doing inspirational presentations all over the USA. I asked for and found many warriors, as Gabriel promised, who would support me on my healing journey.

Lanette recommended Cellfood, a leading supplement on today's market created by a man whom Einstein called a genius: Everett L. Storey. His 'story' deserves retelling. He used a water-splitting technique causing oxygen to split from hydrogen. In the 1940's the American government asked him for his research which he turned over to them. To his horror, it became the critical component in the atomic bomb. Being a humanitarian, he reversed his formula, determined to find something healing. He created an electromagnetic equation of plant food which released vital oxygen and hydrogen into the bloodstream, strengthened the immune system; removed free radicals (a powerful antioxidant); promoted faster injury recovery; nourished and rebuilt the human body. The result of 49 years of research: Cellfood, which includes 78 trace elements and minerals, 34 enzymes, 17 amino acids, electrolytes and nascent oxygen and hydrogen as by-products.

By then, Storey was dying from exposure to the radiation from his experiments. The Cellfood cured him and he lived a long productive life. His formula is now into the fifth generation of development. You add its clear liquid drops to your water jug and drink it throughout the day. From my research, liquid supplements far outweigh the pill form for consistency, potency and longevity. Cellfood actually *improves* with time. I body tested this stuff and my body leapt towards it!

According to the makers of Cellfood, all forms of illness can be traced to two basic causes – too many toxins in the body and too few nutrients reaching cells surrounded by a cesspool of stagnant fluid. Why wouldn't the sick cells mutate into cancer?! Cellfood addresses both health problems, getting the nutrients in and the toxins out. Not only that, it boosts the oxygen levels in each cell and oxygen is the ultimate detoxifier. Where most detox products only target the liver and colon, Cellfood nourishes and cleans *every* cell in the body! How perfect is that?

In addition, Cellfood helps normalize ph levels – integral to proper detoxification and healing. It assists with energy; boosts the immune system and aids in water absorption at cellular levels, thereby preventing free radical damage.

I sound like an ad for this product but for someone in the middle of any illness or disease, including radiation treatments, Cellfood certainly won't hurt you! This is the *only* supplement I took (besides Thyodine, a kelp extract) for six months after my surgery. I believe it was very instrumental in my own healing process (besides whitening my teeth!). After the six months, I body tested Cellfood and found I no longer needed it. My Naturopath's various tests indicated all my vital minerals, vitamins and electrolytes were back in balance and functioning normally. From time to time, I continue to body test this wonderful product. When my body craves it, I take it once again for a few months.

Lanette also introduced me to the Infra-Red sauna. The first time I stepped into the big cedar cabinet with soft music playing in the background, I felt a powerful sense of well-being. I relaxed unto the seat with a great sigh of peace and contentment. Then I 'heard' "**This is your radiation.**" I thought, 'Twenty-first century version! I'm in!' My thumbs went up in celebration.

My guides cautioned me to take one treatment at a time. Detoxing too fast would weaken my healing body. This was good advice. **Never try several treatments at once. One at a time allows your body to adjust to the changes and if you have a reaction, you know immediately what to stop doing**. I completed the Chinese herbalist's detox then my guides told me to take four Infra-Red saunas, one week apart. In my first sauna, what little perspiration I had looked like white milk. By the fourth sauna, I perspired profusely, pushing out a clear but smelly fluid. Lanette and I cheered because it meant my lymph system was finally moving and cleaning itself nicely.

Infra-Red, a radiant heat, does not warm the air, only your skin. It penetrates to a depth of three to four inches, causing the body to sweat at a temperature of 110 to 220 degrees Fahrenheit. Yet it is so soothing, I barely felt it during the half hour treatment.

Don, the cancer survivor, told me cancer cells are not like normal cells, they cannot survive temperatures over 105° Fahrenheit. In addition, the penetrating heat of the Infra-red sauna kills any parasites in your body (Dr. Regehr Clark will be pleased). Infra-Red saunas dilate (expand) blood vessels, which increase oxygen flow (thus killing cancer cells). Consequently, the saunas boost the immune system and support healing of soft tissue and muscle injuries. It certainly helped my incisions heal very quickly.

My radiation indeed! (Now I get it! My guides called it 'sessional radiation'!) Something had bothered me about the radiation my guides had originally recommended. They called it by a different name than what the cancer hospital staff called it. Now I understood. It *was* a different type! It still makes me flinch how close I came to not recognizing the difference. Besides, Gabriel had also told me they would reduce the radiation treatments because I had worked through so much of my healing already.

I loved these saunas so much I went out and bought a portable one, which was, of course, on sale! It folds up like a suitcase I can take anywhere. According to my research, you can take these saunas daily though I believe in moderation of once or twice a week.

Infra-Red saunas also remove toxins accumulated in the body as a result of metabolic wastes and sluggish elimination. Heat stimulates sweat glands, helping remove toxins like nicotine, alcohol, cholesterol and heavy metals like cadmium, lead, zinc and nickel accumulated in the body. These heavy metals are thus released from the cells into the interstitial fluid (the clear stuff leaking out of any wound) and then into sweat glands. Sweating, therefore, alleviates the toxic stress of your overburdened liver and kidneys dumping toxins into intestines for removal. This is why we are supposed to exercise enough to sweat! Regularly!

Consequently, Infra-Red saunas clear the body lymphatic fluid system. I read several health books recommending this new technology from the Asian countries. These saunas also help arthritis, shoulder pain, bursitis, strains and sprains, spinal cord shock, back pain, scar tissue, fibromyalgia, cholesterol and cellulite (subcutaneous fat where toxins are stored).

Our lymphatic fluid volume is much larger than blood volume: 45 pints of lymph fluid compared to 14 pints of blood. And, according to Dr. Bernard Jensen's *Nutrition Handbook*, it is the "most neglected body function in the healing arts today" (2000:100). He says the lymph system must be kept clean, like a clear flowing stream versus a backed up, brackish, sluggish sewage dump. Boils and pimples indicate a lymphatic system overloaded with toxins. He recommends eliminating all wheat and dairy products because they become "quite pasty in the body and can easily clog the lymph vessels" (00:101) I had pimples on my chest, upper arms and legs for years! Now, as I juice, de-tox and take Cellfood, I notice the pimples come back as soon as I eat wheat or dairy or too much sugar. My lesson and my warning message to you.

Dr. Jensen recommends a very healthy diet of proper minerals, vitamins, vegetables and fruits. Remember John Hopkins Society's recommendations of 80% vegetables and no dairy or wheat? Here is further evidence of their power.

Our twenty-first century bodies are constantly bombarded with toxins from our environment, the food we eat plus the cleaners and chemicals we use every day. Our lymphatic system cannot eliminate them fast enough. Since our lymph system has no heart, only body movement, muscle contractions and gravity keep it moving and carrying nutrients to the cells. Lymph nodes are located along the lymph vessel pathways in the joints, armpits, neck, groin and spine. Dr Jensen says the nodes "filter lymph fluid and remove dangerous impurities such as dead red blood cells, debris-laden white blood cells, chemicals, dyes and cellular debris" (00:98). He uses a rebounder (mini trampoline) and encourages walking, swimming, dancing, hiking, yoga, skin brushing and the slant board for squeezing the lymphatic system and keeping it moving. (00:102).

A year after my surgery, the ionized foot cleanse baths were much clearer, except for chunks of heavy metal and dead red blood cells – the results of my body's final deep cleaning and deeper rebuilding. It took almost eighteen months for my liver to function without aches and pains. It finally felt like a normal size, fitting into my right side comfortably. I no longer feel its presence when I bend over.

The lymphatic drainage system is part of our immune system and plays a major role in the body's defences against infection and disease. Once the lymph ducts become blocked, waste products are not effectively eliminated from our cells and they begin to malfunction. It creates a deadly breeding ground for infection and local decay of the cells. Once major lymph ducts become impaired the whole lymphatic system is compromised, reducing circulation throughout the body. Health deteriorates.

According to Dr. Newman in her book, *Make Your Juicer Your Drug Store*, "Every acute disease is merely a healing crisis, a result of the body struggling to free itself from its load of toxic poisons within. A fever is the body's attempt to burn up the waste." It's hard to believe she wrote this in 1970 and still, *nobody listens!*

Research now links obesity with cancer. Obesity is the body's first defence mechanism against too many toxins. The body knows toxins are not food so it links them with fat cells and stores them to protect the body from their harm. **Cellulite is thus the garbage waste dump for toxins.** I had more than my share of it on my thighs. As I drank the juices, cut out the wheat, sugar and dairy, my body slowly reduced the lumpy cellulite on my legs. It took six or seven months for my thighs to return to normal size and structure.

I cleaned my lymphatic system with the saunas, ionized foot baths, Cellfood and juicing. Around this time, I also discovered Gogi berries, or Chinese Wolf berries. They are like magical little dried berries that support the liver and kidneys while they detoxify the body. My guides had me start with five dried berries, which I soaked overnight and blended into my morning juice. They bumped them up to seven for a few months then brought them back to five, which Cliff and I still take today. I also continued to exercise and stretch as much as I could.

For thousands of years, my Aboriginal ancestors practiced wholistic healing in sweat lodges. A self induced fever stimulates the immune system and kills bacteria, parasites and viruses. Negative thoughts and emotions were released through prayers, singing and crying in the darkness of the sweat lodge where no light penetrates. With sweat pouring down our bodies, we waited quietly for the brush of a feather or fur against our bodies and listened for the cries of our Spirit totems who visited us 'In the Silence' of the sweatlodge, the symbol of Mother Earth's womb. Coming out of a sweat lodge, I always felt exhausted yet peaceful, amazed and connected as I lay upon Mother Earth to cool my steaming body. My skin felt incredibly soft and clean for days afterwards. Unfortunately, I never attended a sweat lodge ceremony during the five years prior to my diagnosis. Perhaps I could have prevented the cancer.

Now I faced stressful days, as week after week I fought to stay true to my beliefs, bucking the medical system, finding my own cures and wondering if I was doing the right thing. Once the oncologist found out I refused both chemo and radiation, he called me every day for a week straight. He *really* irritated me. Luckily I have 'Call display' on my phone. I sat and listened to it ring thinking, "There is nothing you can say that I want to hear." His messages became more and more abrupt until he literally talked through his teeth in fury. I ignored them all. Still, they pushed my stress to another level.

He eventually sent me a letter saying I was discharged from the cancer hospital's care and "what a pleasure it had been serving me".

Right. My chart probably reads, 'Difficult, stubborn, argumentative and unwilling to listen to sound medical advice.' In hind sight, I realize Spirit sent me the perfect oncologist who made me so mad I dug in my heels even more. If it had been a gentler doctor, he might have persuaded me to try the treatments despite my inner misgivings.

Then the volunteer from the Women's Breast Cancer Support Group called. Throughout my preliminary tests and surgery, she was very supportive and chatty. When she asked how I was feeling and how my treatments were going, I told her I chose alternative therapies. Her voice totally changed.

"Well" she said coldly, "we won't be following your progress." And she hung up. I never heard from her or the support group again.

I was on my own.

Not that I cared. I had all the help I needed. I continued to read and research everything I could get my hands on about cancer and natural healing. And the good information kept coming.

I asked my guides for stress-reducing techniques. I had just read how chronic stress creates the same symptoms and conditions of a highly acidic disease: lowering bone density; reducing muscle tissue with blood sugar fluctuations; suppressing the immune system and causing obesity. Oh joy!

They gave me the following information – like ideas popping into my head. The brackets are my own thoughts:

1. Compartmentalize – You can only do so much today, do that and it is enough. Let tomorrow take care of itself.

2. Yoga stretches – (deep breathing oxygenates the body, relaxing the muscles and stimulating the lymphatic system)

3. Talk about your feelings – admitting them out loud releases them. (In a public speaking class I took years ago, a stand-up comedian taught me, if you are nervous, admit it to your audience and the fear goes away. It works for me every time)

4. Take warm mineral baths to soothe you, hot as you can stand them, for at least half an hour. (I did this, burning sea salt candles and incense).

5. Take long walks of fresh air and sunshine. They are God's and Mother Earth's healing remedies. (Gentle exercise keeps everything moving and healing).

6. Add the Cellfood to your water jug and drink it all day (I use a 32 oz. coloured sports bottle called Nalgene, one of the few plastics which does not bleed the plastic chemicals back into the water. The Cellfood hydrates, nourishes and detoxifies, bumping up my immune system in the process.)

7. Juicing organic foods is your daily, bread & butter healing.

When I looked at this list, I realized it truly is physical, mental, emotional and spiritual healing advice. How cool!

I phoned my sister-in-law, Elaine and admitted my gut-eating fear and endless doubts. She understood totally. I face tough, life-threatening decisions and they don't come easy! But the more I talked, the more I *knew* I made the right choice. I *knew* this gentle, loving nurturing was the right way to heal myself and I continued to honour it.

She said, "You are already healing yourself. Look at all the help you are given. The synchronicity of it is breathtaking!"

And I *do* have so much help. Each day I get up and learn one more step, one more way to love myself and heal my body.

The milestones are there: I flew through my surgery and incision healing. My dry skin is softer, moisturized and clearing. My hair is soft and curling. I have so much energy. People tell me I actually glow with health. I think about the women who were in the hospital with me and wonder how their health is. If it is about quality of life, I have it in spades!

28.

Dragons and Whales

"If we can have faith and trust in Creator's greater plan then we can begin the process of healing our wounds and gently, over time, expose our true selves to others."

Linda Ewashina, *Spirit of the Wheel Cards*

Is there a connection between the Infra-Red saunas (Eastern technology) and the red Dragon energy from the East? When I refused radiation, I lost the Dragon Skin tribal initiation. With some trepidation, I wondered how Xi would react. I asked Elia, my red dragon to come. She exploded into view, her red cape flying. Enveloping me in a hug, she cried, "Oh, you have been through so much!" She wrapped me in her loving cloak and took me to Xi, her mate. He too hugged me and told me he loves me. He is not angry; he awaited my choice, willing to help me whatever way I chose to heal. He wrapped me in his cloak and I fled into magical dreams.

I dreamt I was in a school, learning again. I ran into an old school chum from my childhood I have not seen in thirty years. We played, danced and laughed. He lifted me up so I could touch the ceiling with an icicle. Why? I don't know! We did it because we could – Life is Because We Can! In retrospect I wonder if this ceiling represents the roof of our shallow beliefs about Spirit guidance and opportunities. Perhaps it needs to be touched with an icicle, a magical wand, playfully explored and expanded – Because We Can.

When I awoke, I asked Xi for his ideas on how to heal from cancer and its aftermath. He said:

"Spiritually: We know cancer is a dis-ease of the Soul. It is a disconnection of God from your spirit and soul. Reconnection through faith, prayer, hope, meditation and loving yourself are key. (I wonder if this is another symbol of the purse, the silver connection and the growing red 'human' heart I saw so many months ago).

"Emotionally, too many emotions have nowhere to go, so they get caught in the body, creating tension, drama and pain. Blow them out the lotus of your head. Imagine a smoke stack and blow the energy hard and wild as you can. We'll waft it away. We have that ability."

I imagined a giant chimney blowing thick grey-white smoke. He swatted it away like a big old bug. We laughed together.

He went on, "Imagine the energy of Mother Earth and her daughters coming up through your legs into your body, mixing with the warm loving energy of your heart and God's energy of light and love coming down. Swirl them together and feel the joy and healing energy dancing within you. Tamoxifen has nothing on this loving stuff!"

"Mentally, learn new ways to heal; talk about it, think about it and incorporate it into your life, but gently, gently with great loving Soul. Be Sacred and Silly – every day. Irreverent and Reverent, this is the balance of God's mental health.

"Physically, heal your body with good food and health practices. Fresh air, oxygen therapies like walks and exercise will relieve the tension and make you loose, warm and joyful.

"Most of all surround yourself with joy: joyful people, joyful pastimes, joyful measures of viewing the world and sharing your wisdom with others. Think to the greater picture and community. You are a part of the healing which must take place, it is about joy, life, giving, serving, doing, being and loving. As you are, so mote it be!"

Still reeling, I asked, "Why did they take six of my lymph nodes?"

He smiled, "A reminder to take care of yourself. You must stick with the 80% vegetarian diet and expand it. The energies coming in will demand this higher vibration of live food. The meat is okay but reduce it."

He tilted his dragon man face, "Do you not see how much clearer and easier it is for you to communicate with us now?"

Surprised, I realized how clearly I could see him, right down to the individual scales on his face. Our conversation seemed so light and easy as if I conversed with one of my human friends. Who was I to complain when I loved every moment of our time together.

I could not ask his thoughts on my refusal of the cancer treatments. I just couldn't. He seemed to be okay with where I was and I was too cowardly to ask why. I hugged him and left. I woke up in awe of the powerful message I had just received.

The next night, I dreamt of my family and friends, getting well, learning from my mistakes and eating more vegetables and fruit, healing themselves in the process. So too shall they adjust to the new energies and survive along with me.

In the dream we were at a picnic near the ocean. Suddenly in the gloom of dark grey and blue skies, I saw a giant helicopter air-lifting a whale by its tail. The whale wriggled, spouting water in all directions as it spun in the overcast skies before drifting forward into full sunshine. He had a mystical air about him, each drop of water magnified, like a Disney movie of water droplets. He wasn't so much real as mythical, magical and symbolic. And most of all – magnificently alive! He was a killer whale, black and white and gorgeous. Imagine, a whale by the tail (tale) in the gloom, coming out to full colour sunshine.

When I awoke, I looked up the symbolism of whale in *Animal Speak*. It is about insulating myself and using my creative energies more conservatively through an ancient knowledge of breath. Whale brings greater reasoning capabilities and creative thinking. It is about going deep within myself. The creativity I awaken can resurrect my life, if I bring it out and apply it. Rather than keeping everything inside, I must bring it out, showing the magnificence and power of my creativity. I am not to mimic what others do but build upon them in new, dynamic ways. I must apply my intuition to old processes and life formulas, imbuing them with power and magic. Whale creativity awakens great depths of inspiration, adding colour and lights to my outer life and making it wondrous.

Oh my Goodness! Instead of mimicking the medical profession's options, I applied old intuitive processes and ancient wisdom formulas, allowing Spirit to infuse them with renewed power and magic! For months after surgery, I stayed home, healing, reading, researching and writing, lost in a world that nurtured me peacefully and wisely. Now as I write this, sharing my intuition, dreams, guides and messengers, their truth amazes me. I received great depths of inspiration, like the dragon advice, adding colour and lights to my outer life, hopefully to yours too, making it wondrous indeed.

I share these dreams hoping you too can touch the wonder of their messages; the magnificence of Spirit's World, so willing to forgive us, love us and teach us how to bring the magic back into our lives. I hope it is so for you. May you find whales in your dreams to help bring out the creative, intuitive, magnificent sides of your soul. May you find colour, light and magic all around you, as I do, every day.

29.

Body Tour

"The noble soul has reverence for itself."
Friedrich Nietzsche, *Beyond Good and Evil*.

Gabriel introduced me to my new Spirit Guide, called Shu (not her full name). Gabriel says I am well on my way to healing and no longer need her care. I humbly thanked her for her wisdom and patience with me and my tantrums. I am amazed at how clearly I can 'hear' and 'see' Shu. She's a fair, chunky lady dressed in a sari-type long billowing dress, which is sometimes turquoise, sometimes pink. Shu took me on a whole new journey.

I had just read in Susan Weed's book about asking the Wise Woman within you to give you a tour of your inner body. I decided to play with this – what did I have to lose? With all the incredible stress, worry and confusion these past months, my sanity was overrated anyway. I just wanted to escape, play a while. I went into a quiet meditation and asked Shu to accompany me on an inner tour of my body. We shrank down to a few inches height (in meditation anyway) and away we went, down through my throat, into my stomach and intestinal area. My intestines are doing well, flowing smoothly; my stomach lining is pink and healthy on my alkaline diet. I suffered ulcers for years when I was in my thirties but now I 'saw' little white patches on my stomach wall – scars I suppose.

We sat on my liver. Shu said it was too dense to enter yet but it is cleansing and healing slowly. I found myself gently rubbing its purple/brown exterior. I saw thick, white ugly veins running all over its surface. They looked clogged, sluggish, like lumpy varicose veins. I asked her if there was anything I could do to help.

She replied, "Drink lots of water. The detox from the Chinese herbalist is pumping major toxins from your body into your liver and intestines. You need to drink lots of water to flush them away. Your liver will need some DNA reconstruction but not yet."

I had no idea what she meant but I would learn in the months ahead.

I asked her, like Susan Weed suggested, to take me to the happiest cells in my body. Shu took me to my brain cells, saying they were learning and growing, challenged by all the new information pouring in from my reading and research. They called to me, "Yo! Hi! How ya doin'?" in deep male voices (I have a male brain? Who knew? Maybe it's the logic thing again.)

We checked out my heart, warm, radiant and growing in delight and compassion – another happy organ.

Then we went to my right breast. I saw the fluid and particles, orange-pink and vibrant, floating around me. So cool! Then we found a small blackened area, burned and charred, opposite the same area on my right breast where the tumour had been on my left breast. Shu explained this was another cancer spot 'they' burned out. I have no idea who did it (Gabriel? the dragons?). It shocked me because nothing showed up on any of my medical tests! She also pointed to the new skin, now pink and rebuilding with all the juicing and nurturing I am giving my body.

Then we moved to my poor damaged left breast. This one has a knife slash through it but I'm surprised how white, bright and clear the area is. She smiled, "It's all the white light you brought in to heal it!" And it *is* healing, cleanly, clearly and sweetly – all healthy pink tissues, not a cancer cell around! I kissed the tissue and patted it gently.

We moved to my arm pit area where the six lymph nodes were removed. I'm trying not to get angry but I remember Dr. Day saying on her DVD how silly it was to remove these lymphatic cleaners. She argued, "If you have an infection in your foot and the lymph glands are swollen in your groin from removing the infection, why would you cut them out? They are doing their job! If there are cancer cells in these lymph nodes, it means they are doing their job!"

Now I see another 'blackened' spot where other cancer cells were 'burned' out. Shu says, "This is a sad story. The nodes are gone that could have healed and cleansed the area. You will always live with some swelling here but exercise, movement and massage will keep it healthy."

We went higher to my shoulder where I felt some pain and a worrisome burning sensation. She explained this area is still carrying some excess acidic fluid from the tumour site, which like all tumours, has an acidic environment. Because my lost lymph nodes can not remove the fluid, it builds and drains off slowly. She claims the alkaline diet will slowly alleviate this problem. Right now, the detox is building more acid around this area but drinking lots of water will help flush it away.

Since the muscles from my shoulder to my breast were cut, some have retracted, the ends often laying in the acidic fluid, hence the burning sensation. Other severed muscles inside my breast also shrank to the bottom of my breast, leaving a bumpy, lumpy texture of scar tissue as the months wore on. A breast is in constant motion so with my heavier breast I ended up with lots and lots of scar tissue. Not a pretty sight but I have learned to love it and live with it all. At least I still have my breast.

Overall, according to Shu, I am doing fine, healed really - just like Gabriel promised! I came out of the meditation feeling so much better and more relaxed. I feared the burning sensation above my breast incision was growing cancer cells. Not so! What I saw truly made sense. I tried different positions and movements which soon alleviated the burning pain completely. I am just fine and slowly returning to health.

Shu went on, "You need quiet healing time for the next month or so to recover from the trauma of the past four months. It is the mind, heart, spirit and physical healing work you must write about."

I can 'see' her puckish face with its short, wavy blonde hair in my mind as she smiles in mischief, "I'm the Queen of Publishing so we'll get this book published too!'

I feel excited now and wonder how much of my own story I will add to this book.

"All of it!" she instantly replies and I cringe uneasily.

Then I dreamt I was a mid-wife to a little baby girl, whose old/young wizened face looked exactly like mine. The books I wrote in the past always showed up symbolically in my dreams as 'babies' that I love and nurture to adulthood (finished and published). Yet with this new book, my latest 'baby, I merely assisted its 'birthing' from the Spirit World. It looks like me but does not *belong* to me. I am the midwife of something much greater, far more wonderful. Our Aboriginal Elders say we are merely hollow tubes for Creator's messages coming down through us. Such images comfort me.

30.

Surrender unto Grace

"Only when we let go, surrender into the infinite, can a thought-free awareness called 'Grace' be revealed".

Albert Einstein

My sister-in-law, Elaine, sent me Dannion Brinkley's book, *Saved by the Light*. He was struck by lightening, died and was left with a tag on his toe near an elevator to the morgue. When an orderly began moving the gurney Dannion suddenly groaned, terrifying the poor man. Brinkley's experience of the Spirit World plus his painful healing journey is an awesome read. He writes how we must breathe deeply because the Spirit World transmits information to us through our breath. I want to laugh out loud at all the oxygen therapies and spirit messages I received about breathing deep. I'm beginning to see how all of us are connected, united in something much bigger than we can ever dream. Connecting to it brings us unprecedented grace and peace.

How we perceive others is how we perceive ourselves. My Dad used to say, "Treat people as if every day was Sunday." So we treat others with the same respect we treat ourselves. It's the old 'Love they neighbour as thyself' adage yet Brinkley adds another dimension to it when he says the Ten Commandments are not God's orders, but his *rules* for happy living.

According to *A Course in Miracles* and other esoteric texts, humans incarnated and Earth was formed the moment we decided to separate from God because we did not trust His wisdom. We decided to run away and build our own homes where we could be completely in charge. Yeah. And step forth the Ego!

If this Spirit Energy surrounds us, this dimension I am always struggling to tap into and understand because its infinite wisdom helped me so much on this journey, then can not God's will and ours be one? Why fight it? We are part of the Whole Energy – call it Universal

Consciousness, call it Source, call it Higher Power, whatever – we are never truly separated from it. Aboriginal people call it the Great Mystery, where all living things dwell.

I asked my guides to explain the difference between soul and spirit. They said Soul is a part of us connected to Universal Consciousness, a part never touched by any of life's dramas. It observes, guides and loves, yet is never truly Earth bound. It's the third eye in our heads, calm, solid and ever serene. Soul is our inner 'seeing', 'hearing', 'sensing' and 'knowing' of truth, the sixth sense we all have. It's like 'The Watcher' of our entire life which knows all, sees all and remembers all, even our past lives. It's the real Blue Diamond! Blue being the intermediary sky colour between God and Earth – the place where all humans and life on Earth exists.

Spirit is the "I am" of personal, individual beliefs, values, wishes and dreams. It is the creative, funny, playful, mischievous, magical, romantic lover of sports, arts, music and people or whatever we feel passionate about. Our spirit is our personality. We may fall down crying or come out swinging. It is the truly human part which makes each one of us unique. Spirit is the Earth bound human connection to our Otherworldly soul.

So illness, my guides say, is a dis-ease created when connection between spirit and soul is weak. We cannot listen, nor heed what our soul tells us. We don't believe and we don't trust our soul's inner voice of wisdom. We seek answers outside ourselves, from others *who will never know us like our soul does.*

Like my guides told me at the beginning of my diagnosis, cancer is a dis-ease of the soul and it must be healed from the soul outward: physically, mentally, emotionally and *spiritually.* Until we reconnect, until we recognize this soul-spiritual connection, all the pills in the world will not heal us. The dis-ease will return until we finally get it right. We must find our inner wisdom once again because it always tells the truth about ourselves.

Aboriginal people are right when they say all we need to heal is within us – the inner physician of wisdom. All answers dwell within our soul, our universally connected soul. It remains our choice to listen...or not.

Sacred Tree, a powerful Aboriginal teaching book, created by the University of Lethbridge's Four Worlds Development, explains our choice:

> "The doorway through which all must pass if they wish to become more or different than they are now is the doorway of will (volition). A person must decide to take the journey. The path has infinite patience. It will always be there for those who decide to travel it" (85:30).

We seek so many answers outside our self, asking every man and his dog for their advice. We do so many things, good and bad, so others will love us. It makes us human. But now in this crisis of illness, we must turn all our love upon ourselves and learn, if we haven't already, how to like and yes, love ourselves.

That night I had a wonderful dream:

I was at an airport, walking through a turnstile, my thoughts busy with my next flight connection to meet Mom and Dad. She passed away in 1996, my Dad in 2001.

Suddenly, I hear, "Esther!" and Mom stands before me. She looks younger than I remember. Her once short grey hair is dark auburn again, curling around her face. She wears a dusty rose winter coat in some soft, silky smooth fabric. Her hood has a brown fur fringe. Dad sits nearby at a small cafeteria table.

I rush to her and hug her in relief. She is, always has been, about nine inches shorter than me. I hold her close, feeling her hood's fabric and fur tickle my nose and mouth. She feels solid, warm and comforting. My Mom! I am so glad to see her, to know I don't have to go anywhere to be with her and Dad.

Another dark haired woman on my left watches us. "We can never get rid of cancer." She looks like the Earth Cancer Spirit I talked to so long ago. I immediately dislike her.

I freeze, staring at her, "You mean it just comes back in another form?"

"Not necessarily," she frowns and I'm pulled away and awakened, my heart pounding in fright. I still have so much fear of the cancer returning.

I want answers and I call for Shu. She reminds me we all have cancer cells in our body. Since cancer is a dis-ease of the soul and we are always growing and changing, we must remain diligent about our health.

It calms me and I fall asleep to dream of a huge glass display case on a wall. The glass door slides open and I see on display a *silver* (truth and purity) coated photo album, huge and thick. A voice behind me says, "This is your future so you mustn't get too close." The album opens on its own to reveal pictures of bright blue skies, green sparkling grass and groups of friends and family, with me, laughing and hugging in the sunshine. The voice continues, "See the earth, you are still here; see all your laughing times ahead. You will get to see your babies grow up.

And when you are the ripe old age of ninety-two, you'll look back on these pictures and say, 'Yeah, those were the days'.

The same voice encouraged me, "Continue to juice for the rest of your life, take your supplements, exercise every day, breathe in, continue your Attitude of Gratitude, your acts of benevolence, write and be joyful and you will be okay."

I awoke excited and awed. I have always called my sweet grandchildren 'My babies'. I also dream of my books as babies so here, it could mean either or both. Best of all, I now *know* I will be okay. I *will* survive this and live a full and happy, busy life. It is what I came here to do and I *will* do it. I *choose* to, not out of duty, but out of joy and abundance and truth. May God be with me always – and he is – because I am a part of him, as we all are. There is no place in the Universe we can escape him. Always he has our best interests at heart. Our work, our grace, is to trust this. We didn't do so great going it alone!

"What you want, wants you."
Gary Quinn, *May the Angels Be With You*, (01:96)

I met a young teenage girl that day. At eighteen, she tells me she is in love with words, knows she has a gift to write and gave me one of her poems. I encouraged her to write though she complained she never finishes her pieces. They have great beginnings but peter out. I told her to write them and save them anyway. As she grows and learns, she can always come back and finish them the way she wants. She said, "I know I can not write to please anyone. I just write the truth and the truth is never beautiful, but beauty is the truth."

I felt so grateful to be there for her, encouraging and teaching her. I am so very, *very* glad to be alive!

31.

To Go Boldly...

"No amount of failure can move God's hand of affection away from me....To live boldly for that kind of love is the least I can do."

Ekhart Tolle, *A New Earth*

I asked about the role of guides and messengers. Angels are sentient beings who agreed to help. The dragons are interplanetary helpers. My spirit guides are here to help me – so many because I need all their messages to write the truth. Archangels like Gabriel, Michael and Rafael intervene only when necessary, to serve and protect, guide and heal, then they are gone. Gabriel was there for me as I healed, then she turned me over to Shu whom I now hear loud and clear. She is funny, bright, sassy and determined. I like that. Now my guides really cranked the information. Sit down for this chapter!

I watched a video on Esther Hicks who channels a group of sentient beings she calls Abraham. She talked about choice between Upstream (against the flow) or Downstream (with the flow) thoughts. Something moved inside me when she said if you are still talking about something someone did to you twenty years ago, or last month, or last week, you're fighting the flow. You haven't moved into the flow of release and RELIEF. It is a relief when we simply let go, forgive, release and move on down the river!

She suggested we think of what we desire and move downstream towards it. (The past is always Upstream). Rather than focus on what we don't have (then you will always not have it), focus on what we want: "I want it. I get it: I want it! I get it!"

Belief and trust are incredible. Doubt is horrible. Pretty clear message!

Several months after surgery, my guides woke me up at 4:30 again to say:

"We couldn't give you the antidote for cancer right away, during the surgery. We had to wait a while for you to recover."

"And what's the antidote?" I held my breath.

"Love." They replied and sang the old Beatles song:

"All you need is love,
All you really need is love,
La ta da ta da!"

Oh my God! I walked around all day in shock, trying to deny it was so easy; questioning everything, trying to find the loop holes in such a simple answer. By the end of the day, I conceded defeat.

Of course! It *is* about loving yourself, healing all four areas of yourself – physical, emotional, mental and spiritual. When you love yourself, you nurture yourself, forgiving, releasing and becoming all you can be. The superficial lies society dumps upon us fall away, and you become who you really are. When you see your true worth, understand and love yourself, you are home. You are the epitome of love in all areas – ready for the new millennium of harmony when the Hopi prophecy is fulfilled.

Got a lump in your throat, your gut, over your heart, in your unforgiving knees? Boldly heal it with love. And the medical profession wants to cut, poison and burn it out! Oh. My. God!

Cancer is a dis-ease of the soul. Ease its causes by nurturing your soul all four ways and Ta Da! All you need is love.

If you never learn to nurture and love yourself; if you never take this wake-up call to address all your old wounds or whatever is 'eating' you; you will never truly heal the cancer or whatever illness you have. It could come back, stronger than ever. So the time is now to think this through and love yourself totally.

Wounded people raise wounded children. How many future generations of your family are you willing to waste? Wounded people dump their wounds upon their children, spouses, friends and community. They are useless to society's harmony until they face the King Kong in their backyard and reduce him to a pet monkey. He may never go away but he becomes a harmless pet needing kindness, care, attention to health.

Yes, you can have the cancer cut out, poisoned out, burned out and take pills forever to prevent its return. But until you address the <u>cause</u> of the cancer, or any dis-ease, are you truly healed?.

What causes something will also heal it. Do your homework; do your nurturing; step up to the plate and bat a home run for yourself, your family and your community.

Make yourself the number one priority and keep it so! This was my toughest lesson on this Blue Diamond journey. When I nurtured and nourished myself in every way possible, I found an inner sanctuary – my home – filled with harmony and peace.

When I learned to stay in that sanctuary, throughout the day, what I gave out to those around me changed too. I gave out peace, joy, excitement and loving energy. It felt like it came down through me and left in the same manner, taking nothing of my energy with it. I felt connected to an unlimited Source of loving, nurturing energy, which never depleted, weakened or compromised my own energy. In this space, I never 'burned myself out'. I carried nobody's burdens. I simply loved them as they were and encouraged them to think it through to find their own answers. We give away too much of our own energy instead of letting the power of something far greater, far more truthful, flow down through our soul and out to others. I believe this was the toxic waste my guides had called me on: carrying the weight of others, trying to do too much for others, instead of *trusting* they have the same guidance, inner wisdom and truth we are connected to from our very souls. Is it not better to teach others how to LISTEN inside themselves for their own truth?

This energy coming through me now is different, easy, flowing out of me in never-ending waves of happiness - comfortable and genuine. By clearing away the crap of who we thought we were, we uncover the Blue Diamond of our beautiful soul. When we clear away our inner junk and get our ego out of the way, the truth simply flows through us and out in wonderful harmonious grace. It touches everyone around us. We truly become one with the Universe. Who would have guessed love is so easy.

32.

Listening for Truth

"It's possible, with a little time and effort, to develop one's own psychic ability to such a degree that an exciting and stimulating new world begins to unfold. As it does so, one's spiritual awareness deepens and life takes on new dimensions. This has happened to me. It is why I am writing this book."

Ruth Montgomery, *A Search for the Truth, 1966*

What I'm writing about is not breaking news. I think the world is just in a better place to LISTEN! Are you wondering how to find your truth in all this stuff I've been spouting? I've urged you to question while keeping an open mind. As you read, think about what you are reading. Most of all trust your Innate Inner Wisdom. It is never wrong about what is best for you and your body. Nobody can write a book that pleases everyone. We are all too unique with our individual thoughts, upbringing, beliefs and lifestyles. Keep what resonates as truth with you, what you *know* deep in your gut is true and let the rest fall away.

Jamie Sams, in her West Shield teachings of her *Sacred Path Cards* offers three paths to finding the truth. The first, as I have already discussed, is about entering the stillness of our Sacred Space through meditation or just going somewhere quiet where you can think uninterrupted. Be willing to receive the answers made available to us through the experience of daily life. Trust they are for your highest good. I have given you many examples of how this works.

The second path is to digest the answers, question them and learn to *feel* which ones apply, which ones resonate with something deep within you. Eliminate those you *know* don't feel right. While 'Looking Within', accept only ideas most nurturing to you. Integrate this wisdom; make it your own truth because it *feels* right to do so. What you release may be true just not *your* truth.

The third path is to take your digested ideas and form a plan to reach your goals, desires and dreams (90:104). Goals based on your personal truth and desires will be approached with joy. They are yours! Not goals others expect of us. When other opinions mix with our doubts and fears, they block us from our potential, limiting us when we forget to enter the Silence and digest the questions so our personal answers can emerge. When someone criticizes what I do, I remember theirs is the opinion of one and I honour them. Who said I had to agree?

Sams continues with a spine tingling message for me about bear medicine. Bear asks me to look at my present goals and think about how they affect my future. Are they from my inner knowing? If not, I need to go back to the Silence and begin again. Bear is from the West Shield, the West direction on the Medicine wheel, the place of hibernation, going within to think things through. If I am afraid of the unknown, it may be time to clear away the fear.

I meditated, back in my inner sanctuary. One of my favourite Elder Wise Woman guides joined me, saying, "How are you feeling?"

I asked, "How should I be feeling?"

"Oh," she smiled breezily, her long white hair swinging gently, "You are fine physically but I wondered how you were doing emotionally?"

I sighed, "I'm getting more relaxed as the memory of the past few months fade slowly."

She nodded, "It was traumatic and you need the time to heal."

I addressed the nagging fear inside me, "Did I make the right decision?"

"For you, yes. Now that you've made your choice and stand firm behind it, we can tell you the rest. The chemo cells would have been endless."

I gazed at her in horror, "Chemo cells? You mean the cancer cells would have mutated from the chemotherapy?" (Later I would find this same side effect on an internet website. The cancer hospital certainly never mentioned it).

She nodded, "They would have never stopped developing and you would have been constantly sick from the side effects."

I *knew* this, especially for my sick liver. "And if I had chosen radiation?"

She replied, "The radiation would have burned the cells out but damaged your breast, heart and lungs. Worse, it would have broken your spirit in a way that you could not have recovered from."

I am weak with shock but it *feels* like the truth. "Maybe losing faith in my guides because I was so sick?"

"Yes."

I had to think about this. Yet I have met women who seem fully recovered from chemo and radiation. I don't know. I wish I could meet more women who have survived. The Breast Cancer support group is totally lost to me. I truly am on my own.

Still, I felt rested. I swam for forty minutes and did two rounds in the steam room, sweating out more toxins. That night my incision hurt, burning from all the exercise I'd given it. The pain kept me awake.

I decided to call in some outside help to soothe me. Using Xi's advice, I focused on Mother Earth energy. She always gives me strength. I pulled her blue energy up through my body, visualizing a lotus flower on the top of my head opening and letting her energy flow out. I then pulled the white light of Creator's energy down, letting the two mix and dance until it flowed out my feet. This beautiful swirling energy put me to sleep in no time....

The next morning, I returned to Jamie Sams' *Sacred Path Cards*. They are chock full of ancient teachings and always have some message I need. I pulled the 'Standing People' card (p.69), the Tree people in our teachings. The message was about roots, about nurturing ourselves through connections to the Earth in order to give freely without exhaustion. The root of the self is where strength is gathered and it should be firmly planted in the soil of our Mother Planet. What a perfect parallel about my energy sources and how to nurture myself and others.

33.

Meeting Marsha

"The spiritual realm is not a realm in which all our troubles are dissolved into some blinding light. The true path to realization is learning to manifest the spiritual within the physical."

Ted Andrews, Animal Speak (04:169)

I dreamt an old Earth Mother Spirit rose up like a small rounded mountain from the dark earth. With her back towards me, I stared at her black kinky hair, partially pulled into a topknot cut bluntly across the back in a short bob. The rest of her hair, coarse and wiry, flowed freely around her shoulders. She wore a long dark dress and warm cape. My guides introduced us, saying, "This is Marsha (apt name?). She doesn't talk to just anyone."

When I wrote my book, *When We Still Laughed,* I dreamt of another Earth Mother Spirit called Mud Woman. I incorporated her into the dreams of the book's main characters, Broken Arrow and the Irishman, Mac. For comparison, here is my description of her: "Out of the swamp she rose: her head a mud-woven hummock; her eyes, two golden oak leaves blazing with light; her hands, gnarled roots of ancient trees and her skirt, a drifting sea of dried grass" (02:316). She, like Marsha, smelled of warm, moist earth.

When Marsha turned around, her Polynesian features looked like images of old wise women I have seen in pictures. She spoke in a deep, hoarse, resonating voice, "Give me your hands child."

When I did, she began to 'read' them, "Ah, you are healing nicely, warm and secure in your passage through time." She touched my palm with long crooked fingers, brown and gnarled like tree roots.

"You are full of sunshine!" she declared, "and that is a good thing! You will be well soon and all is well." She smiled gently. Her Wise Woman face left me weak in awe.

She sat and told me an old Earth Mother story. I fell asleep and woke at dawn, rested and peaceful. BUT I CAN NOT REMEMBER THE STORY! It is gone like a whisper in the wind. My guides say it was a story just for me and not to be written down. I hope my soul remembers it.

Marsha would return another night and this time, I wrote down what she said:

Rules of the Game of Life

1. Stick to it – heal yourself first, then you can help others. You are healing nicely and have healed the cancer. Now you need to heal from the trauma of the cancer, surgery, facing your own mortality and reversing the toxic build-up.

2. Be a class act – walk your talk, do as you are told and tell others the same.

3. Go out on the town – celebrate, be happy and joyous in the aftermath of these past months.

4. Get a grin and keep it – always!

5. Care must be taken to always be who you really are. Worry not what others think. Care only for yourself and what you think.

6. Blessings be upon you and also upon others.

7. Share the Wealth of your wisdom and knowledge on this journey through your stories, verbally with others and of course, your book.

8. Journey to the four corners of the Earth and tell your story for all to hear. We will help you on your journey.

9. Be wise, be calm, be careful always with your health and you will live to be 92.

10. Caution must be taken to always be who you are – a light worker of extraordinary wisdom, kindness, thoughtfulness and joy.

Walk in wisdom.
Dare the impossible. Share the Dream of Wisdom, Kindness and Compassion.
You are who you are!"

Earth wisdom indeed. As I type this into my computer, I am amazed at Marsha's basic truths. She summarized my struggles with such eloquence it humbles me. Can you see the stunning synchronicity between my thoughts, choices and actions and what the Spirit World teaches me? But travel the world? Is *this* my destiny? It wasn't anything I considered before. For now, detoxing work takes precedence.

34.

Detoxing

"We have to understand the body works according to natural law, and, in the reversal process, as the body cleanses itself we find we go back over the same course the disease followed as it developed."

Dr. Bernard Jensen, *Guide to Diet and Detoxification*, (00:47)

According to Dr. Jensen, an internationally acclaimed nutritionalist who has practiced natural healing therapies for more than seventy years, "...if we suppress natural elimination processes, driving toxic material into the body or causing it to be retained, eventually chronic disease will develop" (00:46). To reverse this process, we must detoxify our body, "giving it a rest, taking in more liquids and draining off the catarrh (excessive mucous secretions), toxic materials and accumulations by bringing them to the 'running stage' of cleansing" (00:46). Catarrh is a Greek word meaning to 'flow down' – which is what our bodies do to cleanse our insides. We actually heal from the head downwards, one section at a time. From dry constipation, our goal is to move to smooth, free flowing BMs (nurse lingo for bowel movements). Detoxing is a process of learning, experimenting, adjusting and moving into a healthier lifestyle. It may take up to two years or more to complete. The good news: you can continue with your daily life, just rest more and drink more water.

Why detoxify? The Chinese believe we should clean the interior of our bodies just like we do the outside. All forms of illness can be traced to two causes: too many toxins in the body and/ or too few nutrients reaching the cells. Both weaken our immune system which normally kicks out any bacteria, virus, fungus or cancer cells. Stick out your tongue in a mirror. According to Dr. Jensen, if it is coated (white), it's a sure sign that you are "loaded to the gills with toxic materials. It means the liver is toxic and the bowel is not eliminating properly" (00:48).

Dr. Christine Horner, F.A.C.S is a surgeon who grew tired of cutting tumours out of women's breasts. When her mother died of breast cancer, the doctor vowed her life would not be in vain.

She did her own research, wrote a book, *Waking the Warrior Goddess,* and has a website worth looking into: <u>www.healthy.net.</u> It contains in-depth information regarding many issues about cancer.

From a reflexologist chart I found the following symptoms of toxic indication (author unknown):

1. Small/large intestine: pustules [on the skin], redness, irritations, bloating, acne, heavy creases – caused by constipation or slow digestion /sluggish elimination.
2. Liver: flaking, itchy skin, irritation, puffiness caused by toxaemia (presence in the blood of toxic products formed by body cells or bacteria).
3. Kidneys: bags under the eyes, dark circles, swelling, saggy appearance caused by poor bladder elimination.
4. Stomach: skin blemishes, flaking, irritation, acne caused by slow or improper digestion.
5. Lungs: sagging, congestion, blotches caused by lack of oxygen.
6. Chin & Throat: pustules, congestion, acne, flaking caused by slow digestion

If you have any of the following symptoms, you have a toxic body crying out for help:

Jaundice	Depressed appetite	Pale stool
Metallic taste in mouth	Nausea	Chemical sensitivities
Discoloured whiteness of eyes	Allergies	Digestive complaints
Fatty food intolerance	Mood swings	Drowsiness after eating
	Difficulty loosing weight	
Pain under right shoulder blade	Weak tendons, ligaments and muscles	

Before my surgery I had a swollen liver with pain on my right side just under my shoulder blade and down to my floating ribs. I had a rash across my chest, a metallic taste in my mouth, was often constipated and suffered with a mild headache for years. I struggled with anaemia and breathing problems resulting from the lack of red blood cells to carry the oxygen because my liver was malfunctioning. I suffered from digestive problems like gas, bloating and acid reflux. I went for regular physical check-ups and blood work. NOBODY IN THE MEDICAL PROFESSION EVER TOLD ME I HAD TOXIC LIVER ISSUES!!! Surely my enlarged liver must have shown up on all the tests including ultrasound and x-rays I had through the years and before surgery.

For years the doctors treated me for ulcers. Now I discovered it was my liver all along. When I went back to the Chinese herbalist for a check-up, I told him of the pain in my right side. He examined me and gave me some supplements to help the liver, warning me to avoid alcohol, fatty, fried foods and excessive protein. Within two days, the pain in my right side was gone and so was the faint nausea.

I am still angry at the medical profession. It let me down completely. If I had been properly diagnosed years ago ABOUT LIVER PROBLEMS, maybe the cancer could have been prevented. Getting cancer and being forced to find my *own* answers has probably saved my life.

Detoxing really awakened my whole digestive system. I had BMs to rival all BMs and they smelled horrible - the worst possible chemical mix you could imagine. My stools were yellow, a sign of strong liver bile release – another good indicator of detoxing you should know about and watch for. It took over ten months of gentle detoxing before my stools smelled and looked normal. Then I celebrated, believe me!

Normal stools have a specific colour, smell and weight. Your stool should be a walnut brown – with temporary fluctuations from foods you eat such as beets or dark green vegetables. If they smell foul, you need serious detoxing. Stools should be the consistency of toothpaste – not hard little pellets or runny, watery stuff. You should have quick, easy elimination of stools; straining means constipation. Your stools should settle slowly in the water. If they float, they have too much undigested fat. If they drop like stones, you need more fibre.

What happens if you have only one BM every couple of days, ten days or two weeks? Some people do and consider it *normal* for them. In reality, constipation causes a toxic colon, a putrefying mess of poisons release back into the body, causing no end of problems including obesity. Chronic constipation creates a distorted, convoluted, prolapsed (sags in the middle from the weight of excess material), unhealthy colon. In some cases, it becomes spastic, shrinking to pencil thin widths in some spots, stretching to dangerous widths in others. Stress can cause your poor colon to look like a cartoon version of a hump-back, screeching cat!

If we eat three meals per day, we should have two or three BMs per day. I got so good at this I ate beets one day and eliminated them the next! If you want to know your rate of removal, eats beets. Their red color is unmistakable (looks like blood in your stool so don't panic). Juicing really helped on a daily basis, not only detoxifying but also keeping my intestines 'flowing down' smoothly.

Life went on for me as I detoxed. I went out for supper with Cliff – Greek food – one of our favourites. My guides told me I could have one glass of wine but no dessert. So I did and enjoyed my moussaka and salad. But the next day, they told me I needed to reduce my acid levels. I've noticed a continuing acidic, almost metallic taste in my mouth. My ph tape test of saliva confirms my guides' advice. I should be in the 6.2 to 7.6 range and I'm in the 5's. For my morning juice I added a slice of lemon, carrot and avocado (all alkaline foods) to my apple and grapefruit juice. Oranges are acidic but grapefruits are alkaline.

I swam for an hour with my friend, Louise, but the steam room left me weak the next day. Too much exercise for my detoxing body, especially with the heavy sweating and the liver pills from the Chinese herbalist. So I go slower and rest more.

Diets high in meats, dairy, breads, sugars, salt, Trans fats and hydrogenated oils increase our acid levels and slowly turn our body toxic. Dairy coats our intestines with a mucous preventing digestion of needed nutrients. Meat takes lots of enzymes to digest, which could be used rebuilding cells, tissues and the immune system. Meat is dead energy. It actually has to *rot* in our intestines for our body to break it down and use it. Still, I choose to eat meat, just less now. I have Type O blood, meaning we are the meat eaters of all blood types. I naturally have the digestive enzymes needed. Breaking down these foods, however, forces the overworked liver, our major detox agent, to increase alkaline bile, further depleting our body's calcium, magnesium, sodium and potassium. Their depletion means there is not enough left to jump start enzymes. Enzymes need 4,000 biochemical reactions to keep us healthy. So now, I eat less meat, sticking to more fish and chicken.

According to Michelle Schoffro Cook, in her fascinating book, *The Ultimate pH Solution,* if we eat highly processed, chemically laden, additive filled food, our bodies can not metabolize it properly, resulting in acidic waste. WHAT THE BODY DOES NOT RECOGNIZE AS FOOD, IT LINKS IT TO FAT CELLS AND STORES SOMEWHERE IN THE BODY WHERE IT CAN DO NO HARM. Obesity is caused by such fat stores. It's our body's built-in protective mechanism against high acidity which has the potential to damage every cell in our body.

Research proves heavier thighs actually save our body from harm. In a 1991 Stanford University study of 133 men and 130 women, the bigger their thighs, the lower their heart disease risks! Unfortunately, the risk increases if you have more fat around your waist than your thighs. Dr. Glenn Gaesser, PH.D., in his book *Big Fat Lies,* exposes massive research projects the public knows nothing about. It would ruin the diet industry. He states, "A relatively large thigh circumference, especially in women, was associated with healthy low levels of blood triglycerides and LDL, cholesterol (the bad kind, which promotes heart disease). I too have heavier thighs but no cholesterol problem. Men and women with small thigh circumferences had just the opposite blood fat profile! (96:131). A similar study at Laval University in Quebec used CAT scans to show men with the fattest thighs had the lowest levels of blood triglycerides and highest HDL – the good cholesterol (96:132). In all the studies, the results were the same:

the fatter thighs, the better! More astonishing, "women with endometrial cancer or breast cancer had significantly less thigh fat and smaller hip measurements than women without cancer (96:133)! Well I worked out hard for years to bring my thigh size down. Instead, I should have changed my diet lifestyle and detoxified regularly.

More frightening news: yo-yo dieting actually increases our chances of premature death! According to Dr. Gaesser's summary of thousands of research studies world-wide, "women who intentionally lost between one and nineteen pounds over a period of one year or more had premature death rates from cancer, cardiovascular disease, and all causes, were increased by as much as 40 to 70 percent" (96:160). Unintentional (is there any other kind?) weight gain, on the other hand, had no adverse effects on premature deaths of non-smoking, overweight women. His conclusion: exercise, eat healthy and <u>stay</u> at the weight you are! Your blood and longevity tells the real story, not your weight!

When I read his book, I felt ill. I have yo-yo dieted all my life trying to get skinnier thighs! I never appreciated my slimmer waist, which never gained a lot of weight. Yet I hated my thighs for fighting me all the way on weight loss. My constant dieting simply raised my body weight set point to a much higher weight than if I had *just left it alone*. Well, I'm doing it now and I accept my body as it is. I walk, do yoga, eat well *and leave the rest alone*!

Schoffro Cook explains how the laws of electromagnetism demand that opposites attract so unhealthy cells and their acid attract and bind to healthy cells. The acidic environment and decrease of oxygen to the healthy cells can damage them to the point they mutate. As this mass grows, the body creates a defense mechanism to surround and isolate the tissue to prevent it spreading (08:57). **This is called a tumor.**

She continues: "Even one mineral deficiency caused by excess acidity can throw off a range of body functions and lead to serious health concerns" (08:40). Our bodies have incredible ways to release toxins but they *can not keep up* with our Western diet of fast food burgers and fries, milk, coffee, cake, candy, soda pop, white bread, sugar and salt. Our body is forced to pull alkaline substances like calcium, potassium, bicarbonate, glutamine and magnesium from our organs, bones, muscles and tissues with no hope of replenishment. They in turn become weakened and acidic. It becomes a vicious circle and our body pays the price.

Schoffro Cook writes, "a growing number of groundbreaking studies, published in popular, recognized scientific journals, link a wide range of health disorders to an acidic state of the body. Some of the conditions most commonly associated with excess acid formation include arthritis, kidney disease, osteoporosis, weight gain and chronic infections such as sinusitis and bronchitis. Most shocking perhaps, is that cancer is increasingly being added to this list" (08:52).

I agree with Schoffro Cook who claims Western medicine is simply a band-aid approach, with no recognition of the *cause*. For her, it's like corking a lava flow.

I met medical intuitive Caroline Sutherland who wrote the book, *The Body Knows How to Stay Young*. She intuitively scanned my body and told me I had wheat allergies and high yeast levels. She recommended I get off wheat and sugar to reduce yeast. I experimented, quitting all wheat (which my guides had warned me about anyway) and sugar for three days. I felt much better. Then I one day, I ate wheat and loaded up on sugar (cookies and muffins I baked). The next day, I felt depressed, tired and bloated. My entire body ached and my fingers felt stiff with painful, puffy joints. Then I knew exactly what I had to do if I wanted a healthier body without arthritis as I aged.

Revisit the symptoms of toxicity listed below. By now you should know what causes them:

Low energy	Heartburn	Constipation	Insomnia
Indigestion	Aches	Water retention	Irritability
Memory problems	Headaches	Candidiasis	Pimples/rashes
Gas	Bloating	Weight gain	Bad breath

You can pick up any over-the-counter drugs to suppress – not heal – any of these symptoms. None of those drugs address the *cause*.

35.

What They Don't Tell You

"You won't hear this in the U.S. because the media is practically owned by the Big Pharma these days, but nearly all cancer is preventable. Even the World Health Organization says that 70 % of all cancers can be prevented. I believe the real number is closer to 90 percent."

Mike Adams, *Breast Cancer Deception,* Natural News website:
http://www.naturalnews.com/Report_Breast_Cancer_Deception_12.html

From a different source I found similar reports about the World Health Organization (WHO) saying 4% of the cancers are inherited or genetic. The rest are preventable and linked to lifestyle, diet and environment (08:56).

Then why isn't anyone doing something about this?? I went to one of the top cancer hospitals in Canada and they told me NOTHING about ACID LEVELS, ENVIRONMENT, DETOXING OR PROPER NUTRITION!!!

Their advice to me: "drink all the coffee you want, eat whatever you want, just continue with your regular diet and eat protein every meal - in other words, just follow the Canada Health Food Guide."

Months ago, when they were still talking to me, the Volunteer Women's Breast Cancer Support Group sent me a package of information including the book, *The Intelligent Patient Guide to Breast Cancer.* In the whole 300 page book, only a couple of pages mention nutrition. It states, "A healthy diet includes a wide variety of whole grain cereals and breads, vegetables, fruit, legumes (beans), lentils, nuts and seeds as well as lean meat, chicken, fish and low-fat dairy products" (06:213).

Our medical professionals receive exactly four hours of instruction on nutrition: the leading cause of any disease. Their biggest solution is to pass out drugs and more drugs. Why? Because natural foods can not be patented so nobody makes any money prescribing them. When my medical doctor told me to eat yogurt for a yeast infection, she whispered it!

In fact, Canada just passed new laws which do not allow us to claim any naturopathic, herbal remedies or Wholistic treatments as medical expenses. Now only medical doctor and pharmaceutical expenses can be claimed on our income tax. Who benefits from this legislation? Certainly not Canadians! What will be banned next? Grandma's mustard plaster?

As consumers, we buy into this 'quick fix', the old 'give me a pill to make it better' lies. The real truth: we want instant relief not natural, long term solutions.

On another matter, the hoopla about men's erectile dysfunction is terribly misleading. When men hit their late forties and early fifties, they too have a form of menopause – pause being the operative word. A spokesperson for Ottawa's Centre for Menopause explained how men will begin intercourse, then a window slams, a dog barks and everything stops and wilts. But with a little patience, a little message, everything begins again and finishes in grand style. This is *normal* for our older men! They are neither sick nor ill or lacking in any way. Nor do they need pills!

Here is another sad truth: not one cent of our hard earned cancer research dollars goes to natural cures. NOT ONE CENT! Many of those "pink' products for breast cancer are actually backed by the big pharmaceutical companies. They get money on both ends of the spectrum of research, diagnosis and medication. All their money goes to developing drugs and more drugs. There is a reason why every country in the world has a cure for cancer EXCEPT Canada and the United States, who have the highest rates of cancer in the world. Did you know in the United States, any naturopath treating a cancer patient with natural products can be jailed? The American FDA (Food and Drug Association) has passed a ruling stating disease can only be treated with *drugs*.

I found a cancer killing herbal medicine called Graviola that tropical countries have used for years to cure cancer. The cancer institutions have known about it since the 1940's, have researched it since 1976. Health Science Institute, an independent media newsletter describes the evils of what they call "Big Pharma" (pharmaceutical companies). "But even we were shocked at the shameless greed behind the Graviola scandal (2002), when a major drug company covered up news of the miraculous cancer cure just because it couldn't figure out a way to profit from the discovery" (www.HSIBaltimore.com March 2007, Vol.11, No. 9). Clinical studies have pitted Graviola against chemo and found it is just as potent without the toxic side effects. According to the Health Science Institute, Graviola has unmatched power against a whole army of cancer cell lines: liver, lung, breast, skin, kidney, prostate, colon ...and that's just to name a few (07:6, Vol.11, No.9). YET NOBODY HAS HEARD OF IT!

You can not patent plants. Mixing Graviola with any other chemical reduces its potency. I think Mother Earth is trying to teach them something!

A company in Nevada, USA called Rain-tree harvested the small evergreen tropical tree whose leaves and stems are ground into high quality, easy to swallow capsules. Then a second tree, called Mountain Graviola revealed 26 additional cancer-fighting chemicals. The two plants combined, Graviola Max, offers over 100 cancer fighting components - particularly effective against liver, lung and ovarian cancer with no side effects!. It *kills* the cancer cells, curing within one year. Yet the FDA has gagged Rain-tree from advertising their product! Nor are they allowed to post on their website all the glowing testimonials from grateful customers. You can buy Graviola and Graviola Max at some heath food stores or online. Look up 'Graviola Max' on the internet, the information and research is all there including how it kills parasites. Health Sciences Institute is currently updating its information on these powerful products and the latest research on it.

By now you understand how the liver is toxically congested before cancer occurs. Imagine dumping a whole poisonous load of chemo into it. No wonder the medical professions say liver cancer is usually incurable.

In 2010 Health Canada set up legislation to ban Graviola. WHO BENEFITS? WHO IS MOST THREATENED BY THIS POTENT LITTLE HERB? When did we abdicate the right to take whatever we choose to heal ourselves?!!! We do not live in a dictatorship!

Remember our Canadian biochemist Hulda Regehr Clark who isolated parasites which caused cancer? Did she get a Nobel Peace Prize? No, they jailed her, saying the black walnut oil (yeah from walnuts) in her cure was toxic. I recently learned Black Walnut oil is also a powerful lymphatic drainer! Dr. Regehr Clark continues her research and you can find her books online. Every self-respecting naturopath has copies of her books although the general public has never heard of her.

I read a massage therapist's brochure stating 80% of lumps, cysts and tumours in the breast are found on the right side. 70% show up on the outer quadrant of the right breast. The therapist writes, "The drain fields of the sewer dump in the body are plugged." Seems she knows more than our cancer institutes who simply admit that most women get breast cancer in the right breast. This therapist suggests massaging the area at five or six specific sites around the breast to open up the drains and allow the toxins to flow and be carried out of the body (unknown author).

Another book which emphasized detoxification is called *The Complete Cancer Cleanse* by Cheri Calbom, John Calbom and Michael Mahaffey. This book not only looks at lifestyle, nutrition and detoxification, but also spirituality! It finds many cancer patients have a similar behavioural and emotional pattern known as the Type C personality. Very often they have experienced loss: of hope, an unwanted divorce or death of a loved one - a child or spouse. The individual feels a sense of hopelessness and despair. Also, many people with cancer suppress their emotions, especially anger; they experience loneliness and tend to carry other people's burdens or take on extra obligations. The book offers many practical solutions and easy lifestyle changes. Again, I learned none of this from the cancer institution.

Go on the internet. Do your own research. Look up a website called the *Cancer Cure Foundation:* www.cancure.org/AlternativeTherapy.htm. Their philosophy and research about alternative therapies is worth considering. Another site called Natural News.com. Their March 3, 2008 article claims instead of addressing the causes of cancer – toxins and a weakened immune system – treatments which slash, burn and poison away the tumours and cancer cells further weaken the immune system cancer has already defeated and only *worsens* the condition of the patient. Consequently, the way is paved for the return of cancer or the introduction of another cancer or serious condition. The road to further illness is often made easier due to the damaged immune system and major organs caused by the *treatment of the symptoms*. The writers also believe nature gives us an army of tools to beat cancer and the underlying causes – such as nutritious foods (fresh, organic, alive fruits and vegetables), vitamins, minerals, supplements and lifestyle choices. The website urges its readers to clean their bodies, houses and workplace of toxins like heavy metals, pesticides and polluted air. They believe the bigger your arsenal to fight any disease, the better chance you have of winning the battle. (08:1-3). Why should we be surprised that every tumor is laced with chemicals and pesticides – something nobody at the cancer hospital told me.

Read Suzanne Somers book, *Knockout,* where she interviews Doctors who are curing cancer. She contends chemo really only works for four kinds of cancer: childhood leukemia, some lymphomas, testicular cancer and Hodgkins. For all the major cancer killers, according to Dr. Nicholas Gonzalez – "metastic breast, lung, prostate and pancreatic – chemotherapy does absolutely nothing...zero" (09:95). He cites an independent scientist with a PhD in Germany reviewed the world's literature on chemotherapy used against solid tumours and he found absolutely no benefit to chemotherapy. He published his findings in German and English but the American oncology community got it suppressed in the United States (09:95).

Find out for yourself how many books and lengthy research projects by reputable doctors and scientists in Canada and the United States have been "suppressed" from public knowledge. I found a website by Dr. William Donald Kelley, D.D.S, M.S., http://www.drkelley.com/CANLIVER55.html. *One Answer to Cancer, reviewed after 32 years, 1967 to 1999 with cancer cure.* It states on the first page: ***Suppressed.***

Find out how many doctors on the web are speaking out about the terrible side effects of chemo, radiation and cancer drugs, including the John Hopkins Centre. If nothing else, consider the millions, no billions of dollars raised for cancer research in the past fifty years then realize that **NO CURES HAVE BEEN FOUND – JUST MORE DRUGS.** We are stuck with garbage created in the 1940's and 1960's! Why? According to Dr. Lorraine Day on her DVD, it is "a multi-billion, no trillion dollar business nobody is willing to stop." On the below website, the latest 'miracle drug' called Herceptin only prevented breast cancer in 0.6 per cent of women according to Dr. Ralph W. Moss in an article for New Scientist magazine. He's a cancer expert from the world of conventional medicine. He even published a book about it called *Herceptin – Or Deception?* My Oncologist prescribed this drug for me though I refused to take it. Another website states every person with cancer generates $800,000.00 of income from chemo, radiation and the endless drugs. Who would give that up and offer a cheap natural cure like Graviola which sells for $36.95 for 100 capsules?

Here is a website that will have you gasping in shock. Look up http:///www.naturalnews.com/report_Breast_Cancer_Deception_0.html. The article by Mike Adams, states if you travelled the world in search of treatment or cures for breast cancer; you would find hundreds, even thousands of cures. Many, such as those in Chinese medicine, are meticulously documented and based on *thousands of years of research.* In his article, which he gets no economic benefits from, he says the western cancer industry compromised of cancer clinics, drug-company funded cancer non-profits, pharmaceutical firms, hospitals, doctors, medical schools and medical journals go out of their way to deny women access to the natural cure information and wisdom about treating or preventing breast cancer. He claims the cancer industry effectively keeps women in a state of ignorance about cancer solutions, which could actually cure them. Their strategy to disempower women is symbolized by the pink ribbon which is about male dominated control over women.

He takes it even further stating Black People are not informed they need twice as much Vitamin D/sunlight as white people to prevent cancer. Their dark skin does not allow the sun's rays to penetrate as effectively as white people so they suffer from perpetual vitamin D deficiency. He charts statistics which indicate cancer in white people is decreasing while in black people it's skyrocketing. Yet in Dr. Lee's book, *What your Doctor May Not Tell You About Menopause,* he says cancer has risen over 60% from 1950.

I know how easily statistics can be 'fudged'. People who die before their horrendous chemotherapy and radiation treatments are finished are written off as dying from 'complications' or 'failure to complete treatment'. And those of us who refuse the conventional treatments are simply classified as 'spontaneous remission.'

I remember Dr. Day in her video, *Cancer Doesn't Scare Me Anymore,* saying black people's statistics are not even *added* to the national stats because their numbers would raise the stats too high. Mike Adams says the cancer industry really stands for: "Keeping all women ignorant; enslaving black women in treatments that don't work; exploiting women's bodies to initiate a transfer of wealth to cancer industry organizations; domination of rich, white Big Pharma men over women patients; the use of women to enslave other women into a chemical treatment trap (which keeps them on drugs for the rest of their lives from all the side affects)." If you want more information, read my chapter entitled "What All Women Should Know."

Sound over the top? Then how about the circulating rumours about the Catholic Church and Goodyear allegedly owning the big pharmaceutical companies? I can't prove this but you need to read Mike Adam's article and other websites and make up your own mind.

As a nurse in the 1970's and 80's, I recall a large number of women in Canada who were given hysterectomies and appendix operations. You probably know of such women amongst your own family and friends. We nurses knew many of them had perfectly healthy tissue removed but we were not allowed to say anything – a breech of confidentiality. Was it just a cash cow for unscrupulous doctors and surgeons? When the media got wind of the numbers and questioned it, the powers that be quietly looked into it and quietly put a stop to it. Today these same women are often given Hormonal Treatment Therapies (HRT) which, according to Dr. Lee, a leading doctor in hormone balancing, increases their risk of cancer and blood clots by 200 – 300 %. He quotes a 2002 Women's Health Initiative study showing a 41% increase in strokes for women on Prem Pro or Premarin; a 29% higher risk of breast cancer; 26% higher risk of heart disease and 41% higher risk of stroke (04:262).

My experience and research about the whole cancer industry bears out much of what Mike Adams is saying. He lists 18 things which cause cancer and 22 things which prevent cancer. I have written about similar information throughout this book but I encourage you read as much as you can for your own information. Adams suggests avoiding cancer-causing chemicals in foods and personal care products. Avoid sodium nitrate in processed meats, artificial food colouring, chemicals, chemical sweeteners, plastic food containers, indoor air pollutants, air fresheners, popular cosmetics, skin care products, antibacterial soaps and more.

If you don't believe this, then go to a health food store and *read how many products say, "Free of aluminum, parabens, propylene, LSL or glycol."* This is pretty much in line with the toxins my guides warned me about. On a further note, the media recently announced research confirming a toxic chemical called PBS found in the lining of canned products, beer and soda cans. My guides stand vindicated for their heads up to me in the early stages of my diagnosis and treatment.

A doctor in Vancouver found small tumours in four out of five women diagnosed with breast cancer will disappear if *left alone*! Imagine my horror when I found mine would have too. In hindsight, I believe every person diagnosed with cancer should immediately be put on a detoxification/high nutritional program and possibly given cancer fighting herbs like Graviola before any surgery, chemo and radiation are ever considered! Like Suzanne Somers, I believe people can be taught to manage their cancer while they heal slowly and completely!

Then I hear the horrible excuse about thousands of people put out of work if the cancer industry collapses. I say these same people would be better off researching and teaching people – *including their loved ones* – how to heal, stay healthy and live longer! But...this is just my opinion.

> "Health is a gift; disease is something we earn."
> Dr. Joel Robbins, M.D. author of the DVD *Toxic Colon*

It seems we have also earned the greed and lack of concern for our fellow man, which prevents us from sharing the *real* cures for cancer.

36.

Joyful Good Health

"....our spirit is very much a part of our daily lives; it embodies our thoughts and
emotions, and it records every one of them, from the most mundane to the visionary...
it participates in every second of our lives. It is the conscious force of life itself."

Caroline Myss, PH.D. *Anatomy of the Spirit*, (96:03).

Every thought, every word we generate, our cells are listening! Indeed, many Eastern spiritual traditions understand illness to be a depletion of one's internal power or spirit. The congruencies among major spiritual traditions underscore the universal human experience of the *connection* between the spirit and the body, illness and healing. In the Western world, we have a long way to go before accepting this concept. Our naturopaths and holistic healers remain on the fringe of professional medicine because our society does not accept, *nor will it pay for*, such philosophies. Science has its beneficial place in our society. Unfortunately, its tendency to divide and isolate issues in order to study them negates any holistic healing practices. It creates tunnel vision, not universal awareness. Consequently, very few people in this Western World understand, let alone *have* a truly healthy physical, mental, emotional and spiritual body.

According to Dr. Jensen, most of us have been sick for so long we accept it as normal - just part of aging. He says very few people are healthy enough to actually feel good. He quotes Sir John Boyd Orr, Nobel Prize winner for his work in nutrition states, "If we have perfect health, we get a kick out of life. We are 100% alive. A healthy person is usually a cheerful person, full of the joy of living." Yes and a merry heart doeth good like a medicine. Of course we know the connection between laughter and good health, but we need to look deeper.

Dr Jensen also mentions an English doctor who conducted a study of anaemia in women. When their diets included foods high in iron, the doctor noted the women grew more cheerful, took more interest in life. They became neater and dressed better. Many went out and bought hats (circa 1970).

The road back to health is not easy. We must walk it gently, slowly and with great wisdom. So where do we start? I began this book with some tips on nutrition I hope you are continuing. Here are some more gentle ways I researched to slowly heal:

1. Two daily rest periods of at least fifteen minutes (a good time to meditate or simply sit quietly with a blank mind).
2. A warm bath of 2 ½ cups Epson salts or 1 cup of Sea Salt promotes circulation and detox through perspiration. Besides my daily showers, I nurture myself with a hot detox bath once a week.
3. Rub yourself briskly with a towel after bathing to awaken your lymph system
4. Lighten the work of your overburdened liver with *alive* and easy to digest fresh fruits and vegetables.
5. Go to a naturopath or Natural Medicine doctor. Keep searching until you find one that just 'feels' right to talk with and learn from.
6. If you turn yellow as you detoxify, it is not from the carrots! It is the poisonous release of toxins. (My bath water turned orange one day. My guides told me it was the orange dye from cheddar cheese – one of the major toxins in my body).
7. No peanuts or peanut butter - they contain aflatoxins, a highly carcinogenic mould. Almond or sunflower seed butter, better options, can be found in any grocery store. If any oils or nuts taste rancid or old – don't eat them! They become toxic in our body. I truly believe we need to pay more attention to people's allergies – they provide clues to what is not healthy for *any* human body!
8. Let no chemical, additive, pesticide, herbicide touch your body! Purging your body also means purging your home, garage and shed.
9. Back off on the coffee. I love my coffee, but sprayed with pesticides, laced with acidic chocolate, sugar and cream like in my favourite mocha lattes – AAGGH! Organic coffee is available everywhere. Dr. Gonzales in Suzanne Somers book believes coffee actually shuts down the liver (09:92).
10. No dairy – all are acidic except goat milk and cheeses. Try almond or rice milk as delicious alternatives.
11. Boost your alkaline levels with avocadoes, tomatoes, lemons, limes and grapefruits. Put a slice of lemon, skin and all, in your water and visualize your alkalinity soaring with joy.
12. Make a 10 minute walk part of your daily routine. It doesn't take long, you get the Vitamin D you need and it moves your lymphatic system.

As you can see, these suggestions address healing on a physical level. Other chapters in this book address the mental, emotional and spiritual issues. To achieve balance, you must work on all four areas, simultaneously. It's not easy but I will continue to show you how I do it.

Stress needs its own category. Toxic side effects of stress on Western Women are explained in my chapter called, *What Every Woman Should Know*. Stress also causes depression. According to Michelle Schoffro Cook, depression is so powerful it actually erodes bones in the body causing a great deal of pain. Stress hormones are acid forming. http://www.drkelley.com/CANLIVER55.html.

She witnessed dramatic improvements in many previously depressed people who switched their diet to a more alkaline one (08:62). This makes sense since sugar, flour, butter and chocolate, which I crave when I get stressed or upset, are all acidic.

37.

XI Returns

If we don't change, we don't grow.
If we don't grow, we are not really living.
Growth demands a temporary surrender of security.
Gail Sheehy

I dreamt of walking with Xi along a mountain path. I asked him for his take on cancer. This is what he replied:

"Cancer is a dis-ease of the soul, it's true. But it is much more. In this world of toxins, harsh substances and embellishments of greed, you are bombarded with an environment difficult and harsh to live in.

"The care taken to live a clean, clear life allows only so much freedom of thought and form. The rest is illusion. And all disease is an illusion. It awakens you, shocks you into being more aware of your soul, your very purpose and design for coming here. You are to learn, grow, change and move on.

"Of course we healed you of the cancer ages ago. You saw the burned out areas. Now you are moving into not only healing from the trauma but also into prevention, the final state of this process. You will be okay. We promise you. We love you and care for you and need you to go on with your life and the writing you must do. Convince others to listen to their hearts, their souls and their guides. This is your hardest task but also your most delightful.

"The dream we have for mankind is one day they will awaken to their hearts' delight and move into the flow of this realm, feeling and seeing the vast wisdom of its place and form far beyond the greed and fear of materialism - the true cancer!

"If people but knew how easy it is to cure cancer, it would push the entire pharmaceutical companies out on their greedy little ears. We have the antidote! It is truly about love – love of self, of one another and of this planet. It is that simple and that easy.

"Then they can move on to address the cancer:

1. Physically – the dream world awaits once they move to a more vegetarian life style. It clears their system, heals their clogged bodies and frees them up for the vibration of the twenty first century.
2. Emotionally – letting go of old thoughts, old angers, old revenges, old bitterness, old fears – all wasted because they are past. All they do is hold us back and anchor our freedom. To let go is to have wings to fly in the creative freedom of tomorrow – a life of joy and peace.
3. Mentally – awakening to this moment's awareness, feeding upon the rapture of today – lived with every sense of one's being. This is all we have anyway – today – this moment. It deserves our entire focus, of being in the present but also giving out and receiving a sense of comfort and joy.
4. Spiritually – awakening to the new dawn of the future. We are alive, present in this dawn to experience it all the way to our cleared out, cleaned out soul. We are to feel, touch, taste it, dream it, live it, glory in it and give thanks for this dawn – a gift we can but experience one day at a time.

"Certainly there are losses, they too have purpose. There are gains and they too teach us more about ourselves. We live and that is enough – for this day and every day of our futures. We care not for our past but as a teacher and harbinger of today – this moment we share in a brief space of time.

"Illusion? Of course it is – all is illusion – the dreamer coming alive to dream another day in this vast cosmos of dreams. So dare to dream big, dare to dream it all and live to the fullest capacity of your being. Then let it be enough, for today."

We curled up together and watched the new dawn. I noticed his hand changed to a furry paw. Idly, I asked if he wanted to turn into a bear.

"I might", he said. And did.

Now that's a trick! From dragon to bear?

He pretended to eat me but I felt no fear. I am so done with the fear of any bear. "Go ahead" I invited. Instead, he cuddled me close, making me feel warm and comforted beyond measure.

"Do you have more to tell me in this form?" Then I got it. "So the Dragon planet is part of the Big Bear galaxy?"

He nodded, growing more serious. "You see, we are all connected, you and I. Form is not sufficient to hold all the information of this universe. So we change, we grow and we become more than we ever thought possible. New eyes, ears and mouth give us broader perspectives, warm up our desires to try more, live more and experience more. Why limit ourselves in any way? When freedom allows us to choose in so many ways a different life so all dreams are possible, all endings are possible. We choose and we make it so."

He switched to human form and hugged me. "I love, as you are. I love you forever more. You and I, we are one with this universe and together we experience all its forms of life and laughter. As it is, so may it be."

He has become such a wise friend, I hugged him back. "Can cancer be reversed?"

"Of course," he replied. "Cancer is an indicator of change, of the need to clear out and clean out our environment of toxins, our unhealthy thoughts and memories – our old luggage of ancient emotions – tired and weary and heavy. Clearing en-light-ens, moves us into a healthier space, ready for tomorrow, healed and whole.

"Clean up your environment, eat healthy foods, ease your memories, relax your pent up emotions, dare to dream big and you're well on your way to healing any cancer. Best of all, it is free – a free choice. It is not the Boogey man people think it is. It is merely their wake-up call. Change...or die and learn on the Other Side what you could have changed here. The choice, as always, is yours."

I frown. "I always think it's too simple. It should take more than this. But I guess this is just my ego talking. It always wants *more*."

"Yes, it does. But the truth of the matter is simplicity, where you step into the flow of the Universe and simply be who you really are, who you really choose to be – just go with the flow and Be."

When I awoke, you can imagine how quickly I grabbed a pen and wrote frantically, struggling to recall our entire conversation, detail by detail. Luckily, his thoughts replayed themselves in my memory, clarifying whenever my pen stopped.

I suddenly felt the urge to pull a card from *Spirit of the Wheel*, another of my favourite card series. #25 Ducks Fly Moon, summarized what Xi had told me: Synchronicity, balance and certainty. Change is necessary to return the self to a state of inner balance. Let go of all judgements or ego attachments. Become a bridge between earth and sky, feel the nurturing, grounding energies of Earth Mother while connecting to the divine flow feeding our spiritual essence. When we do this, *magic is revealed through miracles, synchronicity, inner peace and joy.* We know, with complete certainty we are on our destined path. Once we achieve this inner balance, we are called upon to teach others to bring balance to the world around us.

"The cosmos is not chaotic. The very word means order."

Ekhart Tolle

38.

What About the Fear?

"We are frightfully concerned with our own deaths; sometimes so much we forget the real purpose of our lives."

Brian L. Weiss, M.D., *Many Lives, Many Masters* (88:59)

Have you ever noticed we are never allowed to forget about cancer or its terrible consequences? Every day on the news, in the paper, at checkout counters, on bulletin boards, we see the big 'C' word. We are constantly asked to support cancer research, go on walkathons and buy pink products yaddy...yaddy...ya! For cancer survivors, just hearing the word boosts our fear levels - every time. It forces us to live in perpetual fear. Do you really think it's a coincidence? Fear of ageing, obesity, loneliness, abandonment, poverty and most of all, fear of death makes us buy products and do whatever we are asked to do to reduce our fears. Fear is the most powerful marketing tool known to man and it is used *ruthlessly* to make us buy useless junk we don't need. Junk that could even kill us. But our fear rides too high for us to listen to our quiet inner voice, which always tells the truth. Somehow, some way, we need to walk beyond the fear into our true destiny.

In the aftermath of cancer a lingering fear rises up when we are at our weakest, most vulnerable moments. What if IT returns? And the fear grabs our throats, stops our breath and adds tension to our muscles all over again. Fear never really goes away.

How do we deal with the fear of cancer returning?

I hated it, fought it until I realized my very resistance only added to the tension, built the fear and put my ego back in control of my life. I never realized what a mean streak my ego had – making me afraid; putting all the 'What if...? When...' scenarios into my head. They would play like some horror movie; dark and threatening...with no basis in reality, no form other than my racing imagination. They'd catch me unawares as I stared out a window, drifted off to sleep and Wham! They'd play in full color, sending my heart racing and my blood pressure soaring. It infuriated me.

Then I'd do the elaborate 'Well that's not true because...'and I would list all the realities: I'm healing, doing well, my guides tell me so, my psychic friends tell me the same. My dreams tell me I'll live to be an old lady. This I know. But it seemed so nebulous, with no more substance than the imaginings of my mind. I hear, I see, I know, I dream and still I doubt. And doubting is hell. I want solid, concrete evidence the cancer is gone. Yet what would it look like? Even doctors offer no guarantee.

How do we live with cancer?

> "Feel the fear and do it anyway."
> Tamara Mellon, successful owner of *Jimmy Choo Shoes*

I finally admitted to my sister-in-law, Elaine I sometimes had panic attacks that literally took my breath away. I'd break into a cold sweat while my heart pounded like a maniac. I hated to admit this weakness. I should be stronger than this!

Elaine is one who simply opens her mouth and allows Spirit messages to flow out of her. She has no idea what she is going to say, simply trusts what needs to be said will come out.

She turned to me and replied, "Do your yoga pose of relaxation and deep breathing, pulling your head back and up, connect your fingers and breathe. Breath until it passes and you are calm. Then tell yourself, 'There, I've had a moment and it is gone.'" Then her eyes widened as she realized what she had said. At that point, she had no idea I even practised yoga!

I wanted to cry, perhaps at the validation from Spirit, perhaps at the simplicity of just accepting this fear. Sometimes it is still easier to believe someone else's spiritual messages than my own. Old insecurities raise their heads, making me sigh in frustration.

I awoke in the night thinking my heart is beating too fast and I'm afraid. Is IT coming back? Why the accelerated heart beat?

I rolled to Cliff and whispered, "I'm worried." I told him about the anxiety and what Elaine's guides had said to help it. He nodded, "It's normal to feel anxious because usually the medical profession is there to reassure us...but not this time."

He told me to count my heart beats. I counted 60 per minute – actually low since a woman's pulse is normally 60 – 80 beats per minute. This simple exercise reassured me and I fell asleep once again.

Beryl called the next morning. (Thank you Spirit for her timely call). She calmed me with her gentle voice alone. She talked of Elizabeth Prophet's book on the new energy coming to Earth – a healing energy of violet light we must intentionally pull to Earth. And I laughed out loud in delight.

Here was a validation of the fuchsia light I often played with. Consciously healing myself focuses the violet energy: Mother Earth created my physical body (blue), Creator added my soul (white) and I, the soul, am the red energy, loving it and mixing it together to form purple healing energy! It *is* the antidote: Love conquers all!

I learned to just surrender to fear, sit in my emotions and *experience* the fear, accept it as real, valid and normal at this time. I have my moment then I get on with living.

Space - I've heard of the space beyond our thoughts and feelings and it's where I went in mediation – a vast void – like looking at the stars then looking into the space around them we call the universe. If you could touch a star, what is around it but space? One can not exist without the other. Which is more real? Both are part of the universe.

Then it dawned on me. Like the space between planets, I am *not* my fears! They are simply little star parts of me in this instance but *I am* the larger, unlimited space in which they exist. They can drift away but I remain. I AM NOT MY FEARS. I am greater than fear! It does not control me or the I AM of my soul. I can see my fears, sense them, resist them or feel them, accept them or let them drift away. They are *not* the sum total of me – never will be. I breathe deeper. I live through this moment of realization.

What brought my fears up was going back to my childhood home, back to my brothers and sisters and explaining, all over again, why I had chosen this path of healing. Faced with their fear and worry, I doubted myself once again. I had to justify my choices and rethink why I made them. Coward that I am, I could not tell them the full story as I relate it in this book. My family comes from farming stock in cowboy country. I left my childhood home thirty-six years ago and travelled the world. I changed.

My family doesn't understand me or what I believe today. They've never sat in talking circles or sweat lodges listening to Elders. They never received the teachings, the stories and the humor Elders shared. My family has neither the background of education, information, research and dreams nor my experiences with the many people who influenced me. My mother refused to admit we had Native ancestry so we never received any cultural teachings at home. I didn't know where to begin explaining to my siblings what happened to me. My clumsy efforts only confused them. Actually, I was glad to leave. I'm not strong enough to take on their worries as well as my own. I know they are afraid because they love me and that is okay.

I feel so alone. And I am – like a black sheep of this narrow minded society. The medical profession has forced me to do this alone – except for my husband, kids, close friends and my guides. Yet, this is my truth and I walk it, live it as I *choose* and I *know* this is the right path for me.

I still have some pain in my breast and under my arm where the incisions are. My arm and shoulder ache as the severed nerve endings awaken. I asked my guides to rebuild healthy, functioning lymph nodes to replace the removed ones. If people can re-grow tonsils and appendixes, then I can re-grow lymph nodes – same thing. My guides tell me this is 'an unusual request' but they agreed to do this for me though it could take two years of construction. So be it. Consequently, it causes more pain and swelling in the area as my body readjusts, grows and heals. Over a year would pass before the pins and needles stopped running down the back of my arm. Still, I am content. A small cut on my finger healed within two days, proof my immune system is up and running.

Thank you Lord!

I dreamt of abandonment fears. And did this not just play out with my family? Once we make this fear part of our reality, we let no one come too close. Consequently, we 'feel' abandoned; we re-enact it again and again in our lives. Abandonment, if allowed to fester, will create all kinds of internal blockages of energy. Here was another piece of the blockage over my heart.

People who do not love themselves fear all. I met a man with a growth in his throat, which slowly choked him. Out of curiosity, I looked up throat problems in Louise Hays' book, *Heal Your Body A-Z*. She says it is the inability to speak up for oneself, swallowed anger, stifled creativity and a refusal to change (1982-88:102). I know this man had an abusive childhood and is still estranged from his parents. Abused children are forced to think and act under the total control of their parents. Creativity is not allowed. So much pain, so little resolution. People, who do not believe in anything, can not believe in themselves. Worst of all, they will never know true inner contentment until they make peace with themselves, if not with their parents. Forgiveness of the self is all it takes.

I meditated and visualized myself as a little girl dressed in a red coat and rubber boots. She calls herself 'Esto'. I sat her on my knee and talked to her, adult to child. She gave me a memory of not being wanted while still in my mother's womb! I am the sixth child (one miscarriage) of an exhausted farm wife who knew full well the work involved in raising yet another child. Now, as a parent and grandmother, I understand such thoughts and emotions. I've felt them myself. I adore all my babies but they *are* a lot of work. I also remembered how well Mom loved me, cared for me, clothed me (handmade clothes and blankets), fed me from her huge garden and worried over me when I was sick – like she did with all my brothers and sisters. She was always there for us and never shirked her responsibilities as a parent. I always knew she loved me. In my heart, I thank you Mom. You loved me well and I am eternally grateful.

Do you see how easy it is to acknowledge such feelings, accept them as valid and real and let them go? For the man with throat issues, Louise Hays offers these affirmations: words we can say over and over to ourselves *until* we believe them: "It's okay to make noise. I express myself freely and joyously. I speak up for myself with ease. I express my creativity. I am willing to change" (88:102). Behind such positive thoughts always comes a sense of truth...and peace. I must say these words out loud too.

How closely we are all connected! How similar our experiences and feelings. I have talked with other women who through hypnosis, dreams or flashbacks also recall their mother's thoughts from the womb. The mind forgets but the soul does not. Now is the time to heal from the soul outward: understand it, accept it and release it.

I worked hard to stay positive, upbeat. I refused to watch the news or any violent shows. Instead, I laughed along with comedy shows and sweet movies like Walt Disney's children shows – anything and everything positive, funny and loving. Laughter heals like tears. Laughter also releases fears. I noticed whenever I laughed a lot, I started to cough, another sign of clearing away the dark stuff from my body.

Yet fear has deeper, gut level roots which require recognition. Sometimes it helps to think about how we dealt with fear in the past. Let's play with it. Let me tell you a story about *real fear*, the day my son and I found ourselves in the eye of a tornado. Get a cup of tea, juice or lemon water and find a cozy chair, couch or bed while I share with you a chapter of my life from the summer my son turned nineteen:

We were attending an Aboriginal sweat lodge ceremony on the prairies. My son along with three other teens tended the fire outside the lodge. Their job was to keep the rocks heating in the fire and then carry them with forks into the sweat lodge when the Elder called for them. In the house, nearby, I put the finishing touches on the ceremonial feast for everyone when they came out of the sweatlodge. They were on their final round of prayers and singing.

It was a hot muggy day, the same as the previous five days, with thunderstorms lashing the hills around us every night. Taking a breather, I sat on the house's south step watching two clouds from different directions converge above the open prairie below me. One massive cloud had an ugly green cast I had never seen before. As they met, I watched in awe as huge walls of water from the bottom of the cloud exploded upwards before falling into the middle of the storm. A tiny finger of grey fell out the bottom of the cloud, touching the prairie with a tentative finger, lifting off and coming back for more, again and again. In fascination I watched it swirl like a tiny teacup with a saucer of dust flying out around it. I thought the storm was moving west to east, far south of us. Instead, our hillside home sat directly in its path.

Though it was mid-afternoon the sky soon darkened as the black clouds loomed overhead. We called the eight children playing outside to come into the house. I took them to the back bedroom to play, far from the living room and kitchen windows facing the storm. Rain fell softly, quietly. Looking out the bedroom window at the forest of white poplar behind the house, I felt the silent stillness of the land. An old outhouse in the backyard suddenly toppled without a sound.

FFOOM! A rippling explosion of air flattened grass and bent the trees to impossible angles. The wind screamed down upon the house, every window and door chattering. An eight foot square wooden bin by the east porch see-sawed drunkenly across the back yard, slammed into my car and flew away in the wind.

In dawning horror, I watched the wind pick up my car, rock it over on two wheels then set it gently down, only to begin the process over again. Hail blasted windows in the living room and kitchens so loud I expected them to shatter any minute. The children whimpered around me, sensing this was no ordinary storm. When I saw pieces of shingles, tarpaper and boards flying off the house roof to smash against my car, I knew without a doubt we were no longer safe.

I felt my way through the blackened rooms to the kitchen where a trapdoor led to the basement. Together the mother of the home and I struggled to lift it. We were the only adults in the house, the rest were in the sweat lodge. I ran back for the children who wailed openly when I told them we had to move to the basement. A little four year old held out her arms to me and I snatched her to my chest, stumbling over furniture in the blackened rooms. Just as we reached the trapdoor, fists pounded on the east door in the kitchen.

I set the little girl on the kitchen counter and opened the door to two terrified, mud spattered teens barely clinging to the porch railing. They say I braced myself against the door jamb, grabbed them by their shirts and hauled them in with one hand. They were as big as me. I don't remember doing this; I only wanted my son who had been with them at the fire. I searched the howling fury behind them, vainly trying to find my son. The two teens babbled about the wind flinging them into the trees while sheds smashed around them. One of the boys had a heavy bruise on his forehead from ramming headfirst into a tree. They had no idea where my son was.

I looked out upon a world gone mad. The wind screamed so loudly it deafened us. It surrounded the house with a solid wall of grey, slashing water. Ropes of spinning rain, swinging parallel to the ground, spun around the house like circling prey. And still the wind grew louder, taunting me, inviting me to take one step beyond the door. I knew I'd die if I moved. All I could do was whimper, "My son, my son, my son!" But he was not there.

Ten children behind me needed a safer place to hide. It broke my heart to shut the door knowing my son was lost in the shrieking malevolence. It took all my strength, with my foot braced against the doorframe to pull the *screen door, with no glass,* shut against the sucking vacuum from without. Luckily, the heavier wooden door swung inside the kitchen and I latched it easily.

When I turned to face the children, I was so close to tears I couldn't utter a sound; I just pulled the little girl back into my arms and held her tight. The other mother quickly marshalled the children and sent them down dark steps into the dirt basement. Suddenly, shrieking with terror they raced back up screaming, "A lizard! A lizard!" A little five year old girl climbed me like a tree, strangling me in terror. I locked my arms around both girls and felt the bone in my arm actually bend from their combined weights. One was a chunky 60 pounds; the other topped my burden to around a hundred pounds.

One of the teen boys threw the poor little two inch lizard into a corner and the whole wailing group ran back down the stairs. Wading through muddy water in my sock feet, I climbed onto an old high stool, cuddling the little girls against me, kissing their cheeks and trying to comfort them. One never stopped wailing, the other never made a sound. I lifted my filthy feet to the stool's rail, surrounded by a rippling river of mud pouring down beneath the front step.

And the wind screamed louder. It roared like thunder, louder than a freight train, bellowing down the chimney and vibrating through the furnace until the shivering ducts rumbled to life. Two baleful eyes glared at us from the mud, a shimmering reflection from tiny windows at each end of the basement. Giant rocks slammed against the shuddering house and timbers cracked and broke in the rooms above our heads. Suddenly the basement windows disappeared, frame and all. Icy mud, sand, grass and water sprayed our faces. The children screamed in terror. Then I heard the worst sound of all: a wooden house grating and sliding off its cement foundation. Grabbing the little girls' heads, I slammed their faces into my chest and ducked.

Holding my breath for what seemed like hours, I heard the house stop moving.

Cold and terrified, we waited in the darkness. Gradually the wind calmed. Was it the eye of the storm? Or was it over? Slowly, cautiously, through endless minutes, the wind softened, easing to a sigh. Aching muscles relaxed as we heard the rain turn to a gentle patter on the broken window sills.

A door slammed upstairs and someone called out. The other mother climbed the stairs while I stayed back with the children. I burst into tears when I recognized my son's calm voice as he spoke to her.

The little girl who never spoke a word throughout the storm put her hand on my cheek and whispered, "Don't cry Auntie, your boy is okay." I simply rocked the little girls and cried.

When we trouped up stairs I didn't know my son. He was coated in mud and sand so thick, only the whites of his eyes showed. His hair, matted with mud and fuzzy insulation from the attic stood on end like a bizarre wig. But he was fine, fine, fine. I couldn't stop touching and hugging him, crying in relief and laughing at his wild appearance. Once he knew we were okay, he hurried outside to check on the six occupants still in the sweatlodge.

When they all returned, soaked and shivering from shock, but unharmed, we pieced together the rest of the wild tale. I recalled my nursing instructor saying, "When you are in a crisis, put your emotions on hold; deal with the situation as logically as you can. People cope best if you restore their lives to as normal as possible. When it is all over, then deal with your emotions." We had no power but I pushed heavily sweetened lukewarm tea I had made for the feast into everyone's shaking hands. I donned rubber boots and started mopping the flour while people babbled out their stories.

The sixteen year old girl hugged my son and sobbed in relief, thanking him over and over for saving her life. When the storm hit, my son and the three teens tending the fire were instantly surrounded by swirling hot ashes from the fire. They screamed in pain, batting away the burning coals. When the wind picked up the two boys and flung them into the trees, my six foot five son somehow managed to tuck the teenage girl under his arm and hang on. Her father reached out from the sweatlodge, grabbed one of her flying feet and hauled her into the lodge. They couldn't find my son who had disappeared in a black wall of hail and smoke.

While two large nearby sheds the size of granaries smashed into the trees, my son turned and calmly walked to the lee side of the house out of the wind. He tried to get back to the lodge to help the others but when he stuck his head out, a giant rock bounced off his cheek. Just as he ducked back to the shelter of the house wall, a twenty foot holiday trailer flew past him and landed upside down in the shattering trees. He waited out the storm just under the eaves, watching the roof disintegrate over his head. When the wind died down, he came in the east door to see how we had fared. Through the entire storm, he heard my voice frantically screaming in his head, asking where he was.

We staggered outside unable to believe the carnage from a storm lasting less than half an hour. All the trees behind the house were broken off near the ground, any remaining bark stripped away. Half the house roof was gone, leaving bare rafters. The living room ceiling gaped open to the sky while muddy water dripped to the floors below. Huge rocks, picked up from the open prairie left gigantic holes in the outside walls of the house. One missed the picture window by inches. The house lay skewed off its foundation. We found out later the tornado's rise to clear the hillside probably saved us from total disaster.

When the tornado dropped back down the hill behind us, it tore a house trailer right off its cement pad. The home was never found, only wreckage strewn for over twenty miles. Luckily its occupants were with us and remained unharmed.

Rocks and sand delivered unbelievable damage. One rock shattered the back window of a truck parked in front of the house. The trucks and cars parked outside the house were so full of sand and mud, none of the engines would start. Every vehicle needed new windows and paint jobs from the blasting sand, rocks and roof materials.

Some incidents still defy explanation. Despite one collapsed portion, the little sweat lodge made of flimsy willows remained intact throughout the tornado, saving all six occupants from harm. Of the eighteen people there, only one lady, the owner of the house trailer, had a small cut on her finger. I tore all the muscles in my left arm, shoulder and upper back. Whether from carrying the little girls or pulling the teenage boys into the house, I don't know. Yet while the tornado flung buildings, holiday trailer and vehicles into the air, my son walked, *unharmed* to safety. He had one small bruise on his cheek from the flying rock. Inside the house, water, mud and sand blasting around the closed window frames coated everything in a sea of dirty water. The kitchen counters and sinks carried two inches of muddy sand and grass. Yet, not a foot away, the table, loaded with the feast I had just finished preparing for ceremony, *had not one drop of water or grain of sand upon it!* Strangest of all, before the storm hit, the Elder placed his pipe outside the sweat lodge on the horns of an ancient buffalo skull. Except for its bowl turning upside down, the *pipe never moved through the entire storm!*

My son dreamt he looked into the eye of a tornado. He knew if he wasn't afraid it would not harm him. If he grew fearful, it would kill him. In his dream, seven suns at different positions arced across the sky. It was seven days from his dream when the tornado struck. Throughout the entire storm he remained calm. In the kitchen after the storm, he showed me his quiet palms while mine shook like a leaf. He knew and he believed, acting out his truth. He would later name his first child, Kistin, a Cree word for "Big Wind."

****

Now I called up my memories of that raging storm. It taught me how to cope with fear, do what I had to do and move on. It was time *I* moved beyond the fear. I did it once, I could do it again. In meditation I turned and attacked the emotional fear of cancer:

Muscle knotting, pain screaming I grabbed my guides and dove into the snarling tornado of dark threatening hate, ugly, black, green depths of fear. It ate me, swallowed, digested, swirled, drowned, smothered, smashed, hurled, haunted, hauled and disintegrated me. I see black boiling mass before me and fly into its eye. It snarls around me, flings me into the depths of the ocean and smashes me upon its rocks, scraping my flesh on coral reefs. Swallowed whole by a whale it spat me onto hundred foot waves in a screaming, broiling sea of the blackest night. I ride the waves alone, a small dot on a seething black ocean of fury, flung to the highest peaks and slammed into the depths so deep my feet touch sand before it drags me up again.

I scream at the elements, scream out my name, scream out my fury. I dare the world to do its worst. I imagine my body with a hundred tumours, pop, Pop, POP! I imagine my deformity, my worst pain, worst anger, fury, grief, horror, betrayal, loss, denial, disgust, shame, hatred and I feel it, feel it, *feel it!* I scream at the swirling fear around me and snarl into its face. "Do your worst! Is this it? Is it the f-------best you can do? Come on!"

I fling myself into that black storm with its roiling depths of heart palpitating, endless fear, a monster unchecked. I become part of it, become the fear, dive in again, make it swallow me, eat me, chop me into fragments and hurl me into the vicious black hole until I am nothing, nothing, nothing but fear.

Yet I breathe, feel my breath, *feel* how little this touches my soul. Feel myself as I am. All that I am. I feel it, feel it and *feel* it, this thing that knots my back, screaming, frenzied, violent, shattering pain and I force the fear to tie itself tighter, harder, fiercer until my back grinds into a thousand clumps of agony. I clench my fists so hard my fingernails curl. Fury rides me so harsh and malevolent I barely breathe and still I sneer, "Is this it? This best you can do? Harder! Harder! Make it worse, worse until I hate, hate, hate you with every fibre of my being! And still I live! Still I breathe! I shook my fist in its snarling face, "Screw you! SCREW YOU!" I scream it through my teeth.

I flew to the Earth Cancer Spirit who sneered at my fear so long ago. I dug her, screaming, struggling body out of the ground.

"Give me Earth Cancer Energy! Give it to me! Show me what it is!" I was so wild; I became the black hate, a swirling monster consumed with fury. I BECAME the fear and I grew ugly, vicious and malevolent – a storm, a seething tornado of black energy spinning out of control. Vengeful, depraved, I wanted her. I WANTED HER! I wanted her energy NOW!

She cowered before me and I hated her. She dared to scare me with her thoughts? I felt like Dorothy uncovering the truth of Oz. In scorning disgust I watched her shallow weakness and it blew my mind in rage.

"Why?" I screamed in her face, my jaws clenched in madness.

"I wanted to control you!"

"Why?" My rigid body shook in bone-deep hatred.

"I wanted your energy."

"Why?" I shook her in a two fisted frenzy.

She babbled, "I wanted you to be less. To never fulfill your destiny."

"And what is that?" I roared in her face. "I am as I am and I hate you! I can destroy you!"

I flung her into the air above me, caught her and slashed her to ribbons with my curled nails, then slammed her weeping mess into a mountain wall. "You f------- coward! You damned bitch! You lousy, muckraking, screaming miserable coward. You filthy abomination! You disgust me. You can't have my power. You can't be me! You can't have what I have. You can't have what I never gave you! You can't be me! Find your own damned soul! You can't have mine. I will never give it up! I take back my power! I take back everything I am. I will *never* be less than I am. You...can't...have...me!

I hurled her so deep into the earth it left a furrowed hole. Out of its depths rose a black cloud. A young man's face took shape in the swirling mass drifting towards me.

I held my ground, fists ready, snarling, "Who the hell are you?"

"I am the coward's way." He called to me in a calm voice. He had no form other than his shifting face.

"And what is that? Life or Death?" I ground me teeth so hard they ached.

"Hiding from both."

Ah hell.... Isn't that what fear really is? I deflated like a balloon and came back to myself in a weakened muddle of spent sighs.

I drew a long slow breath, letting my tension release. So...I just embraced death in all its forms of fear. How do I now embrace life in all its forms of joy? Damn! Why does it have to be so sensible and sane? I faced the fear, went head to head, toe to toe, and still I lived, breathed my way through it all, breathed, breathed, breathed. Fear, fury and truth are all part of life – especially mine right now....

My afterthoughts:

When fear dogs your every thought, your only recourse is anger. Fight for your life! Fight for a life without fear, beyond the coward's way. Dive into fear; make it do its worst to you. Imagine the worst case scenario, the worst storm, the blackest night. See it for what it is: just a lesson in facing truth and the emotions swirling around it. When you face the fear in all its forms, breath in its storm of emotions and own them, something changes inside you. You become the fear, the fury, the horror and the truth of who you really are. No illness, not even death can take that away from your soul. You are who you are, full measure. And still you breathe on this day. Eventually you drift into the peaceful aftermath of acceptance. Let tomorrow be what it will. For now, you have earned the strength and courage of a survivor. Be proud of it. Walk in dignity always.

Perhaps the Cancer Earth Spirit was simply a test about my inner strength. Fury lent me power I never knew I possessed. It seemed like the final test of my commitment to simply be who I am, and all that I am. What I fought and won is priceless. Beyond the fear, I found the dignity and pride as a survivor and I shall never relinquish either! In the background, I hear my ego wail for it has no power now. I reduce it to a turquoise bubblegum ball and drop it into my pocket for another day.

"The decision to make the present moment into your friend is the end of ego."

Ekart Tolle

This journey into wisdom is not always delightful. Stand in the truth of who you are at this moment and be not afraid of Life.

39.

Healing Crises

"The body works according to natural law....this conforms to Hering's Law of Cure: All cure is from the head down, from the inside out and in reverse order as the symptoms first appeared."

Dr. Bernard Jensen, *Guide to Diet and Detoxification* (00:49)

Months after surgery, my liver hit a healing crisis. I had read enough to know congested liver issues cause cancer, so no surprise that it would need healing. How ironic people are told the cancer spreads to their liver. Actually, it probably *started* there! My liver became very sore – painfully so at times. I 'hear' the word, "overburdened". Yes, my overworked liver must produce over 13,000 different chemicals, maintain over 2,000 internal enzyme systems, filter blood, produce bile for digestion, break down hormones, regulate blood sugar *plus* change harmful toxins into substances that can be safely eliminated from the body. This information comes from Brenda Watson, N.D., C.T. and her brochure called, *Do You Suffer From Liver Problems?* Here too, is another clue why we must stay away from sugar as we heal. Sugar/glucose spikes just add another burden to our struggling livers. With my detoxification regime, I was dumping fifty-seven years of toxins back onto my liver. It had every right to complain.

I aided it by stopping my beloved coffee (one cup was still too much), reducing the starches, cutting out all deep-fried foods, existing on juices, soups and *some* wholegrain breads – five small meals per day.

One morning, as I awoke, I 'saw' an image of rich creamy milk pouring into half a coconut shell. I never questioned it; I just started making breakfast smoothies with coconut milk and fruits. Yum!

When I visited Dr. Anne Mageau, NMD. DNM, RMT, RNCP, D.AC, she laughed when I told her about the coconut milk. This Doctor of Natural Medicine, licensed in both Canada and the United States said it was the perfect food for me right now. Coconut milk is very supportive of the liver and will nurture it during this crisis. She encouraged me to cook my eggs in coconut oil as well. When I told her my healing regime, she reassured me I was doing *everything* right! My guides were right on target with *all* the information they had given me. Finally, a physical, medical validation of my messengers. So perfect!

I met Dr. Mageau when I signed up for her course on Detoxification at a local college. Like me, she had cancer and cured herself too. Best of all, she just 'gets' me, accepting my body testing technique and the assistance of my guides. She felt like a friend I had known forever and we just 'clicked' when we met. Later, I would discover she has Ojibwa/Anishnabeg roots like me. I can not emphasize how important this connection is with whomever you see in the medical profession. If you don't like them or don't trust them...don't go back!

According to Dr. Mageau's extensive urinalysis, I am healing well. The juicing with fruits and vegetables helped me detox gently but now I need more protein, my iron levels are lower than they should be. Anaemia is an ongoing problem with me, again, because of chronic liver issues. Dr. Mageau suggested Salba, a plant protein with high contents of Omega 3's, fibre and antioxidants. My vitamin D, potassium and magnesium are also slightly low. I know mineral deficiencies can cause cancer, so no surprise. I had no base numbers from before my surgery (doctors never tell you any results) so I just carry on, hoping these deficiencies are decreasing with all the healthy stuff I'm taking. Also, the fungus I have in my right ear could be linked to bowel issues. Any fungus is systemic, the result of other issues in your body. Here too is a sign my lymphatic system is not running as fluidly as it should – yet.

As an aside, I threw away two of my beloved houseplants around this time. I have plants, which are twenty years old and more. Yet one developed bugs, another a root fungus. Another coincidence? Or maybe just a symbolic parallel for my body.

Dr. Mageau also recommended Thyrosol to support my low functioning thyroid. I have always suspected my thyroid was low yet nothing showed up on medical tests. Dr. Mageau says the archaic tests they still use in the labs are based on 1940 bodies and do not accurately read our twenty first century sensitivity. Now, for the first time ever, I recorded my temperature twice a day for a month before I went to see her. To my surprise my temperature was three to four degrees below normal and fluctuated wildly – menopausal issues still working their way out. My sugar levels and my heart rate are also below normal. When I body tested the Thyrosol, my body rocked sideways, something I had never seen it do before. When I asked my guides for the dosage, I 'heard' "two or three." After taking Thyrosol at home a few times, I found it started to increase my heart rate so I stopped taking it. Later it dawned on me; I *really needed only two or three.* Next time I'll LISTEN AND ASK for more information. Might save me some money too.

To test my iodine levels Dr. Mageau simply painted my inside wrist with iodine. If your body needs iodine, it will absorb it immediately. The iodine took over six hours to absorb and fade from my skin so my iodine levels are still low. The iodine patch should take 24 hours to disappear from your skin.

Dr. Mageau also recommended ½ teaspoon of Turmeric in my daily juices. As I write this, I realize I forgot to take it! Recently, I read how Turmeric is a powerful anti-cancer agent. I immediately went to my kitchen and body tested this spice. My body shows no reaction to it at all. Perhaps I did not need it then or now.

This naturopath also told me if I had taken chemo and radiation, I'd have a lot more problems than I do now!

Sometimes I am still amazed at the incredible guidance I receive both from Spirit and from the people who come into my life when I need them the most. I asked my guides what they wanted to be called and they said (archly), 'Guides of Wisdom'. It made me smile and I added, 'Love'. So I thank my guides of Wisdom and Love for their magical, wonderful assistance.

Dr. Mageau explained colitis, an inflammation of the liver from the major detoxing. I ran full tilt into this problem as my liver healed in slow increments, cycles where my liver ached, bubbled and gurgled. I felt weak and had yellow BM's. After a few days, the pain eased and I felt healthy again. Dr. Jensen was right; I gradually healed from the top to the bottom of my liver. At first, the pain was high on my right side in front and just beneath my shoulder blade in back. As the months went by, the pain moved slowly downward until only the bottom of my liver hurt, then ached, then slowly returned to normal. Sudden weakness or dizzy spells (liver cleansing side effect) lasted only momentarily. They worried me of course, yet I *knew* I was healing.

Dr. Mageau gave me a hot castor oil remedy to relieve the colitis. I smeared castor oil on an old tea towel. Then I wrapped it around my right rib cage. Covering it with another thin tea towel, I then pinned a bath towel over both and placed an electric heating pad on top. I sat with this hot oil pack for an hour and a half. It felt so soothing and wonderful, I often fell asleep. I used these packs three days in a row, took a three day break and spread the area with olive oil. Whenever my liver felt sore, I repeated the packs, usually a few months apart. As the months passed I noticed the colitis attacks became further and further apart.

One morning, in my waking vision I 'saw' bran flakes, raisins, tomatoes and stewed prunes. Whole grain cereals provide calcium and magnesium; raisins have iron while tomatoes and prunes offer potassium. So again, I added more whole grains and nuts to the strict fruit and vegetable diet I tried to maintain while my liver healed. I avoided all fried, greasy foods, caffeine and alcohol. I reduced my meat to relieve the daily duties of my liver. I added tomatoes, a wonderful alkaline treat, to my afternoon juicing. In addition, the stewed prunes cleaned and cleared my intestines from the entire 'plumbing' backlog that I saw in the dream. Amazing how this fits together!

I used several techniques to help my liver and gall bladder flush. My guides told me to drink as much water as I possibly could right now. I went for another Infra red sauna and foot bath too. I considered trying a two day liver detox with apple cider, lemons and olive oil but sensed, somehow, it would be too much of a shock for my recovering body. Then, one of my more powerful psychic friends, Sue, called me saying she was very worried about my liver. She says it is in a fragile state, requiring gentle, loving care right now. She agreed with me about not doing any harsh liver cleanses. Oddly enough, I had searched but never found apple cider in *any of the five stores* I went to. I laugh now because my guides know me too well and probably hid it from me.

Real detoxing takes time, so expect it and be patient with your body. Allow it to gently process at its own pace. Eat well: five small meals a day, mostly vegetables and fruit. Juice regularly and rest often. As your body flushes a lifetime of accumulated toxins, don't think it will be easy. Expect itchy skin, dry scalp, flu-like symptoms, joint and muscle pains, stomach upsets, diarrhea, brain fog, tiredness, weakness, depression and all kinds of emotional upheavals. Expect a pressure and bubbling sound under your right rib cage – it's your liver at work. It feels like it expands then releases. Consequently, your liver pays less attention to other body functions, so of course you feel weak and tired for a while. Rest often until the crises passes! Don't eat anything after dinner so your liver has at least 8 – 10 hours of rest before breakfast. All the junk you stored in your body, you now must face on a daily basis as your body flushes it away. *Don't think it will be easy.* As long as you have regular BMs, often with a yellow colour from the bile released by the liver, know you are healing and moving forward into wellness once again.

I had bought Milk Thistle, a well known organic liver supplement, before my surgery but never used it, knowing it was too soon. Now, I body tested it and felt my body surge towards it. It is so good tasting with its mixture of dates and other fruits. I felt it soothe my liver within a few hours.

These healing components are good enough for now. If I'm tired and weak, I sit, read, meditate or sleep. I do nothing my body is incapable of at this time. So be it. It is my healing journey and I do the best I can for me.

I bought some chocolate treats to celebrate my healing body after seeing the naturopath. I didn't enjoy them. After being away from sugar for so long, I disliked its bitter aftertaste. My guides tell me 'no sugar or starches right now' just to help my liver heal gently and lovingly.

Also, no oranges, just grapefruits right now. I body tested oranges and it was, 'Nope'. I am a Type O blood type. Oranges are too acidic for our bodies yet we can tolerate the alkaline grapefruits with ease.

I listen as hard as I can to my body– like I never did before. Everything in our life is a lesson and this is my journey – redirecting my life to a healthier, happier, brighter direction. I am so grateful for this second chance to get it right.

40.

My Body's New Renovations

"I've heard it said that prayer is an act of talking to God, while meditation is an act of listening."

Elizabeth Gilbert, *Eat Pray Love*, (06:132)

Remember how the mind thinks and dreams in symbols? Many months into my healing, I dreamt of living in a clean but older house, which needed renovating. I pulled two layers of curtains off high tiny windows and looked at the narrow bathroom with its old 1960's flooring and fixtures (I was a teen through the 1960's). The toilet works fine but the tub is gone, just a blackened hole with a chunk of black and white toxic stuff (in the shape of a liver) around the drain in the floor. My dreams changed now, giving me wonderful symbolic images of my body's healing progress.

In this dream, I saw platters of healthy food arrayed on a kitchen counter. The food was for Cliff, me and other women in the house who were helping me. I know I did not prepare the food. I just paid for it. A whistling, cheerful, energetic young man did the renovations while I supervised his work and paid the bills. He says, "You're too beautiful to cook."

A man in a grey business suit comes bustling in, talking about an itinerary to Thailand and how things are going to happen quickly so I need to be ready to go. I'm determined to have these renovations completed before I leave.

I want to tear out a wall to modernize the bathroom. I know the structure of the house is sound, it just needs remodelling. Yeah, just like my nearly sixty year old body!

And here is the sweet symbolism of this dream: This house represents my body, cleaner now, older but sound, just needing a few renovations. But I don't have to do the work! I simply oversee it, provide good food and let it happen. In the bathroom, the functioning toilet means my body is 'flushing' well. Yet the plumbing from the absent tub still needs scraping and cleaning. I suppose my intestines are still dealing with the backlog of toxins so I must keep 'washing' them down until they are clear too. I know, even in the dream, it will all drain away, clean and clear. It just takes time.

I asked my guides what the toxins at the drain were and I 'heard', "Cheese, greed, fury, housing guests, fury, curds, care worn grief, sorrow, nasty news, shared consulting, care worn blood, nerves, sorrow" - rebuilding now, releasing now, grieving, coming, dreaming, sieving, slumbering, laughing, loving, relieving, sowing and being me. I live on...in this healing body. I worked on these feelings, releasing my frustration from the long healing process, building stronger boundaries against people who still try to use me and move into the joy of life.

I'm not sure what the man from Thailand represents. I dream of Asian people a lot. Maybe they'll help me market this book.

I recall another dream I had after a meal of too much meat and fat. I went to bed tired, in pain and worried about it. I just prayed and surrendered into it. I didn't know what else to do. I dreamt of Cliff and I caught in a heavy snowstorm. Our four-wheel drive pulled us slowly but easily through the drifts. I saw the road, bare and dry just beyond the next drift. We almost slid into the congested traffic around us. We stopped to help a young Asian couple with two little girls and a holiday trailer. They were trying to pass us, going in the opposite direction.

I chatted with the friendly mother who told me they planned to go through the mountain pass before stopping for the night. I advised her, "It is five or six hours away and you don't know what the roads are like. You would be safer to get a room here and tackle the roads in the daylight." I envisioned a nice hotel room with waterslides for the girls to play in while their parents relaxed by the pool. When the husband joined us, a cheerful young man, I told him the same.

My dream interpretation: Asian couple – again! Why do I dream of them all the time? Even as I write this I don't understand.

Cliff and I were in a clogged, cold, drifting road and it is night – the darkest, hardest hours. We were on our way home and I saw bare and dry roads ahead. My advice to the couple was to stay, go no further, just relax and enjoy their evening. Tomorrow will take care of itself. It was too dangerous to continue and they were exhausted from a full day on the road. I needed to take my own advice! 'Don't push so hard, relax, enjoy the evening and let tomorrow take care of itself. I am almost home, almost healed.

In archetypal symbolism, the car like the black horse of my earlier dream is something which carries us from one place to another, from one place in the psyche, one idea or thought or endeavour or situation to another. Our car, like my body, would pull us safely through the storm to bare, dry roads ahead, beyond the clogged, congested traffic. I see this as eventually moving beyond this clogged, congested, dark detoxing era to a smoother, clearer life ahead. Times are hardest in the dark night when we are exhausted with no vision of tomorrow. Yet I felt safe and knew we would make it home without mishap.

When I asked my guides in the morning, they said, "You will be okay. This is a minor mishap on the road to health. Your journey is not complete and much healing must take place. Your journey to wellness goes well. **Know the liver is the heart of the soul. Know it needs healing from the soul outward**. You are moving north into wisdom and growth and you will survive this holocaust of snow, debris clearing and wealth of new information and health to wellness (Yes! In the dream, we *were* moving north!). The careworn attitude is a restless one because you have been sick for so long. The care given to your body must continue. Go slowly, dream often and know you are taken care of. You have much to learn and say and speak and write. The truth of this journey is your path to wellness and health and it lies straight ahead. Go with God and be at peace. You will solve this riddle easily and well. Again, we say to you, we are with you always. Your health is important to us because you have much to do yet. And you will be well. We honour you and your wishes and we care for you. You will be well and all is well."

"P.S. We love you" – from the Angels of Light and Mercy.

Oh how I need these validations! You may think I sound like a broken record but the fear creeps back in the night and only these incredible messages keep my faith. This road is not easy, especially when I'm exhausted, at my weakest. I am so *tired* of being sick! They had the careworn attitude pegged. I must be patient – not one of my strong points. I took years to get sick; I can not heal in a few months or even a year (sigh).

North is the place of wisdom in our Aboriginal teachings. It is the place of the white haired Elders, and our beautiful white buffalo, the symbol of gratitude, innocence and purity. She teaches us we do not have to struggle to survive if the right action is joined by the right prayer. By uniting the mundane and the divine appropriately, all which is needed is available. This comes from Ted Andrew's *Animal Speak* (04:254). He also reminds us God helps those who help themselves.

A few days later, Shu and I did another internal meditation tour of my liver. We sat inside it this time – a hollowed out domed space, clear and clean as we watched the blood pulsing overhead. Some of it looked dark and dirty red, while other places were cleaner, clearer, pinkish brown and white. She said the dark was the 'bad blood' still washing away. She encouraged me to drink lots of water the next two to three days and flush it even more. We stayed in the dome for some time, watching the blood pulse. It reassured me because during the first body tour months ago, the liver was too dense to enter, clogged with toxins. As a further validation of my shrinking, swollen liver, I could now wear my normal bra size. Before this date, I had to wear a bra ten inches wider around my ribs – evidence of substantial swelling after the surgery.

Shu also showed me some white stuff in the corner, like seeds, similar to the stuff I saw on top of the bathroom drain in my earlier dream. I asked her if it was cancer and she replied, "No, just seeds."

"For what?" I asked but awoke without an answer. When I asked again, I 'heard', "Seeds of love, returning strength, wisdom, goodness, kindness, joy and care. We can plant the seeds in the dome, but not yet, not until the toxins are gone." Cleansing before rebuilding makes sense.

41.

Burying the Tumour and Celebrating

"Let each day be a stone in the path of growth."
Elizabeth Kubler-Ross, *Death, the Final Stage of Growth*, (75:167)

I awoke with high anxiety, fear riding high. I surrendered to it, sitting in my nagging worries. I meditated, imagined myself 'going with the flow', floating my boat downstream, no paddles, just trust. I thought I was doing quite well until I looked back. My ego, which I 'see' as a little white egghead like Humpty Dumpty with legs, sits behind me, eyes enormous. And he's got my tumor, wrapped up in a thick cloth, tied on a long rope bouncing along behind my boat! I need to deal with this.

I lean back and cut the rope. I reinforce my determination that cancer will not define me; it can not control my every thought. I am much more than this aberration! So I sit down in my boat and look back. My ego has tied the tumor back on. It likes the fear, feeds off it and grows in power. Damn!

I cut the rope again, untie the loose end throw it in the water. I duct tape my ego's mouth shut and sit down, serene once again in my downstream thoughts. I look back and there is the tumor, tied back on *again*, bouncing along behind in the water. I tell it, "I forgive you. I release you!" and throw it back in the water. No good, it just returns.

This time, I sigh, remove the tape from my ego's mouth, pull up the tumor and float into shore, resting in the sunlight. My anxious ego, no longer in control, asks me what I'm going to do.

"Nothing." I reply, resting tiredly in the sun.

I close my eyes and pray, asking, "Is there a loving way to dispose of this?"

I hear, "Yes, there is. This tumor was a part of you. You must honour it in a loving way. Hold a ceremony and with honour, respect and gratitude, bury it."

I slant a wary look at my egghead ego, "You okay with this?"

It gulps and nods nervously, "As long as I can revisit it."

I see where this is going! "You can revisit it, on occasion. But you can never, ever dig it up. Promise?"

Slowly, sadly it nods its head.

"And no symbols, replicas, pictures, etc. shall you hold – ever!" Reluctantly, it agrees. Self worship and martyrdom I do *not* need! I've watched too many women cradle their illness, draining every last drop of pity and sympathy from those around them. They will never be well as long as they cling to their past, loving the attention it garners.

Yeah, I know my old ego well but I'm holding the lines now. I hate its negative thought patterns, reminders and sly little 'slip-in' fears it uses to dog my life. Enough!

I thought about inviting my friends to the burial ceremony but it seemed too gruesome. My ego and I will do this together, in a loving, honourable way.

I examine the rope and tumor. The rope has bright multicoloured strands with white woven through it. Rainbows are always associated with Spirit, the bright promise after the storm. The tumor is thickly wrapped in a sky blue and white patterned cloth. Why?

The cloth reminds me of clouds in the sky, drifting upward in a beautiful diagonal pattern. Flat-bottomed, these clouds reach for new, rounded, dreamy, fluffy heights. White, the colour of purity, sharing and truth, is also the colour of the crown chakra, giving us access to universal wisdom. I see the white clouds as Divine messages filled with love and wisdom floating down to me.

Blue reminds me of the blue diamond, always there under the self-imposed crap. Yet no diamond resides in this bundle, just old, stale air and decayed flesh, ended now. Blue also represents happiness, calm and truth according to Ted Andrews (04:50). The bundle is egg-shaped like all my visions of the purple tumor inside. The egg shape intrigues me, carrying the potential of death or fertility. Rebirth – the symbol of resurrection.

Bundled up in thick layers of cloth to protect me, the tumour is something no longer needed or useful. Its job is done; its passion spent; its purpose fulfilled, empty now of design or reason. It deserves an honourable burial.

The brightly wrapped tumour is a gift. It shocked me into taking better care of myself, opening my heart to all the love around me and pushing me into expressing who I truly am - permanently and lovingly. I learned to give and receive love equally, full rainbow circle, a rope of love from Spirit to me. I also learned a new way to express myself with a clearer connection to universal wisdom. It started the resurrection of my heart, mind, body and spirit. What I learn, I share. Of course! My tumor must be buried in these colors to honour its gift for me. How perfect! How amazing! How loving!

I came out of meditation to write this down before I lost any of it. Looking out the window I notice a white cloud, which looks like a roaring, snarling bear on its hind legs. But as I watch in fascination, his mouth closes and he holds what looks like my bundled tumor in his claws! I write this down, remembering the bears I faced months ago and how they symbolised my fears, courage, strength and determination. When I look outside again, the tumor is gone and the bear looks like a busy beaver, slowly drifting forward.

Yes I do have much work to do and it is time to release, grieve, give thanks and move forward. What a lesson today. Next time I looked up, it's just a cloud, shining more brightly than the grey ones around it, a small spot of sunshine in the warm, flowing air....

Back in mediation, I discussed with my guides a burial ceremony for my tumor. Since I don't have the tumor physically, I must perform this ceremony on a spiritual level, through my *intentions*. I refused to even think of burying it on our acreage. It is too close for my ego's reminders. So we decided on a spot near our family cemetery far, far away. It is a beautiful, serene area on the top of a distant, isolated riverbank.

We also discussed what I wanted to bury with it. I wanted to get rid of old negative thought patterns from childhood, the 'scare me with the Bogey Man stuff; the 'if only' and 'what if's... leading to wasted emotions and useless drama. I imagined a large wicker basket and lid and put in little, colourful 'worry dolls' to represent these old childhood patterns. I also added my lack of self worth, in a clear glass jar and lid shaped like a star. Pretty but empty. I kept a big shining star of my growing, glowing self worth made from love and nurturing – mine for eternity. I buried criticism and judgement that I 'should' be pretty, fragile and empty. Now, I love myself down to my soul and back outwards. I held onto my forgiveness and understanding. Finally, I gently placed my tumor inside the basket. It is huge, almost to my knees in size because it has so many protective layers bundled around it. I honoured its gift, recognized, accepted and healed – forever more. I kissed it good-bye and closed the lid.

We buried it deep within a hillside, far from anyone or anything, returned to Mother Earth from whence it came, ashes to ashes, dust to dust....

I thought I might visit it occasionally in remembrance and gratitude for the life changing journey which led me closer to Spirit and my own purpose in life. Yet I never returned in meditation – had no desire or need to do so. Two years later, my bird totems took me there in my sleep, we drifted above the spot but all signs or remnants are gone back to Mother Earth, as it should, as it was meant to be.

My guides told me, "Clean your house". In our Aboriginal beliefs, we begin with ourselves in the healing process. Then like ripples on a pond, we reach out to heal our homes, our families, our community and our earth. Cleaning my house also required a spiritual, emotional and mental cleansing. It meant clearing and cleaning the energies of my closest relationships into a renewed sense of love, honour, respect, joy, abundance and peace. It also meant backing away from toxic people while wishing them well on their journey. Yeah! These are the final little chunks of 'bad blood' on my dress.

I dream of my parents now and feel so happy to see them once again, if only in my dreams. I loved Dad, my wonderful musical, boisterous, funny, loving Irish father who taught me so much about life. I admired and loved Mom, respecting her actions and determination to be a good mother and she was. I am not blind to either of my parents' faults. I simply cherish who they are and what they gave me.

I accompanied my guide, Shu on another tour of my body. The happiest cells were my breasts with the tiny new lymph nodes surrounded by green and white energy – colours of healing and light. The oldest cells were in my stomach lining, doing well, sighing with pleasure with almond milk, alkaline protein. The busiest cells were the liver, kidneys and pancreas. The liver cells were the youngest, rejuvenating and truly kicking the toxins into the bile ducts and out into my intestines. My kidneys were busy doing their share while rebuilding themselves too. The islets of Langerhans – insulin making cells of the pancreas are doing well but demand NO SUGAR for the next two days. Sugar spikes will damage their growth.

I'm getting there! I'm healing, growing and rebuilding now. I dreamt of an apple, orange and kiwi in a row and heard the word 'excoriation'. Random House dictionary defines it: 'to strip off or remove the skin from" (80:461). This sounds drastic but truly depicts my liver stripping dead cells away and building new healthy tissue. For the next several months I used this combination of fruits every day in my juicer. A year later, I would read a magazine article by Norma Hope, a certified Colon Hydrotherapist. Although all fruits are acidic, she writes, "The fruits that are okay are apples, berries and kiwi" (09:7). Oranges, according to Michael Van Straten's book, *The Healthy Food Directory*, strengthen the walls of tiny blood capillaries, provide 110 percent of Vitamin C, plus thiamine, folic acid, B6, magnesium, phosphorus, riboflavin, calcium, iron and more – all perfect for my healing liver. "Drinking orange juice with a meal can increase iron absorption by up to two-and-a-half times (99:25). He says the pectin in apples joins up with heavy metals such as lead and mercury and helps the body get rid of them (99:18). Kiwi, while providing twice as much Vitamin C you need per day, is also good for the immune system, skin and digestive problems (99:43). My body tells me the truth once again!

I continue with the castor oil packs when needed and my mainly vegetarian diet. Such hard work! Yet I know it is the right path back to health. I dream endless nightmares of violence, danger and attacks but through it all, I am uninjured, unharmed. All the things which created dis-ease must leave and the darkness they represent can often be experienced in dreams. It's what true detoxing 'looks' like symbolically.

A year later, I dreamt again of my 'house', the renovations complete. The kitchen had new white cupboards and beautiful hunter green countertops, the colors of cleansing and healing. The bathroom contained a gigantic three-cornered silver-green tub with a shower stall in another corner. All is in working order. Cherry hardwood floors covered living room and kitchen floors. Silver-green wallpaper with a faint fleur-de-lis, elegant French provincial furniture and soft fabric lamps created a cozy, welcoming atmosphere. In the basement, bare concrete floors continually flooded with clean rain while the upper floors remained liveable and dry. I see dirty towels and laundry still needing washing; the detoxing continues. Months later, I walked into a show home with the exact colours of my dream. It was so stunning I wanted to buy it.

The excoriation continues. I 'see' the white bulging veins on my liver shrinking, replaced by new, smaller, pinker, healthier ones. My liver gets a major overhaul now. I am to continue with the apple/orange/kiwi juice in the morning followed by the coconut milk smoothie of blueberries, strawberries and bananas before noon with soups for meals and another green juice in the afternoon. Such is my healing program and I take heart it continues as 'planned'.

I called in my bird totems and they flew me to a red dawn – new energy blowing in on the wind. K... is angry with me and my lack of faith and crowding doubts. But his mate understands my human failings. Still, my stubborn faith keeps me fighting. They showed me a room filled with stacks of books I will write. Yet I must get beyond the paralyzing criticism and condemnation to write them. His mate tells me the renovations out to the skin is necessary to prepare me for the listening and channelling I will eventually do. I am already channelling but it will come clearer as my body releases the toxins, past emotions and memories now blocking the energy flow. When she finished K... came back and whirled me up into his arms, loving me and holding me close.

I felt so good but my treat of pecan pie and coffee went horribly wrong. I felt sick afterwards, my liver was in agony for the next day and a half. Ouch! My poor healing liver can not tolerate coffee or sugar. I need to tell my ego to take a back seat and get over its whining for treats and coffee! I'm back to drinking fennel and fenugreek tea (sigh). Then my massage therapist casually mentioned coffee is very dangerous to a detoxing liver. Really?

After many months, I went off the Cellfood; body testing proved I no longer need it for now. Milk thistle continues to soothe my healing liver. I finally 'hear' the excoriation is slowing. I 'see' a mango added to the other three fruits for my morning juice. Van Straten says mangoes are a "great combination of antioxidants, in a very easily digestible form....good for convalescence, skin problems, the immune system and cancer protection" (99:42). And I give thanks to my guides' truth once again.

In celebration of my returning health, Cliff and I planned a big fish fry for our friends. A couple times each year, we buy pickerel (walleye), the best tasting fish in the world and invite all our friends to bring the trimmings. I worried about my energy levels with the house cleaning, preparation, party and clean up. It is lots of work for more than forty people. We've had up to eighty because friends bring friends, etc. Luckily Beryl flew in to help me. One of my friends called from Saskatchewan, visualizing me still languishing weakly in bed, was shocked to discover Beryl and I staining the new deck Cliff had just finished in time for the party.

I prayed for strength to get me through the upcoming day. My guides replied, "You have looked at this with fear, now look at it with love." My entire perspective did a one eighty. All my worries faded away; my mind calmed into blank, peacefulness. It carried me through the day, easily, slowly and joyfully focused. I allowed each moment or crisis to work itself out. Instead of trying to do everything myself, I delegated – big step for me! I even slipped away for a quick nap in the late afternoon. In the evening, I slept again then rejoined our friends for a midnight campfire until 3:00 a.m. The pace soothed me, not stressing my body in any way. After months of solitude and quiet healing, it felt so wonderful to laugh and joke and tease with our friends once again. I did it all and I am so proud of myself.

A week later, we took our three grandchildren camping. Again, my guides tell me, "You'll do well". My 'babies' love and joy heal me like fresh air and sunshine. We had a wonderful week of wading in creeks and lakes, gathering rocks for our water fountain, squealing with laughter and enjoying beautiful scenery around our evening campfires. It was worth every moment, despite the twelve loads of laundry when we returned!

I dreamt of my house again. Only this time, I am outside planting flowers and shrubs – an outward beauty. So I tried a new hairstyle and streaked my hair. I bought new semi-precious necklaces and bracelets. I threw out old plants, old clothes, old papers and junk. The rest I saved for a Garage Sale for our canoe club.

Cliff and I helped create an Outriggers paddling Club for Aboriginal families. Our Hawaiian forty-eight foot canoes have a floating amah on the side for balance. We paddle with our grandchildren and members every Sunday afternoon. Yes, my incisions pull but I paddle anyway and love the exercise. We fly through the sunshine across sparkling waters, our faces brushed by gentle winds, keeping pace with the loons, pelicans and Canadian geese families. Life gets no better than this!!

I asked Shu about my underarm incision aching from the paddling. She says it is 'waking up from the numbness, so the pins and needles and occasional aches are normal'. When I asked about the line of black energy running down from the incision, she explained that the cut blocked energy flow - an omen I never realized until several months later.

42.

DNA Healing

The sins of the father are visited upon his children and their children and their children....

Passed through our DNA, old issues, old memories play like broken records through our minds, leaving us bewildered and bemused about where such ideas came from. I knew my family's history, wrote stories about it. Now I encountered a whole new level of pain, grief and anger billowing up from every cell in my body...and it wasn't mine!

When I weighed myself I had dropped another seven pounds. I worried about losing weight like so many terminal cancer patients do but sensed something deeper. Fear of starvation probably lingers in everyone's DNA from ancestral hunger and deprivation. For some it could be more recent, like the hungry 1930 Depression years my parents lived through. In this time of my intentional abundance, I wanted to release this ancient fear. I imagined telling my ancestors 'we have arrived! We have achieved our goal of abundance in all things. There is enough for all." I release the fear of death; guilt and shame of starvation – a failure to provide. I reach back in time and forward in time to release it all.

I met a cheerful, talkative lady, Sandy, who finally gave me further familial strife. Her gift is psychometry, the ability to hold a personal article and gather insights from the owner's psyche. When she held a necklace Beryl had gave me, she described my sister, though they had never met, right down to her physical appearance, her age, personality and the personal issues she struggled with.

Sandy then described two ladies in spirit around me. From her description, I recognized my maternal grandmother, Blanche and her mother, Mary Louise Day, my Ojibwa ancestors. Both were pleased with all the work Beryl and I do plus how we choose to honour our Aboriginal roots in our daily practices and beliefs. Sandy reiterated what strong women these two were, way ahead of their time in their beliefs and actions. I could only smile. I know I come from a long line of strong women. Sandy also said Mary had been a chief, a shaman and a medicine healer in past lives. If she were alive today, she would probably be Prime Minister according to Sandy! Creator made this woman sturdy: physically, mentally, emotionally and spiritually. This gift she passed to me. Sandy encouraged me to try and contact Mary who had been with me all along and who so badly wanted to communicate with me. "She has things to tell she won't tell me!"

That night I meditated and 'saw' her immediately, a young giggling girl in her early thirties. She was a pretty woman with a wide mouth, a strong sturdy build and braids wrapped in a coronet around her head. A white hand-knit shawl wrapped her arms. Somehow I knew it was her favourite. When she smiled, she looked like my daughter and one of my cousins, also her great-granddaughter. Something about the thickness of her upper lip between her nose and her mouth reminded me of Mom's. Mary raised Mom, who often talked about her. Then Mary gave me images of her life that shocked me silent.

Mary Louise Day was born on a small farm, on the outskirts of Sault Ste Marie, Michigan. She told me her grandmother came 'from the land of castles, Versailles, France. Fearing for her life, her grandmother ran away from her abusive husband and found shelter with the Chippewa (Ojibwa) First Nation People. There, she met a gentle warrior she fell in love with and had several children with, including Mary's mother. Mary learned much about medicines and herbs from her Métis (French for 'mixed') parents. The oldest of four children, Mary accepted responsibility at a young age. Her Ojibwa name, similar to Running Deer but with a harder edge to it, grew stronger from all the challenges life threw Mary's way.

She was barely a teenager when men with guns came to their quiet farm when Mary's parents were away. Unlike her girlfriend who ran and hid, Mary stayed, naively innocent of her danger. By the time she was afraid, it was too late. A man dragged her from the closet and raped her repeatedly. In horror I saw them lying in the middle of her parent's freshly sanded floor in the new home they were building. I could see the bright rafters over her head and smell the fresh sawdust. From above, I watched Mary's beautiful auburn hair spill out behind her, as she lay there bloody and exhausted, beneath her panting tormentor.

When she became pregnant with his child, the community forced him to marry her. His name was Jake, my great-grandfather. According to our family records, she was only thirteen.

How could anyone build a good relationship with that kind of beginning? In the mid 1800's, society accepted no other solution to their situation.

When I asked her if she ever loved him, she snapped, "Never! And he paid and paid and paid his whole life."

Jake's Dutch family originally came from a 'holler' in Virginia. A Blue Ridge Mountain hillbilly 'twang' coloured my relatives' vocabulary through the generations. They were all short stocky men who loved big women. Jake was a tough little guy with fair, distinguished, gentlemanly features. Sandy said he had a gift too. He 'saw' things and 'knew' things before anyone did. Too bad he never envisioned the life he forced into existence. But seers can not see their own path, they are as blind to it as the rest of us to ours.

Jake became a Soldier of Fortune, fighting for whoever paid his salary. When the Civil War came, he signed up. I have an old tin type picture of him in full Union uniform; Mary sits before him with their oldest son, Jacob Jr. upon her knee, her wide mouth flat and angry.

When Jake went to the front lines he took Mary with him. She said he feared she would leave him. On the quiet days, she cleaned camp and washed clothes for the soldiers. She had a gun and knew how to use it but the men objected strongly to her fighting and firing beside them. Her knowledge of healing herbs and medicines were a great boon to the doctors and wounded soldiers. Whenever they moved camp, I 'saw' Mary sitting in the back of a wagon, making healing possets and herbal mixtures for the sick and wounded.

She became one of the few women to ever receive a lifetime army pension from the American government for all the lives she saved. When most people worked a month for room, board and $5.00 wages, Mary received $50.00 a month in pension.

One day, while racing to help a wounded soldier, Mary's foot caught in a pile of rocks. It wrenched sideways when she fell. Her knee was never the same. Eventually she walked with a cane when arthritis set in. I know pain in the knee is about forgiveness, or, in this case, its lack.

As a soldier, Jacob seldom came home so his wife and nine children looked after the cattle ranch they built in South Dakota. They had little time left for schooling. Whenever Jacob did return, he was usually 'pretty high on the bottle' according to Mom's stories. Drunk, abusive and mean, Jake beat his wife then his children when they interfered. Once in a fit of rage, he grabbed Mary's pet canary and threw it into the fire, cage and all. His family hated him and were happiest when he left. He lost an eye in one of his wars, replacing it with a glass one. Here too is another parallel with his loss of 'vision' and insight.

Jacob eventually died from either the liquor or war wounds in 1900, just four months before his last son, Wesley was born. I have two large individual portraits of Mary and Jacob in their later years. Her eyes are troubled, angry and wise. His are filled with sorrow, a deep impenetrable angst.

DNA memories carry down the generations. All my life I've felt a bone deep ache in my left knee, the same knee Mary injured. No traumas in my life could explain the pain that never goes away. Sandy says I am empathic enough to 'feel' or perhaps to 'remember' my great grandmother's pain. Beryl and two of my other sisters also have unusual knee issues. I believe our coded DNA message means *Judge without forgiveness.*

In another meditation, I sensed a heavy ball of dark energy drift from around my right ovary and coalesce in my hands. I focused on it sensing another DNA code – a history of rape, passed down from generations of women with similar experiences. I don't believe in coincidence. Our feminine DNA code reads: *Men are not to be trusted.* I want this one removed too. I have been surrounded by good men, trustworthy men all my life and this code serves no purpose. I can sense men's attitudes towards women as soon as I meet them. I trust my instincts and am not afraid.

During a massage session with my friend, Teresa, we found another traumatic DNA memory. We discussed ways to release these codes, which serve no purpose in my life, my children's or grandchildren's. I knew we had to go back to areas of my body still holding this energy. When we did, I suddenly saw another shocking image:

> *A slender young woman with red hair, wearing a leaf-green dress with a white fringe between her shoulder blades, stood in a village square, surrounded by shouting people. She faces a gallows where her brother hangs for a crime he did not commit.*

The power of this young woman's grief, revulsion and fury slammed into me like a blow to my solar plexus. I knew she was my Irish great-grandmother, Margaret Emmaline Syer. I sensed this incident became the catalyst in her leaving Ireland for Canada, far from the horror before her. I have never heard a family story about this incident.

Here was another DNA code: *The Irish suffer endless injustice, prejudice and violence.* Perhaps these deep seated reasons pushed me to write long and loud on prejudice, injustice, family violence and its need for healing. All my books, including, *When We Still Laughed*, contain every one of these ancient DNA codes, so subtle, I never recognized them until now.

Not all our DNA codes are bad. I also inherited the strength, determination and wit of my pioneering ancestors to stubbornly carry on, despite all odds. These qualities, along with a dry, sometimes black humour, carried me through many tough times in my life. Because of them, I am still standing today.

So I simply sat with these emotions. With great love and compassion I allowed them to blow through me while I massaged the physically sore areas they were hidden in for too long. I rubbed my right hip and the muscle which wrapped it, so sore I could barely touch it. I gasped in pain, sobbed, ground my teeth and released, released and released the energy, allowing it to flow out my feet and the top of my head. I massaged my knee and did the same. I gently palmed my stomach over the right ovary, repeating the words, "I am strong, healthy and independent. I fear no man, trusting my instincts to warn me of any danger." I actually winced, feeling something shift and move beneath my fingers. When it finally stopped, I felt nothing but peaceful silence and a quiet sense of identification and pride in all my family ties. I prayed for the pain of our DNA codes to be released from my ancestors, our families and our children and theirs and theirs.

Was this whole thing just my imagination? Again? The next morning, still in my pedagogic state, I suddenly 'saw' Mary leaning over me, peering into my face. With a girlish giggle she ran into the sunshine, her long, heavy plaid skirt flying while her soft moccasins flipped in and out of view. Several feathers, white dipped with red, dangled merrily from her hair. I hope she is free at last.

As I sit and type my story into the computer, I realize I can walk easily for miles now, my hips in balance and free from pain. My left knee feels strong and healthy like my right.

43.

Second Chance? Or Next Step?

"There is always opportunity in crisis. Find the good, find the lesson and you will heal."

Ancient Chinese Proverb

About eighteen months after surgery, life took a new turn which shocked and infuriated me. The final pieces of the cause and cure for my breast cancer revealed themselves and Divine Intervention rocked me to the core. Thus began one the roughest periods of my life.

While in Oahu for a much needed vacation I noticed a red rash on the bottom of my left breast, well below the incision. It scared me. Was the lymphatic system clogged because of the missing lymph nodes? So I exercised more, swinging my arms, pumping them high as if walking very fast. But the rash never stopped. Worry ruined my beautiful holiday. I remained silent refusing to ruin Cliff's break too.

Before I left home, I dreamed of seven white figures in the sky, standing together in the clouds. Suddenly they stood before me, four males and three females, all dressed in white. I cried out to them in welcome, "You came! You came!" They replied, "We are the Elohim and we have come to take you home and teach you what to write." While in Oahu, I dreamed of each guide, one at a time as they came to me, introduced themselves, explained about the past lives we had together and how they had agreed to come and help me now. When I asked if I was leaving earth, they all shook their heads but told me no more. Then they went away and never returned for seven months.

My Naturopath, Dr. Mageau recommended a Thermograph which detects abnormal physiological changes and tumor growth. Cancer cells generate a lot of heat as they divide, creating their own capillaries and blood supply. Dr. Christine Horner, F.A.C.S, a well-known surgeon in the United States, recommends thermograms in her book, *Waking the Warrior*

Goddess, Harnessing the Power of Nature and Natural Medicines to Achieve Extraordinary Health. These digital cameras and computer-software systems are so sophisticated their high-resolution images and precise heat-variation calculations detect cancer "as early as five to ten years before cancer can be seen by a mammogram" (07:21). Cancer's hot metabolism shows up as white/yellow/orange on the full colour computer screen. Normal breasts usually display cooler shades of red, blue and indigo. A study done in the January 2003 American Journal of Radiology concluded this technology could help prevent most unnecessary breast biopsies (07:21).

Most doctors, including mine, know nothing about this technology. Many are told the individuals running the cameras are anything from plumbers to psycho-radicals. Well people used to argue the world was flat too. Yes, a trained technician runs the test but the results are sent to Toronto where qualified professionals read them and submit their findings – just like blood testing!

But I couldn't go. I just could not go and take the test. I had worked so hard to heal myself I lived in denial. I just did not feel strong enough to deal with any bad results. So I bought myself some time through the summer, continued my nutritional regime, paddled with our outrigger club, grew my garden and rested. But the soreness never went away.

By September, I knew I was in trouble. My arm and breast were sore, inflamed and swelling while the rash had spread, covering the old incision too. I waited three agonizing weeks for the thermogram results, my mind racing in fear half the time while the rest of the time I hoped it was just scar tissue. I learned that around the two year period after surgery, many women experience pain because the numb nerve endings awaken. As the nerve endings under my arm and across my left side came alive, they caused my breast muscles to actually spasm. I hoped that's all it was but I somehow 'knew' better.

When I met Tanya, the pretty Siberian lady who did the thermogram test, she 'felt' like an old friend. I 'knew' she would help me heal. Her qualifications included a Bachelor of Science degree. While she ran the test, we chatted easily. She mentioned she also did biofeedback analysis. This word had been popping into my head for some time. I immediately signed up for the computerized health scan.

Biofeedback originated in NASA when the scientists wanted to analyse astronauts on a cellular level both before and after they were in space. This diagnostic tool has been around for twenty years or more, becoming more sophisticated with growing computer technology. Every doctor should have one. Even the FDA approves of them, upgrading them recently from biofeedback to *medical* biofeedback tools. Electrode straps wrapped around your head, wrists and ankles are hooked through an adaptor to the computer program. Every part of us has a frequency, as do all diseases, including cancer. This machine can tell you what bones are out in your back, what scars, damage, viruses, parasites or worms you have; what your various personality quirks and moods are plus any hormone, vitamin, mineral deficiency or illness you may have. It even shows the colour of your aura, which I love because mine changes often. I was heartened to know the cancer numbers were still within normal numbers. Yet it registered a 'skin condition' (unknown cause) on my breast and an inflammation.

Waiting for the thermogram results put my nerves on edge. One day, I had a total meltdown. I was so furious with my ego and its endless 'what if' fears running non-stop through my mind. I went into meditation, grabbed a wooden mallet and pounded my ego into the ground, screaming at it for lying to me and scaring me endlessly. I pounded and pounded and pounded venting my fears, worry, doubts and helpless inaction. Finally, I threw the mallet away, falling on my knees in defeat. I felt no better, just ashamed of my outburst, and humbled by the truth of how little control I really had over this whole issue. Still, it blew off a lot of emotional garbage and calmed me with no harm to anyone or anything.

I spent a day in penitent release. I let go of everything I owned, worked for, accomplished or cherished. I released it all. I released everything connected to me; I released every little detail, family issue, whatever I could not change – not mine to do so. I surrendered it all, gave it up. I gave it up to God. Whatever was delivered upon me I returned to the people who sent it. I released it back to the world, back to God because I had no power left to change it. I released my past, all the way back to my birth. I released it all. I gave up all control. I cried for hours in the releasing and accepting whatever lies ahead. Eventually, I felt the peace come in. I prepared myself to die with no ties to hold me to this life. My heart felt broken in grief.

Two days later, Elia took me to the Dragon Kingdom. Xi stood before his parents, petitioning the Dragon King and Queen for additional benefits for his squadron of dragons. When he saw me, he bowed to his parents and ended their discussion until later.

He came and hugged me, leading us to a small room off the throne room. He knew about my meltdown but said, "You're not going anywhere. You still have work to do – thirty some years of it."

When I admitted I still sat on my pity pot wondering what to do next, he offered no sympathy, scolding me instead. And I took it, too humbled and sad to argue. He gestured angrily at me, "Look at you! You don't even know what you are!"

I looked down at the beautiful aqua dress wrapping me in filmy layers of chiffon, shimmering, feathery and light from my shoulders to toes. Thousands of tiny one inch square holes covered the fabric but with so many layers I felt totally covered. Over the dress, I wore a stunning white cloak, rich warm and woollen-like. Down the draping sleeves, embroidered peacock feathers flowed to the floor. There I stood, dressed like royalty, amongst Kings, Queens, Prince Xi and his wife, Elia, whom I had 'raised' from an egg!

Xi crossed his arms and nodded as I stared mutely at him. "I see a woman struggling to set boundaries in her relationships, struggling to heal herself. I see a woman who has learned to love and respect herself on all levels: she loves herself but still does not see herself as others see her: A visionary of the First Water, a Seer in the making and so she comes." He smiled as Elia hugged me and took me home. It would take me months to understand the significance of his words.

When I awoke, I dug out Ted Andrew's *Animal Speak* which says the peacock is a protective and powerful bird. The blue-green iridescence of its feathers creates a sense of awe, its colour often associated with royalty. The "eyes" within the feathers symbolize greater wisdom and vision, as well as a sense of watchfulness. This wondrous bird most resembles the legendary phoenix, rising out of the flames of its ashes, more magnificent than before. Even in Christianity the peacock was a symbol of death and resurrection of Jesus (04:182). I'm done with death and waiting the resurrection.

The thermogram came back without detecting any mass or tumor but the high heat of my breast suggested further testing immediately. Dr. Mageau sent me to my regular doctor who took one look at it and said it was full of cancer. This time when I drove home, I felt quite calm, thinking deeply, trying to understand what this was all about. The blood tests showed me in perfect health (halleluiah!) with a slight elevation of my red blood cells. My white cell count was normal. The biofeedback indicated a problem but not cancer. Again I felt reassured. But what caused the inflammation?

I kept asking my guides if the cancer had returned and they shook their heads. They gave me a date when all would be revealed to me.

My doctor sent me back to my surgeon who also pronounced my breast full of cancer. I stared at her calmly, unafraid, investing no energy into her fears. I have been through too much to be upset now. I wasn't in denial; I *knew* I would be okay. My lack of emotion distressed her and she cried, "If you don't do something about this *you will die!*"

She sent me for more tests: mammogram, ultrasound, bone scan, abdominal CT scan and finally, a biopsy. The ultrasound people zeroed in one spot under my arm. The girl ran out of the room and brought back a doctor to show him. He asked me if I had any suture work done since my surgery. When I shook my head, he growled, "Well I will be talking to your doctor!" I wondered if some sutures were left behind. The area felt incredibly painful after the focused vibration of the ultrasound wand. Several nights of pain killers finally settled it down.

So, back to my surgeon who casually said, "Those aren't suture, but four clips left in permanently. It is standard procedure."

My jaw dropped! I never knew this! Nobody told me! When I asked her what they were made of, she replied, "Titanium."

I closed my eyes and groaned, "My family have terrible metal allergies to gold, silver, you name it, we're allergic to it." (As an aside, did you know fey folk are allergic to all metals?) I can wear gold if air flows between it and my skin. Cliff gave me a special wedding band with holes designed in it. A plain wide band causes instant eczema. I asked for specially designed vents in my blue diamond ring for the same reason. I don't have pierced ears because all my sisters had nothing but problems. Hypoallergenic posts are a joke to all of us.

Then I became furious, "Why wasn't I told about these clips? I would *never* have agreed to them knowing my family history! We break out in eczema from metal touching our skin." I wondered if I noted metal allergies on my surgical medical sheets. I've just learned to avoid metal touching my skin for prolonged periods. I *thought* I was just getting dissolvable sutures, not *metal* ones. I never missed any of the pre-surgery information sessions and *nobody* mentioned metal clips. I would have remembered believe me!

The surgeon explained how titanium is a pure metal and thus hypo-allergenic. According to her nobody reacts to it.

"So," I asked, "What would a two year reaction to metal look like?"

The surgeon pointed to my breast and growled, "That is not eczema!"

"Okay", I replied calmly and walked away unconvinced.

The internet proved titanium is rarely found in pure form, often mixed with alloys like nickel. Even surgical instruments are not pure. Nickel is poisonous to my family. My daughter once wore loose nickel bangles and developed eczema from her wrist to her elbow. I asked my dentist about the metal implants in two of my teeth. After six years they are still inflamed and bleed profusely when the hygienist cleans my teeth. Sure enough they are titanium. I went for a titanium metal allergy test. From zero to one hundred (being the extreme), I scored a ninety-eight.

The next day, the day my guides said all would be made clear to me, I realized my dilemma. My breast had been inflamed from the surgery onward by the titanium clips. Even a low grade inflammation is a hotbed for cancer cells to grow and here were the 'seeds' right in the old bed of the tumor. I never stood a chance despite all my detoxing and healthy living, cleansing, purging efforts. So I prayed that night, oh did I pray!

The next morning, in that pedagogic state, I heard, "The clips are now hermetically sealed. It is too dangerous to remove them. The inflammation will drop immediately."

Groggily I asked, "Can the clips be removed later?"

"Perhaps."

I asked Dr. Mageau what 'hermetic" meant. She explained how the clips were now sealed away from my blood and tissue, where they could not harm the DNA. But what about the harm from two years of exposure? She encouraged me to trust my guides, they had never steered me wrong before. My breast truly felt much cooler.

From her office I went for my weekly biofeedback treatment with Tanya. The inflammation numbers had indeed dropped by thirty points from the week before! I found this very reassuring.

I constantly received physical confirmation about my guides' protection throughout this nightmare. Whenever I drove down a freeway approach, they always gave me a half mile clearance before the next oncoming vehicle – always! No matter how many times I approached a freeway in one day, that half mile clearance was there. Green lights opened up before me like a path cleared for me to move forward. Parking spots appeared exactly where I needed them regardless the busy traffic around me. Such constant physical manifestations of their protection somewhat reassured me. I learned to quietly say 'Thank you' each time.

Yet an old, old issue of trust for my guides' wisdom goaded me into doubt. Did I believe them? Or was it just my ego trying to comfort me? My guides say I don't have cancer, the doctors say I do. *Who do I believe?* The growing physical evidence won. My mistrust caused a blockage from Spirit World; messages soon lacked clarity and focus. I could no longer detect the difference between my ego's lies and Spirit messages so I ignored both. I tried meditating, linking with my deeper self – a still out-of focus lady in red who said, "We tell each other lies." We linked hands and stared into each other's eyes. She whispered, "You are a Healer of the Tomes." Meaning I heal others through my writing.

Yeah? Then how the hell do I heal this?!!

The vicious pendulum continued swinging through four endless months of tests, waiting for results and more tests: Yes its cancer, no its not…yes it is. And the long dark days of winter closed over my head. It was so hard to stay positive while the rash grew unabated, encompassing more and more of my breast, making me whimper in fear whenever I looked in the mirror. It felt like hives from the inside, painfully itchy and hypersensitive to touch. I wanted to reach inside my breast and yank out whatever irritated it.

I realized I just moved forward another step. Yes, I could listen to the wisdom of my guides, or my ego, but did the message *resonate within me*, within my innate wisdom? If not, then I threw it out. I talk so much about my guides but what about my inner spirit and soul? Outside wisdom, regardless of where it comes from, must *feel* like the truth in my gut. I had to trust myself, all the way to my soul first and foremost.

What we think is what we manifest. The Law of Attraction books by Esther Hicks resonated with me now. All my doubts, fears and pain I focused on were manifesting – exactly what I did *not* want. This is my soul work now, getting re-connected to my inner wisdom. I discovered an inner warm resonance with good thoughts and feelings and dis-ease with negative ones. Inner harmony meant *feeling* truthful vibration from whatever I experienced. I worked hard to release the negativity, old thought patterns still hanging on – inside my breast. I relaxed, accepted my thoughts and emotions, understanding then releasing them, feeling the dark heavy energy flow away and out my feet into the earth. I refilled my breast with loving white light from above. I watched the swirling colours mix with my heart and soul's love and revelled in the uplifting energy it created. I finally understood the idea of being one with the universe, feeling part of its energy, like a mist around and within me.

Biofeedback measures your energy and returns it to you for good health. For the first time I actually *felt* the wonderful energy I gave off. No wonder strange dogs and cats came running and jumped into my lap, gazing up at me with soulful eyes. Why a gigantic buffalo bull lumbered up to me in his pen and stared into my eyes for the longest time. I remember rubbing my heart in unease. Then with a snort and a deep bow of his head, he walked away. While fishing, I sent silent greetings to the fish below, promising I would let them go if I could only connect with them for a moment. I caught the biggest fish of the whole ten fishermen around us. I whispered, "Thank you, Sir Trout" as I touched his scales then gently released him. I sent a similar cheerful greeting on a whale watching expedition in Hawaii. Suddenly a humpback whale lifted his massive head out of the water beside our boat and stared at me from a few feet away. I wonder what he saw. Now the biofeedback fed my energy back to me and it was wonderful! Wonderful!

After such a treatment, I drove home singing at the top of my lungs. I danced about my house, singing, laughing and touching my cherished possessions, loving my home, loving my life, loving my family and friends. I felt the energy vibrate through me until I shuddered in awe, in ecstasy and heart deep delight.

That night, I dreamed I stood before archangel Michael and Gabriel. He is a handsome man with dark wavy hair almost to his shoulders. He laughed at my exuberance for life, enjoying my delight, his hand held out as if to say, "Look at her happiness!"

I studied Gabriel's cloak alive with swirling colours of blue, green and gold. This time I looked at myself and noted I also wore a cloak of turquoise but without dancing colours.

She smiled at me and nodded, "Yes, you are one of mine."

Then both archangels backed up and parted, revealing a tall, cubical column of pure white mist behind them. It was so bright, it should have blinded me, but I saw the purity. Out of this mist, higher than my head, two human eyes appeared, shifting from brown, to blue, green, hazel, almond and all the colours human eyes can be. Two large hands came out of the mist and clasped mine. A gentle male voice said, "You are my eyes, hands and feet as you walk upon the Earth and spread my word."

He took my arm and wrapped it around his forearm, saying, "Come, I want you to meet your new guides who will help you with the next stage of your journey." Walking through this white world of mist, I noted other people walking by dressed in colourful cloaks, bent upon their own missions, ignoring us completely. We walked up to the seven Elohim I had seen in my dreams so long ago! They were all dressed in white except for the outside male, a visionary with four turquoise eyes, who wore a brilliant scarlet cape.

I awoke with such a sense of being loved, so profound and deep I shall never forget it nor be afraid of dying – ever. Are we not all God's eyes, hands and feet as we walk this earth? After this dream, I awoke one morning to the words, "It is leaving now; its work is done." All the pain and itching disappeared from my breast like a mission accomplished and done. It remained quiet and calm for some time but I wasn't through it yet.

Whenever the old dark thought patterns came in, I chanted my mantra, "I am loved, I am strong, I am healthy", until I felt the love flowing through me, felt its vibration soothe me, resonated with my good health all the way to my soul.

Xi and Elia teased me, saying I now have real dragon skin as my breast tissue hardened and thickened, grew scaly and dried. I laughed half-heartedly at the different perspective.

Suddenly the air around us roared with thunder and the Dragon King appeared, eyes full of fire. He declared me one of them now. The dragons are returning to Earth and I will help them. The skin on my breast is really a shield over my heart as I aide the dragons but it will retain its soft underbelly, a protection for the Dragon Master. My breast actually feels like a shell, hard and thick with a soft inner core. It feels numb and weird. I wondered if it would kill me. He assured me it won't.

He placed a helmet upon my head, like a virtual reality video screen. I saw the Earth from space and he told me it would soon "right itself". The dragons will hold the energy while it does. The axis will shift slightly and the climates will too. Our area, in central Canada, will have milder winters with very little change in our summers. Unfortunately, many will die and we are to help the survivors. These are big changes coming in the next few years. This is 2010 and the ominous predictions for 2012 loom in my head. I wondered if this was just a doom and gloom scenario but it *felt* real and I felt the power of the Dragon energy around me. I know their work – holding the energy of the Earth. I've seen them do this too many times in my dreams, including the squadrons of Dragons lined up on the fields like fighter planes.

Then I awaken and wonder where it's all going and who would believe me anyhow. Maybe I'm truly losing it. The stress has been too great – four months of tests, fears, worry and hell. Maybe my elaborate, imaginative scheme to deal with the cancer issue has finally made me crazy.

After much soul searching in the long dark nights I finally accepted my situation. Whether I die or I live, I win. If God wants me home, I'm ready. I've healed as many issues in my life as I can. If God wants me to stay and write, okay too. If I die, I go home to the Masters and learn once more at their knee. If I live, I stay and listen to the Messengers, sharing their information with you in all my upcoming books. I still see an entire room of stacked books waiting for me to write. Either way, *I am okay*. I will always learn, grow and 'see' all I can. Life isn't about destination but the richness in the journey. What I have learned, nothing can take it away, not even death.

Some days I just wanted to die and get it over with. I wanted to renege on whatever stupid Life Plan I created before I came here. Why put myself through this endless nightmare? *What the hell was I thinking!?*

I dreamt of walking down the road with Dad while we visited, just like we used to do. He hugged me and told me to be strong. I asked him if I could come 'home' now and he replied, "No, at least not for a long time." When I awoke I chuckled to myself. Mom always hated yellow, we never knew why, but she wouldn't allow Dad to wear the color either. In my dream he wore black dress pants - over much slimmer hips than I remember - and a cheerful yellow shirt, bright as sunshine!

I tried some new gel on my breast to soften the scaly skin. I made the mistake of putting my bra on before it dried completely. At bedtime, I removed my bra and ripped an entire layer of skin with it! The next day, the fragile skin grew a hole that wouldn't close, oozing blood and fluid. I lay down on my bed and wept my heart out. Cliff comforted me but I was inconsolable. I felt so lost, confused and scared. Even he blanched he saw the raw, oozing mess my breast had become. We knew it wasn't eczema.

As we waited for the final biopsy results, I alternated between faith that I would be okay -loved, strong and healthy – and absolute despair, losing faith, worn down and angry. Oh I had lots of anger at being promised good health and watching my breast rapidly deteriorate. Within a week I had three oozing lesions (open holes), within a month, I had eight. Then I would hear, "Help is on the way" and get furious all over again.

I asked, begged, pleaded, demanded and yelled for help. I refused to block any emotion or suppress it. What I felt is what I felt, denying none of it and refusing to feel guilty for all the crazy thoughts and emotion running rampant through me. This is me, as I am and as I feel. I felt raw, strong, energetic, sometimes loving and compassionate, sometimes not. I learned to lean into my emotions, allow them to bubble up from my gut and feel, feel, feel, without judgement or explanation. I simply worked on being aware, feeling where the tension was in my body, focusing on it until the emotion it held moved, shifted and changed as I understood it fully. I fed myself daily on emotional nourishment, the healing way to good health.

Can you imagine my devastation when the biopsy report indicated the cancer had come back, probably never left fully because of the clips? I had a breast full of it and I felt its deadly encroachment on my life force increasing every day. I sensed if it continued unimpeded, I would die.

I was furious with my guides. Why did they deny it was cancer? Why not tell me the truth? I vented to Dr. Mageau who replied, "See the lesions as a blessing. As the dead cells liquefy, it is much healthier for them to drain out your breast than spread throughout your body. Maybe you aren't asking your guides the right question. Your body reads and deals with cancer as an infection. Sometimes the guides' interpretation is different from our own."

So I asked if I had an infection/inflammation and their immediate reply was, "Yes, and a bad one."

Duh.

I demanded to know why they kept saying they healed me while the cancer continued to grow. They replied they helped heal me on many levels: emotionally, spiritually, mentally and yes, physically too with all the detoxing, cleansing and clearing of my liver and internal organs. I assumed they meant physical as in stopping the cancer. Not so; not yet. Their stupid 'word game' drove me wild.

The Elohim came silently in my dreams. I screamed at them, "What?! You came to stand around and watch me die? Help me out or leave!"

I really unloaded on Gabriel the next time I saw her. I felt cheated, betrayed, lied to and abandoned. I totally shut down. I just wanted to curl into a ball and let the darkness close over my head.

My daughter finally stopped my ranting when she said, "Mom, all that cleansing, detoxing and nutritional changes couldn't be for nothing. What if you needed the past two years to heal your body and make it strong enough to face the cancer head on? "

Sigh.

Then I learned about Graviola Max and its power to heal a broad spectrum of cancers including liver, lung, breast, skin, kidney, prostate and more with no side effects. My guides encouraged me to stick with the Graviola Max so I did. I had nothing to lose.

A Nevada company called Rain-tree harvested the evergreen trees and makes high quality Graviola and Graviola Max in capsule form. Buy it at your local Health Store or on the internet. Type in the name and all the research and information is there. Yet the FDA gagged Rain-tree from advertising their products or posting on their website any testimonials from grateful customers.

Well I can! I tell everyone about Graviola Max. I hope you check it out too. The Naturopaths also know of more cancer killing herbal remedies called Myomin and Angiostop. I have done no research on them but you can.

Within one week of taking Graviola Max, my body went into a healing crisis, suddenly awakening to the danger growing in my breast. Cancer cells are a part of us so they fly under the radar of the body's vigilante healing team. I have an inflammatory type of cancer, one in four recovers from it. It heated my breast, arms and hands so hot even my lips chapped. But Graviola Max stopped the heat in one week. My lips returned to normal and I stopped craving endless, endless water. The skin rash stopped spreading. I felt the changes, felt the healing begin from within along with an incredible sense of well being when I awoke each morning. I've learned Graviola also kills parasites and alleviates depression. I knew like I knew *like I knew* I would be okay.

One day, a word popped into my head. I walked around repeating it out loud, "Apoptosis, apoptosis." It drove me crazy wondering what it meant. My old nursing dictionary offered no explanation. I finally asked Dr. Mageau who immediately replied, "It means death of the cancer cells."

I wanted to laugh out loud.

Back at the cancer hospital, a new oncologist (I refused to see the other one) admitted the cancer type I have comes back even with radiation and chemo. It is a very aggressive, inflammatory type although my surgeon still claimed I had the type that grew slowly and didn't spread. Not so! With it now covering most of my breast, she declared it inoperable for a mastectomy. Not enough healthy skin remained to create a flap without using massive skin grafts from my body.

I felt secretly relieved!

The oncologist prescribed Arimidex, an estrogen blocker because the cancer is hormone sensitive, fed by estrogen. It's a tiny white pill I take every day for the rest of my life. He assured me although they can't cure this cancer, they can manage it for years and years on this medication – the sum total of my treatment. He claimed the only side effects were hot flashes and a slight loss of bone over many years.

Right. I *knew* the Graviola would heal it completely – within the year.

Online, I checked out Arimidex. Common side effects also include back, bone, breast, joint or pelvic pain, constipation, cough, diarrhea, dizziness, flu-like muscle aches, tiredness, headache, hot flashes, loss of appetite, nausea, sore throat, stomach pain or upset, sweating, tingling or burning sensation, trouble sleeping, vaginal dryness, vomiting, weakness and weight gain. The list of severe side effects was even longer.

The oncologist explained since I *never* had chemo or radiation, I would do even better on this medication. He shook his head saying, "People who had the conventional treatments don't do well on this drug."

Right.

Two women I know of who took the conventional treatments had strokes after taking Arimidex. One died. Another dangerous side effect is blood clots. Chemo destroys the body's soft tissue found in the oesophagus, heart, chest wall, intestines, abdominal wall etc. and the body never fully recovers. In my research I found people with cancer have thick blood – maybe from all the toxins – causing blood clots. Some people were prescribed blood thinners making weakened blood vessels more vulnerable to bleeding/strokes.

I asked, "Why wasn't I put on Arimidex from the beginning after my surgery?" He said it was available for five years.

"Oh, because we like to kill the cancer before it can spread by getting rid of it as soon as possible. It is our strongest line of defence."

"But if this type of cancer does not respond to chemo and radiation, why did the oncologist still recommend these treatments two years ago?"

The condescending reply, "Well we wouldn't want people to think chemo and radiation doesn't work."

I wanted to bang my head against the wall.

Dr. Mageau gave me an entire protocol of herbal remedies to help support my body as it healed. Arimidex leeched so much calcium from my bones at night that I moaned with pain in my sleep. I wondered if I would have osteoporosis within a year. I took Cellfood, high intensity bone calcium replacement capsules at night and drank liquid calcium in the middle of the night. It soothed the pain and countered bone loss.

Several weeks after starting Graviola Max, I added Arimidex. On the biofeedback machine Graviola tested 100%, Arimidex tested 73% but together, they registered 90% compatibility with my body and breast. My breast oozed a smelly yellow gunk and occasionally bled a little. I flushed the area daily with a sterile saline solution and wore comfortable sports bras (two sizes larger for support without restricting lymphatic flow). Nurses at the hospital taught me how to bandage the lesions. By measuring the size and depth of the lesions we knew they were shrinking. I went from ten (which my guides told me I would have before the spreading stopped and the healing began) to five in five weeks. I often talked to my healing breast, honouring its sorrow and suffering, loving it for its truth, part of me, part of God and the Universe.

Cancer takes a long time to grow and should take a long time to heal. It must be done in stages as the body gradually recovers. Graviola slowly kills cancer cells while chemo causes instant death of the cells. Too many dead cells mean the body can't flush them away fast enough, creating a toxic overload. Tissue rots, causing secondary inflammation and infection in an already sick body. With a compromised immune system, the body has no way to fight the infection. Now I understand why so many people die of secondary complications after chemo. My breast had little blue/brown lumps or pockets under the skin as the cancer inflammation receded. Dr. Mageau explained when the cells die and are flushed away, the pockets slowly refill with saline, clean and clear until new, healthy cells can fill in the pockets. It will take a year to heal fully my guides tell me.

A book called *Strong Women, Strong Hearts* by Dr. Miriam E. Nelson, PhD and Alice Lichtenstein, D. Sc, offered another clue about inflammation. "Blood flow can also be impeded as an indirect result of inflammation. When an atherosclerotic (hardened) artery becomes inflamed, plaque becomes unstable and can rupture, precipitating the formation of a blood clot – and a subsequent heart attack or stroke" (2005:15). Was this why other women on Arimidex did not fare so well?

I would never have found out about Graviola, Arimidex or the shocking information in the following chapters without facing the cancer once again. Biofeedback indicated my immune system and organs, especially my liver, were in excellent health this second time around. Standard medical tests proved the cancer had not left my breast. After two years of healing my body, I now addressed the final causes of the cancer. This time I felt strong and healthy. I just had a sore breast! I maintained my health food regime (juicing and 80% vegetables) and a normal range of activities, housework, shopping, exercising, etc. I rested when tired but otherwise felt perfectly normal. **True healing from cancer should look like this!**

I humbly acknowledged my guides' help throughout this dangerous maze despite my drama and temper tantrums. I apologized to Gabriel for my ignorant behaviour and anger. She merely shrugged it off saying I was entitled to feel the way I did. It took me much longer to forgive myself. My lesson: never feel guilty for emotions.

She introduced me to Archangel Michael who will work with me in the next phase of my life. As the soldier angel, carrying a sword and shield, Michael is the <u>angel of mercy</u>, of careers, courage, achievements, ambitions, motivation and life tasks. He is the great prince charged to defend the people. Angel of repentance and righteousness, he can be invoked in the North for motivation and empowerment in your work. Call on him to protect you day to day. I definitely needed Michael's help to survive this cancer. Remember my Get Well card from the angels of love and mercy? Michael was one of them!

Working with the Elohim guides, I noticed their gender-balanced relationship: two visionaries, male and female; two healers, male and female; and two warriors, male and female. The seventh guide, I shall talk about in another book because his work has no place here.

I chatted with the male warrior guide. He told me we shared many lives as friends, brothers and soldiers, once fighting together in WW1 in England. His nickname name for me as a fellow soldier was Booty because I forever shined my shoes (I still do religiously) and because my last name was Boudell. We died in the trenches together.

I asked him, "So why do I have two new warrior guides?"

He calmly replied, "Because we are taking on the medical profession."

Hooboy!

Judgement is not about destruction of a current system but setting things right. My book outlines the latest available research and spiritual perceptions channelled to me. Experiencing cancer, minute by painful minute, helped me understand what others go through. I am not alone. I am healing a breast full of cancer – without chemo or radiation. People need to understand the truth about cancer and their options for treatment. Now I see why Archangel Michael came to help me. Our conversations remain stilted, not smooth flowing like Gabriel's and mine. Still, he is a warrior angel and acts as such.

My body sent me images of my healing breast from the inside - a domed area with wet, blackened tobacco leaves hanging from the roof. I watched a line of little white angels move from my liver into my breast. They carried tiny water tanks on their backs with hoses to flush the dead leaves away as they fell from the dome above. Eventually, only newer brown leaves remained and they too fell, one by one. Occasionally, one of the angels tipped over but the others quickly righted it and continued working. I never smoked in my life. Yet for years, second hand smoke surrounded me in the offices I worked in through the 70's, 80's and 90's. Back then, people still smoked at their desks and coffee rooms maintained a steady blue haze. Another cause of the cancer revealed by my body's images.

Then the image changed and I saw an assembly line of black, wet rhesus monkeys, wrapped in white mesh sacks strung on a long pulley line, like you see in a slaughter house. The monkeys faced away from me, fully formed but dead. Further along the pulley line, they grew smaller and smaller down to a single a cell – all dead and leaving my breast. Here was the flushing of the dead cells, in little pockets!

Why a monkey symbol? Imagine my surprise when I re-read the first chapter of this book about reducing the cancer King Kong in your home to a monkey and shipping it to Timbuktu. Monkeys are also unpredictable, mischievous even deadly. Later, I found out metastasizing cells are called ras cells. Close enough for me. The empty dome gradually filled with soft white and pink healthy tissue which breathed and moved with me – just like Dr. Mageau reassured me it would.

Three months after starting the Graviola Max, Archangel Michael pulled a reluctant but alive rhesus monkey from a hole in the left side of my breast – below the surgical incision – the hottest part of my breast. I felt my breast actually throb in agony. As the bewildered monkey crouched at his feet, Michael explained it was the original 'monkey' cell which caused the cancer – removed permanently. I asked him about the cells which had already divided from it.

"They will die and no longer have a pattern to follow."

Michael tried to reassure me saying I could now continue my writing projects. He showed me a huge bronzed trophy I will eventually receive for my writing. I stared at it, numb with soul-deep exhaustion, feeling nothing at all. I have fought too long, too hard to be appeased with a trophy. Later, I felt guilty for my lack of enthusiasm before one of the most powerful archangels in Heaven.

I revisited my sister Beryl in Palm Springs. She took me to her favourite psychic. This Jewish lady immediately claimed I would have an excellent year, on the verge of breaking out into my full purpose. What I think, I immediately manifest so I must think positive thoughts about what I truly want. This is a year of recuperation for me (I never said a word about the breast cancer). She said I am a natural healer, rescuer and intuitive. Apparently, I spent many lives in temples and monasteries perfecting my wisdom, intuition, faith and healing abilities. This life is the most important one of all as I remember my full past and pull it all together – a deeper meaning for this book.

She also explained how more and more archangels are coming to help people with the work they are to do. Archangel Uriel who protects the throne of God is around me now. Wisest of all angels, spirit of ministration and peace, he turns our worst disappointments into greatest blessings [Oh I need this one!]. He is the Archangel of salvation, the ruler over magic, devotion, alchemy, sudden changes, universal cosmic consciousness, divine order, distribution of power and universal flow, enlightenment and insights. Uriel means "God is my light' and the sharpest sighted spirit in Heaven according to Gustav Davidson's *Dictionary of Angels,* (1967:298). I am to invoke Uriel to help me with the winds of change and clarify any questions I have.

So I asked this cheerful psychic what the word 'Elohim' meant.

She leaned forward, her eyes wide in shock, "You mean *El-o-heem?"*

I nodded tentatively; it sounded like the same word, mine an English version. I explained where I had heard it.

"Ah', she replied in excitement, "It is Hebrew for 'God'. A few very special chosen people are hearing that word today. It means you have a direct communication link to God and his work you were sent here to do." She shook my hand in delight saying, "It is such an honour to meet you! I knew there was something different about you."

I stared at her dumbfounded. I thought everyone had a direct link to God. Yet my dream of meeting the white light figure who told me I was his eyes, hands and feet as I spread his word on earth now made my hair stand on end.

"But I still don't know what I'm supposed to be doing!' I protested.

She laughed, "It will manifest for you physically and very soon. You will actually see the changes; even your DNA is changing this year. It will happen, just go with the flow and let it play out. You are very close to understanding exactly what you will be doing." She smiled into my eyes and nodded complacently.

She was right. I watched my breast heal daily. Within four months from the second diagnosis of cancer, all the lesions closed, leaving pink, healthy, *cooler* tissue behind. My breast slowly softened to normal, losing none of its shape or size. I slept on it comfortably once again. A miracle! My miracle! Thank you God!

The oncologist was thrilled with my progress. Again I asked why women are not given Arimidex as soon as they are diagnosed.

He replied, "The only way to cure cancer is to cut it out. Chemo and radiation do the rest. And women want it cut out right away."

I sat there, with my two breasts intact (healing) and stared at him. No woman I know 'wants' her breast cut off! When is she given alternatives? I wasn't and I *asked* for healthier options two years ago.

"Do you recommend detoxification for any of your patients?"

He shook his head. "There is no evidence it helps."

I looked into his eyes and merely said, "Really.... Interesting."

I have learned our medical professions must follow a very rigid protocol when treating cancer. It's all they know. I believe far too much information like what I share in this book is not available to them. Their hearts are truly in the right place so I forgive them.

Then my guides sent me into a whole new realm of research and healing every woman in North America should know about.

44.

What Women Need to Know

"When estrogen becomes the dominant hormone...it becomes toxic to the body."
Dr. John R. Lee, *What Your Doctor May* Not *Tell You About Menopause*

Hormone replacement therapy (HRT) is the most deadly widespread hoax visited upon women of North America. In July 2002, a ten-year clinical trial on Prempro and Premarin conducted by the National Institute of Health studied over 16,000 women. The study was abruptly halted due to life threatening side effects from these two drugs openly prescribed to women since the 1960's – with little research to back up their necessity! By now, I hope you realize the information, books and research coming my way are no coincidence! I found a whole nest of shocking information leading to my breast cancer and its deadly potential for younger women.

The above study found blood clots in the lungs of these women went up by 114%; heart attacks and cardio deaths increased 29%; breast cancer increased by 26% and strokes by 41%. "After forty years use, Premarin, the most widely used form of estrogen is now considered unsafe" (Dr. Kalish, Natural Health Solutions (2007:1), www.drkalish.com/a_female_hormone.)

Dr. John R. Lee, in his above book, originally written in 1996 and updated in 2004, sites this study and another about the danger of HRT. These drugs cause other terrible side effects like weight gain, fatigue, depression, irritability, headaches, insomnia, bloating, low thyroid, low libido (sex drive), gallbladder disease and blood clots (04:36). A study from the Breast Cancer Demonstration Project, part of a nationwide breast cancer screening program, "showed that estrogen-only hormone replacement therapy (ERT) increases the overall risk of ovarian cancer by more than three fold" (04:38). Dr. Lee insists the medical profession has known for over twenty years about the unopposed estrogen cancer promoting properties on a women's reproductive system. He says giving only estrogen to women without a uterus should never have happened!

Dr. Lee, a distinguished Harvard medical doctor with over 30 years of practice, pioneered the study and use of hormone *balancing*. Along with Virginia Hopkins, M.A., a Yale University graduate, Dr. Lee has written many books you can probably find in your library such as *What Your Doctor May Not Tell You About Premenopause; What Your Doctor May Not Tell You About Breast Cance*r. His book became my bible as I slowly unravelled the final causes of the breast cancer.

From the 1960's onward, we grew up hearing about estrogen and its necessity for life. When menopause hit and our estrogen levels dropped, well we just needed more of it to stay healthy. Enter the HRT solution touted by the pharmaceutical companies as the next best thing to sliced bread. Doctors happily prescribed it to women complaining about menopausal symptoms. *Yet nobody tested the women to see what their <u>actual</u> estrogen levels were! THEY STILL DON'T!*

Normal menopause is now treated as the onset of an estrogen deficiency disease. Yet Dr. Lee cites a study by Dr. Jerilyn Prior, researcher and professor of endocrinology (study of hormones) at the University of British Columbia in Vancouver. She insists no study proving the relationship between estrogen deficiency and menopausal symptoms and related diseases has yet been done!

According to Dr. Kalish's website article, *Female Hormone Balancing*, from his newsletter, Natural Health Solutions, a Dr. Peter Elison of Harvard University pioneered the use of salivary hormone testing. He found women from industrialized countries have estrogen levels at the *high extreme* of world wide levels and should be considered abnormal (07: 2). Dr. Elison studied people from all over the world and found several contributing factors between hormone levels, diet and exercise. Inactive women who eat more calories than they use will have high estrogen levels. Those who exercise lots and eat less have lower estrogen levels (but there is a catch, read on). Everyone knows obese women have a higher risk of breast cancer. 61% of Americans are overweight and I doubt Canadians are far behind. Our Western diet rich in animal fats, sugars, refined starches and processed foods doubles women's estrogen levels compared to women from other countries who eat a simple agrarian diet.

Estrogen also leeches from herbicides, pesticides and dioxins (DDT, PCB and hormone injected meat). Xenoestrogens, chemical by-products of petrochemicals fill our world in plastic water bottles, food containers, bags and Styrofoam especially if heated in the microwave or left in the sun for prolonged periods. Plastics, once they enter the female body create an estrogen-like effect increasing estrogen levels. Xenoestrogens also suppress the immune system. Dr. Lee found evidence proving exposure to Xenoestrogens may be a significant causal factor in breast cancer, male sperm decline, testicular and prostate cancer (04:45).

High estrogen levels also result from treated water. Urine from women on birth control pills spills estrogen into our water treatment plants which do *not* filter it out, recycling it back into our drinking water. Detergents, dishwashing soap, cosmetics, toiletries, even diaphragm jellies, condoms and vaginal gels add to the Xenoestrogens mix.

So buy the 'green' products and help clean up our waters for all the children who come behind us. Dr. Lee mentions one study found children raised on organic foods have 1/6 the concentration of phosphate pesticides compared to children eating pesticide sprayed food (04:68).

Yes. Time to go organic and ride the Green Band Wagon. The more we consumers demand organic products, the more they will be produced. We do have power!

The most shocking cause of high estrogen levels in North American women rocked me to my soul. Dr. Lee calls it the Yin and Yang factor. For men, their yang/masculine factor of the warrior and protector allows them to survive quite nicely in the work place wars of politics, business and competition. For women, their yin/feminine factor tends toward nurturing, peaceful living and home fires. But our Western women must enter the workforce and compete with men for livelihood. Stressed out women in their 30's and 40's juggle career commitments with a husband, children, housework, extended family and community.

I did this dance for over thirty years: studying nursing in my mid-twenties with two young children, going to university all through my thirties, juggling classes, part-time work and full-time wife, mother and housekeeper. After graduating I worked full time. Stress was my middle name.

The terrible price we women pay for our hard work is the loss of the balancing hormone, progesterone. It is produced in our ovaries during menstrual ovulation (egg release from the ovary) and in the adrenal glands (at the top of the kidneys). A new study discovered dropping fertility rates in Western woman. We've known for years athletic women are often infertile. But this study found the *average* woman also does not ovulate regularly. Estrogen increases when the uterus prepares for the egg but progesterone is only produced *after* ovulation. If no egg is produced, the estrogen climbs while progesterone lowers, month after month. At menopause, when the ovaries stop making progesterone, the adrenal glands must pick up the slack for normal body functioning. Unfortunately, prolonged stress fries the adrenals (which also produce adrenaline) into overload. Many Western women's adrenals become so depleted they can not produce enough progesterone to make corticosteroids. Dr Lee believes lack of corticosteroids are contributing factors in chronic fatigue, mineral imbalance, trauma stresses, inflammation, immune dysfunction, hypoglycaemia, allergies and arthritis (04:156).

I suffered chronic fatigue in my thirties (the biofeedback machine indicates its presence as inactive). I also had mineral deficiencies and immune dysfunctions. I wonder if my tubal ligation at twenty-five also affected my progesterone levels.

Dr Lee writes, "The most common age for the initial stages of breast or uterine cancer is five years or more before menopause, well before estrogen levels fall but coinciding with a drop in progesterone. This fits my timing perfectly. Medical staff told me more and more woman who eat right and exercise regularly are getting breast cancer now. High estrogen is toxic to the body. Athletic woman also drink water from plastic bottles. What are their stresses? Is the resulting low progesterone *our terrible connection to breast cancer?*

Dr. Kalish states, "the balanced ratio of estrogen and progesterone maintain healthy body functioning" (07:2). He explains how estrogen promotes movement of salt and minerals into cells while progesterone protects the integrity and function of cell membranes, the outside lining of cells. According to a chart in Dr. Lee's book (p.86), progesterone increases fat-burning metabolism; balances our weight and sugar levels; maintains proper cellular oxygen levels; protects against fibrocystic breasts; normalizes blood clotting and is an antidepressant, natural diuretic and anti-inflammatory. It prevents cyclical migraines, facilitates thyroid function, enhances libido, stimulates new bone formation and helps prevent breast cancer to name just a few of its abilities. He sites a twenty year long term study done by John Hopkins Medical School starting in 1981. It tracked one group of women with normal progesterone and one group with low progesterone. They found the incidence of breast cancer increased by 80% in the women with low progesterone (p.279-280). We definitely need this magical hormone in our bodies!

Dr. Lee says estrogen *normally* drops at menopause (up to 50%) but progesterone may be depleted to almost nothing. Five years into menopause the body adjusts to the lower levels of estrogen but most women have no balancing progesterone to maintain good health.

Unfortunately, Western Women now face menopause with abnormally *high* levels of estrogen and extremely *low* levels of progesterone. When progesterone levels become too low, the body becomes what Dr Lee calls **estrogen dominant**. Symptoms include all our menopausal complaints: weight gain, water retention, headache, low metabolism, hypothyroidism (low), mood swings, fibrocystic breasts, unstable blood sugar and sluggish mornings with cravings for caffeine, sweets and carbs. He says excess estrogen also causes blood clots. "Estrogen replacement therapy, according to a study done by Grady et al in 1997 increased the risk of venous blood clots by 200 to 360%" (04:262). Women suffering from the above symptoms seek their doctors. *How will increased estrogens in HRT help?* Dr. Lee contends these symptoms can be alleviated by <u>increasing progesterone</u> *not* estrogen along with good nutrition, detoxing and regular exercise.

I exercised regularly and ate well yet suffered many of the above symptoms including hypothyroidism (low thyroid). I learned a low functioning thyroid, can be caused by low iodine and high estrogen levels which throw the whole body out of balance. Dr. Lee says Iodine deficiency *also* increases the risk of breast cancer (p.324). Iodine stimulates the metabolism of another hormone which kills many types of breast cancer. Two servings a week of Broccoli, celery, cauliflower and brussel sprouts will give you the iodine you need. Iodine in the health supplement I use, Indole 3 Carbinol capsules, also removes excess estrogen from your system. Paint your forearm with a one inch circle of iodine. If it disappears within 24 hours, your body is iodine deficient.

We need a test to determine what our hormone levels *actually are* and whether they are metabolising properly. Dr. Kalish admits the difficulty in determining low progesterone because it fluctuates with a woman's monthly flow. Since I'm menopausal, blood tests, urine tests and the biofeedback indicated my estrogen was twice as high as my progesterone, which was so low it never even registered in a urine test.

Yet the media <u>still</u> promotes HRT and without hormone level testing <u>first</u>! I recently picked up a 2010 Health magazine recommending HRT to deal with menopause symptoms. It says current research shows benefits of short-term HRT outweigh risks of heart attack with lower overall death rates for women 50 to 59. **Not so!** The 2002 study previously mentioned tested women aged 50 to 79! The magazine article blithely goes on to say HRT prevents bone loss, dementia and colon cancer. The article does *not* say, *"Get your hormone levels tested first!*

Dr. Lee contends estrogen does not increase bone density *but progesterone can by 30%*. He argues osteoarthritis as an estrogen deficiency disease was "fabricated by the pharmaceuticals companies with no scientific evidence to support it" (04:184). He did his own study giving his osteoporosis patients a natural progesterone skin cream without estrogen and found excellent results. One of his patients, a seventy-five year old with osteoporosis who broke her arm lifting her sick husband, was given progesterone cream and she lived well into her nineties in good health. Another patient with osteoporosis increased her bone density with progesterone to the point she returned to skiing in her seventies!

He states most women do not need supplemental estrogen to have strong bones except slim women (estrogen is stored in fat and used postmenopausally), or those who have had hysterectomies. They may need a *little* estrogen to achieve hormone <u>balance</u> (04:192). Even these ladies should demand their hormone levels be tested first.

"A doctor guides a patient on their path, a doctor <u>doesn't</u> heal. Only nature heals."

Paracelsus, an ancient Greek physician.

Don't you think they should do more research about estrogen stored in our body fat? What is our body trying to do? Protect us? Provide storage for slowly releasing estrogen throughout our old age? Why are menopausal women condemned as being obese? What truths are being withheld from us in this world of endless dieting?

Be also aware not all so-called natural estrogens and progesterones are the same! I checked some internet sites, horrified to find them advertising *synthetic* hormones (not found in nature) as natural and healthy. The body does *not* read or use synthetic hormones like Progestin or Provera. According to Dr. Lee they can cause side effects like loss of mineral electrolytes in cells, intracellular edema (swelling), depression, birth defects, more body hair, blood clots, allergies, acne and skin rashes (p.111) to name a few.

Dr. Lee, who travels all over the United States lecturing on hormone <u>balancing</u> suggests specific types of progesterone made only from natural ingredients. He recommends a transdermal (skin cream) with at least 400 - 450 mg. of progesterone per ounce of cream. Diosgenin does *not* equal progesterone but is often added to the cheaper progesterone creams. The average dosage, ¼ teaspoon of natural cream should have about 15 – 20 mg. of progesterone. Several years after he wrote his book, Dr. Lee developed an excellent cream called Progesta-Care through Life-Flo (©2008) in Phoenix, Arizona. Call 1-888-999-7440 or check out their website: <u>www. life-flo.com</u>. This cream, which I use, has a pump for the exact recommended dose. I believe progesterone is the long term treatment that will prevent the cancer from returning. I plan on taking it for the rest of my life. I am currently looking into bio identical hormones for further hormonal balancing.

After researching hormones and their delicate balancing act, I believe all women of the twenty-first century should understand what their body needs to maintain good health. Our ancestors never lived as long as we do. Menopause is simply another step along the way to longevity and our hormones need assistance to keep pace with our twenty-first century bodies.

A whole new area of research is opening up about bio identical hormones the *natural – not synthetic* balancers for Western Women. Some doctors are getting involved, testing and retesting women's hormones through several months of blood tests until they are balanced. The tests take several months as they track the rebalancing and what hormones need 'tweaking'. Dr. Lee formulated a natural mix of hormones to help women but some doctors prescribe a specific mix for each woman to keep her hormones balanced with excellent results over a long period of time. Compounding Pharmacies, springing up across the country, will blend individually prescribed hormone compounds for each woman.

Yes, we have come a long way in honouring ourselves as unique women with unique bodies. We control of our bodies and what we put in them.

45.

Our New Red Running Shoes

"There is a specific pattern to the loss of instinct. It is essential to study this pattern, to actually memorize it, so that we can guard the treasures of our basic natures and those of our daughters as well."

Clarissa Pinkola Estés, *Women Who Run With the Wolves* (92:214)

I dreamt of feathers – two award feathers – one for me and one for Joyce, my beautiful friend who walked beside me this entire journey (and edited my book). When I asked if my sister Beryl can have one too, they replied, "She already does." I want to share my victory with others. Every feather earned marks our victories, our determination to walk in faith – our way. Yet one problem remains. Once we recapture our feminine instincts how do we keep them?

I went out to meet my guides in a dream; they clapped and cheered my victory. When I looked down, I wore new red running shoes, the slip on type. To understand their symbolism, I turned to my favourite mentoring author, Clarissa Pinkola Estés, PhD and her sassy, rippling prose of *Women Who Run With the Wolves*. I highly recommend this book to all women and young girls searching for their inner voice and intuition. Pinkola Estés, a *cantadora* or storyteller in her culture, analyzes the loss of feminine instinct resulting in the starved, wild woman in Hans Christian Anderson's tale, *The Red Shoes*.

The tale is about a young motherless girl who was so poor she had no shoes. So she gathered bits and scraps and gradually sewed a pair of red shoes for herself. She wore them proudly for they were hers and hers alone. An old woman in a golden carriage offered to take the girl into her home and treat her like a daughter. Once inside the home, however, the old woman burned the girl's clothing including her treasured red shoes. The young girl then learned how to behave, be polite, be nice, kind and good.

The saddened young girl longed for her handmade red shoes. When she saw a pair of red shoes at the shoemaker's she secretly bought them. But when she put them on and began to dance, she could not stop dancing. The strange shoes took control and danced her out of the village and into the dark forest. Finally, exhausted, terrified and alone, she begged the shoemaker to cut her feet off. When he did, the feet continued to dance while the girl remained crippled and unable to walk, struggling to survive.

Pinkola Estés reveals the danger of losing the wild instinct – the serious problem young people still face today. The original red shoes the young girl sewed represent our innate, ability to grow - even without proper nurturing - to piece together and walk with the inner wisdom we are born with. An old woman offers to adopt the little girl. It seems like a good choice: to be cared for, warm, fed and comfortable in exchange for following social rules. This gilded cage traps many women. They are taught to be nice, kind, nurturing and giving while *their* needs, *their* creative, feminine instincts are ignored, suppressed or burned away like the young girl's beautiful handmade red shoes.

Red, white and black symbolise the three stages of womanhood, dating back to Celtic Goddess traditions. White represents our maiden virgin and childhood. Red symbolises menses, motherhood, family and community responsibility. Black is for our wise women: the crone, the elder, the mentor. The Catholic Church reversed our feminine colour symbols. They place our Wise Woman black on the backs of their young priests while cardinals wear our red and an old man sits in our virginal whites.

Red, my favourite colour, is about love, passion, anger and strength – all the emotions lost/suppressed with the burning shoes. In this tale, according to Pinkola Estés, red is the color of life (birth) and sacrifice. The young maiden loses her red before she is able to understand its power and responsibility. The old woman, smothered in social rules and blind to her own instincts, can not teach the girl how to honour the feminine intuition. The tale represents the multi-generational loss of the wise innate wisdom within every woman's body. The girl's vibrant and beloved red is lost, a blood-loss rather than blood-life of the inner power to rule her life, her way. "This sets up a yearning, an obsession and finally an addiction to the other kind of red: the one of fast-breaking, cheap thrills, sex without soul; the one that leads to a life without meaning" (92:222).

Now do you see the trap our young girls face?

Here is the inherent danger of not following our deep instinct of preservation, not honouring what we *make/create/dream for* ourselves. Our yearning leads us into dangerous territory, the gilded cage of false platitudes, where other people control our lives, telling us what is best for us. I call it the killing 'shoulds', which ignore our inner truths and needs for fulfillment. The endless dance of the 'shoulds' becomes our downfall, our self-destruction. Sooner or later, our suppressed inner needs seek fulfillment, often in deadly ways. At first women try to sneak what they need: ant-depressants, sleeping pills, alcohol, food, illegal drugs, shoplifting, sexual affairs, gambling or secret meetings with secret societies, all of which endanger a woman who no longer hears her inner voice warning, *"You have gone too far!"*. She loses her inner wisdom telling her to walk or *run* from any situation not in her best interests. Truly caged, she dances for someone/something else, her life beyond her control.

Gilded cages have many forms: the endless rushing busy-making duties of wife, mother and employee leaves no free time for what our hands yearn to create; glossy books/magazines bedazzle us from writing our stories; endless diets prevent us from seeing our true inner beauty; illicit affairs interfere with loving ourselves first; drugs/alcohol numb our ability to run where our Wise Woman runs. In the tale, a youthful yearning for something else, something 'more', drives the girl on. She sneaks the false shoes to replace her handmade wisdom. So she dances, a wild, obsessive, addictive dance losing control over her life. In the end, she begs for drastic, crippling measures to survive.

How many lies do we tell ourselves every day? Where did we lose our passion, our drive to succeed? When did fear, the 'I can't do' stop us cold? When did we stop *listening* to our handmade inner wisdom? When did we allow society to lock us into gilded cages of proper conduct? Who burned away our faith in the precious gifts we were born with? When did conformity mean more than intelligence and creativity? Where did we lose our heart and soul's red vibrancy, our love, passion, anger and strength? When did we bargain away our very life blood? And what measures will revive the inner wisdom we lost so many years ago?

Blue Diamond Journey is our wake up call to find our red vibrant heart and soul, who we really are and what we came here to do. When we *listen* to our inner voice, we stop being naïve and uninformed. We narrow our eyes and draw a long bead on the lies around us. We stop pleasing people; stop being a doormat. We put on our red shoes and run! W*e decide* what is best for our wild, red soul. We take our life back! Then we can dance across the mountain tops and fly across the sea with real joy, excitement and passion. Only a free, wild spirit can stop whenever *she chooses.*

Pinkola Estés assures us it can be done "... there is a simple door waiting for us to walk through. On the other side are new feet. Go there. Crawl if need be. Stop talking and obsessing. Just do it" (92:252).

"Regaining lost instinct and healing injured instinct is truly within reach, for when a woman pays close attention through listening, looking and sensing the world around herself and then by acting as one sees others act, efficiently, effectively and soulfully. The opportunity to observe others who have instincts well intact is central to retrieval" (92:253).

Where do you want to walk or run or fly to? Take bold action, dream big! Commit to your dream. Unleash your adventurous side. Take risks, be daring. Trust your gut instincts. Meditate and LISTEN to your soul's truth. Better than anyone else, you *know* what is right for you. Do what *feels right down to your very bones.* Reveal your inner wisdom, show good judgement and follow *your* path. Let your instincts heal and guide you for the rest of your life.

"Set your goals in life as if you have already attained them. Do not make false divisions between idea and reality, desire and actuality.
Gary Quinn, *May the Angels be with You* (01:112)

Once we find our red *running* shoes, we *will never let them go!* Then we can share our wisdom, becoming mentors for those who walk beside us and behind us.

46.

Turquoise in the Final Analysis

"Do not go where the path may lead, go instead where there is no path and leave a trail."

Ralph Waldo Emerson

It seems a hundred years passed since my guides ripped the blue diamond from my breast and sent me on this incredible journey. Recently, I 'saw' myself jump off a guard rail, fly across a valley and over a mountain top. I flew so fast my turquoise gown and navy cape crackled in the wind. I'm free at last! Turquoise symbolism throughout this journey offers deeper meanings. A blue diamond is really blue-green or turquoise. The beautiful white buffalo necklace I wear has a thunderbolt of turquoise on it; my black opal ring from Australia that I wore for *seven* years is actually iridescent turquoise. What about the angels' turquoise greeting card? Why a turquoise jumpsuit for healing? Why do I wear turquoise in my visions, so similar to Gabriel's who claims me as one of her own? Everything in our path has reason and purpose.

I needed turquoise to get me through this journey. Judy Hall's *Crystal Bible*, summarizes it perfectly: "turquoise enhances the physical and psychic immune systems, regenerates tissue, supports the assimilation of nutrients, alleviates pollution and viral infections and heals the whole body....It reduces excess acidity, is an anti-inflammatory, detoxifier and pain remover." Turquoise promotes self-realization, assists in creative problem solving and calms the nerves when speaking in public (04:306). I 'see' myself in the future, giving lectures at a podium about this book and others.

Dorothee L. Mella in her book *Stone Power* says our Aboriginal people honoured Turquoise as the "universal stone, believing their minds became one with the universe when wearing the Turquoise (86:111). My journey connected me to Universal energy, whether I wanted it or not. Despite my doubts and determined fact-finding research, my innate inner wisdom constantly led back me to turquoise, purposefully, flawlessly.

Chakras, the seven spinning energy centers within our bodies, which quantum physics proved exist, adds another piece of the puzzle. The throat chakra is blue, covering the throat, the nose, ears, mouth and thyroid (all my expressive issues and hormonal blockages). Blue, the colour of sky, oceans and tears, helps us to heal physically and evolve emotionally. It relaxes the mind and helps us express our true thoughts and feelings to ourselves and others. The green heart chakra represents my raw, personal journey into healing and writing. Blue and green create the turquoise Gabrielle, the archangel of communication wears. She insisted I write my story, angry and truthful.

My guides claimed the antidote to cancer is love; *all you really need is love*. With their help, I learned the power of love, nurturing myself daily, changing my brittle, plastic, fearful heart into a warm, radiant, loving, humanly compassionate heart. They say, "You heal because you choose to heal. Your work was necessary for the healing: your writing, researching, eating, dreaming, dancing, cleansing, wishing, wanting, desiring, loving, hearing...all was needed. We see you as a full entity; healing must take place as a full entity. Cancer defines only the physical but yours was also spiritual, mental and emotional. Cancer is a dis-ease of the soul; does that not define it big enough?

"Disease is an uneasiness, the emotions of self-hatred, loathing of imperfection, DNA memories, not loving, not wanting, not wanting to live, unhappiness, not dreaming fully, lost on purpose, lost from caring for the self. Where did cancer come from? Not loving, not nurturing, not protecting, not wishing or dreaming fully. Not = lack; not = distress = disease from sorrow and anger. Not or lack requires pure love to change it, to see the whole picture. Cancer is a wake-up call, cleaning, clearing, nurturing, loving, protecting, guiding, standing up for the truth, the injustice, seeing what purpose is, what needs to be done."

Their turquoise greeting card lovingly encouraged me on this long arduous path. I released old thoughts, feelings, judgements, fears, beliefs and DNA coded messages, which no longer served me. I listened, I learned and I healed. Writing this book gave me the courage to express myself from my soul for all the women who come behind me, lost and afraid like me. Whenever I say, "I am loved, I am strong, I am healed," I feel something inside shift into place: *click, click, click* and I am content.

My highly psychic friend Sue (see the Forward of my book) gave me the final piece for my book's ending. She awoke one day to the word, "Isra" (phonetic spelling) and knew it was connected to me. She felt he was one of my angel guides. In my Dictionary of Angels, I found Ezra, the celestial scribe of the Most High (67:109). My guides showed me an image of a very slim faced, distinguished looking older gentleman with short white hair. I recognized him immediately! I just never knew his name. He periodically appeared in my dreams for the last twenty years, more so during my University era. Usually he stands at a classroom blackboard lecturing and I am the student listening. I vividly remember a dream of him fifteen years ago standing in the classroom where I studied a course on Ethics. Written on the blackboard beside Ezra were the words: "What Women Need to Know." With dawning wonder, I realized I had just completed my chapter in this book and gave it this title! My guides also say Ezra is a healer through writing, a proponent of human rights and justice for humanity. Why wouldn't he teach in a classroom for ethics!

I have struggled with ethics and written about human rights, women's rights and the practice, or lack of them throughout my life. How fitting, how awesome to know Ezra has been with me that long, helping me weave the tapestry of my life, designing purpose and meaning to this book. It just proves how much love and guidance we are given throughout our lives – whether we know it or not.

Trying to justify myself with my anecdotal stories made me finally admit my slow, life-long evolution as a reluctant seer. I *do have a gift*. I cannot stop what I 'see'; I can only accept it and use it for the greater good. The guides now call me a 'Seer of the First Water' (not sure what the water means but one day I will). As I wrote, I learned to appreciate myself as I am. Webster's Dictionary describes a Seer as "a person endowed with profound moral and spiritual insights" (80:1192). The turquoise opal I wear, the one I was guided to find, "enhances cosmic consciousness and induces psychic and mystical visions. Stimulating originality and dynamic creativity, it aids in accessing and expressing one's true self" (Hall, 04:209). My turquoise gown and white peacock embroidered cloak represents the nobility of truth and honesty a seer must walk in every day. The little square holes in my gown depict the many dimensions I can 'see' into now. Peacock feathers symbolize my new 'eyes' and the glorious responsibility involved. The peacock is associated with the ancient Phoenix which crashed and burned, rising from its funeral pyre bigger and better than ever. The bird guide which tore the diamond from my breast is also connected to the Phoenix. Taking my life to the brink of death made me fight back, made me trust my visions, made me stand alone again and face the world on my own again. I *needed me* as I am today.

Illness taught me to honour my handmade creations and accept myself as a spiritual being and messenger willing to teach others through her writing. Loving each day and all the people I share it with; meditating, dreaming, listening and writing is my natural high. Soon I will publish *Wind Walker*. From the depths of my healed soul, another book awaits, recounting my dreams and messages from a giant stone with an ancient grandmother face. My gift of the language of stones sent me on another journey with this ancient Mother Earth spirit called Shedoah. I sense more words churning deep within my womb, within my soul.

Now, I fly my turquoise colours because I *earned* them. Fifty of my family and friends recently helped me celebrate my 60th birthday. I smiled in the mirror, finally understanding why people smile back at me. I appreciate my thick, shiny curly hair, smooth glowing skin and healthy, mature body - a wisdom keeper. I wore turquoise of course and loved every minute of my day, receiving hugs, flowers and gifts. This is my speech to everyone:

"In my 60 years of life, the wonders I have seen:
I've swam the waters of the Atlantic, the Pacific and the Caribbean.
I've travelled coast to coast in Canada and from Alaska to Florida to California.
I've heard the thunder of a glacier falling into the sea.
I've watched a sunrise from the highest mountain in Maui and
slept in the crater of an ancient volcano in New Zealand.
I've touched the shell of a giant sea turtle as it dozed at my feet and
stared into the eye of a humpback whale from a few feet away.
I've eaten chocolate ants, chicken feet, whale blubber,
pig's knuckles, moose nose and kissed a live cod in Newfoundland.
I've watched the northern lights unravel off the wingtip of our plane at midnight.
I got drunk on shooters, lemon gin and roller coaster rides.
I've snorkelled the magic of a coral reef and
touched the massive red rock Uluru in the middle of Australia.
I've survived the eye of a violent tornado in Saskatchewan and
shot the wild Kanaskis River in a white water raft.
I've watched the ghost of a cheerful woman walk through my tent in broad daylight.
I've never met another man I'd rather marry than Cliff.
I've birthed two children and coached a third into the world.
I've waded every Rocky Mountain stream I could find with my grandchildren.
I've loved all my grandchildren from the moment I met them.
I've kissed my parents good-bye in their caskets and mourned the loss of many more loved ones.
I've scratched the bellies of a newborn foal and endless calves, baby pigs, bunnies, puppies and kittens.
I've planted gardens, flowers, trees and rocks.
I've dined with the Mayor and gossiped with a Premier's wife.
I've danced the night away and floated across a city in a hot air balloon.
I've written poems, short stories, songs, manuals, my family's history and several books.
Along the way I have gathered friends and family, the bright shimmering
threads in the tapestry of my life.
And I love each and every one of you for how rich you make my life.
Thank You.

I am home now; comfortable in the house of belonging I call soul, celebrating my strengths, good health and special gifts. I walk about my acreage and give thanks for the day. I listen to the wind and cherish its caress across my cheeks. Song birds call in the golden morning sunshine, awakening the trees to another day. Our neighbour's dog claims me as his pet and guards me while we walk the countryside. He trots ahead then politely waits for me to catch up. Like a kindred spirit, I *feel* his dancing joy in simply being alive. He asks for nothing else. Why should I? I am not special. I was just curious enough to ask and keep asking, to seek, to listen, to open myself to my dreams and believe in the gifts awaiting us all.

In the final analysis, cancer ripped my life wide open, revealing my true inner diamond. I need the Spirit World and it needs me to spread its messages. I needed to hear its truths, seek its healing, and regain the purpose I came here to fulfill. I finally 'see' my connection to the realm of guides and angels with their quiet humor and consistent messages. I asked out of fear and doubt. They answer gently, lovingly with great unwavering truth. They are as real as the cancer.

May my book bring you hope and choices by addressing the dis-ease that took us down and the options that lift us back up. Cancer, like any chronic illness, takes a long time to form and *should* take a long time to heal. I healed from a breast full of cancer, imagine what you can do! I hope my information helps you *manage* any illness. Every good Naturopath will tell you the best healing uses a combination of conventional and homeopathic remedies. One deals with the physical the other deals with the whole person. Both are needed for good health.

Rather than a King Kong in our living room, cancer is really just a monkey on our backs needing resolution. On a scale of pain, I give it 2 out of 10. Perhaps chemo and radiation cause the agony. Cancer is merely a wake-up call. Change...or die and learn on the Other Side what you could have changed here. The choice, as always, is yours. Clean up your environment, eat healthy foods, take your medicines, ease your unhealthy thoughts and memories, release your tired, weary ancient emotions and sit with your innate, inner wisdom. Clearing en-lightens us, moves us into a healthier space, ready for tomorrow, healed and whole. I believe we will one day look back in horror for treating cancer with surgery, chemotherapy and radiation.

After considering all the ways you and I healed together on this journey, we can go gently into the night, *whenever we are called*, knowing our work is done here and new beginnings await. I 'hear' the word, "Counterpoint". It means the art of combining two or more melodies to produce a satisfying harmony by the interaction of all parts. What a beautiful description of inner balance because we walked this path together! Be at peace my *Anam Cara*, soul friend!

Our Aboriginal Elders are right. We, the people who walk the Earth right now, must do the loving work, healing ourselves first, then projecting our healed inner harmony outwards. We create peace in the world when we project our inner peace outward. We do this wholistically, simultaneously: emotionally, mentally, physically and spiritually – one day at a time.

I see the changes on this planet, the gifting and giving; the caring, forgiving and service to others and I smile in delight. We are getting there, just as the dragons said we would.

The secret of life, of all success and happiness, is feeling *part* of life, *inside* life's energy, every day. Our ego makes us think we are still outside, wanting, needing *more* but we are already there! Celebrate your accomplishments, the abundance in your life and be at peace. Peace means accepting ourselves as we are right now. Dawn will come tomorrow with new challenges and more abundance. Peace means feeling soul deep connection to all parts of yourself, to all parts of the world around you: the Universe and Universal consciousness or whatever you may call it.

So be Sacred and Silly – every day. Watch five year olds play soccer and you will discover how easily, effortlessly they do this. In the middle of a game, they take time to hold hands, pick the flowers and roll on the grass. Irreverent and Reverent is the balance of spiritual health. Live each day, experience each precious moment with your heart, mind, body and spirit. Be one with it all and feel the contentment. Nothing more is expected of us. We are here and we live NOW.

Blessed be.

Bibliography of Works Sited

Andrews, Ted. *Animal Speak*, the Spiritual and Magical Powers of Creatures Great and Small. St, Paul, MN: Llewellyn Worldwide, 2004.

Andrews, Ted. *How to Heal With Color*. St. Paul, MN: Llewellyn Publishers, 2003.

Ban Breathnach, Sarah. *Romancing the Ordinary*, A Year of Simple Splendor. New York: Simple Abundance Press Scribner, 2002.

Bays, Brandon. *Freedom Is*, Liberating your Boundless Potential. Novato, CA: New World Library, 2006

Beck, Leslie, RD. *Foods That Fight Disease*, A nutrition guide to staying healthy for life. Toronto: Penguin Group (Canada), 2008.

Beliveau, Richard, PhD & Gingras, Denis, Ph.D. *Cooking with Foods that Fight Cancer*. Quebec: McClelland & Stewart ltd. 2007

Black, Allida D. ed. *Courage in a Dangerous World*, the political writings of Eleanor Roosevelt. New York: Columbia University Press, 1999.

Bopp, Judie et al. *The Sacred Tree*. Lethbridge, Alberta: University of Lethbridge, Four Worlds Development, 1985.

Calbom, Cheri, MS. *The Juice Lady's Guide to Juicing for Health*. New York: Avery Publishing Group, 1999.

Calbom, Cheri; Calbom, John and Mahaffey, Michael. *The Complete Cancer Cleanse*. Thomas Nelson Inc., 2006

Cheung, Theresa. An Angel Called My Name. London, England: Harper Element, an imprint of Harper Collins Publisher, 2008.

Ciruelo. *The Book of the Dragon*. New York: Sterling Publishing Co, Inc., 2000.

Davidson, Gustav. *A Dictionary of Angels*, including the fallen angels. Toronto: Maxwell Macmillan Canada, 1967.

Dyer, Dr. David S. *Cellfood*, Vital Cellular Nutrition for the New Millennium, USA: Feedback Books, Inc. 2000.

Elsbeth, Marguerite, *Crystal Medicine*. St. Paul, MN: Llewellyn Publishers, 1998.

Ewashina, Linda. *Spirit of the Wheel*, Meditation Deck. Stamford, CT: U.S. Games System Inc., 2006

Farmer, Steven D. Ph.D. *Power Animals*, How to connect with Your Animal Spirit Guide. Carlsbad, California: Hay House, Inc. 2007.

Gaesser, Glenn A. PH.D. *Big Fat Lies*. The truth about your weight and health. New York: Fawcett Columbine, 1996.

Georgian, Linda, *Communicating With the Dead*. New York: Simon & Schuster, 1995.

Gilbert, Elizabeth. *Eat Pray Love*. New York: Penguin Books, 2006

Goldberg, Natalie. *Writing Down the Bones*, Freeing the Writer Within. Boston: Shambala, 1986.

Hall, Judy. *The Crystal Bible*, a Definitive guide to crystals. Cincinnati, Ohio: Walking Stick Press, 2004.

Hay, Louise L. *Heal Your Body, A – Z*. Carlsbad, CA: Hay House Inc., 1998.

Henderson, Bill. *Cancer-Free, your guide to gentle non-toxic healing*. Second Edition. USA: Booklocker.com, 2007. His website:http://www.Beating-Cancer-Gently.com

Horner, Christine, M.D., F.A.C.S. *Waking the Warrior Goddess*, Harnessing the Power of Nature and Natural Medicines to Achieve Extraordinary Health. Laguna Beach, California: Basic Health Publications, 2007.

Jensen, Dr. Bernard. *Guide to Diet and Detoxification*. Los Angeles: Keats Publishing, 2000.

Jensen, Dr. Bernard. *Nutrition Handbook*, A Daily Regime for Healthy Living. Los Angeles, CA: Keats Publishing, 2000.

Kubler-Ross, Elizabeth. *Death, the final stage of growth*. New Jersey: Prentice-Hall, Inc., 1975.

Lee, John R. M.D. with Virginia Hopkins. *What Your Doctor May Not Tell you About Menopause.* The Breakthrough Book on Natural Hormone Balance. New York: Warner Books, 1996, updated version, 2004.

Mella, Dorothee L. *Stone Power*, New York: Warner Books Edition, 1986.

Millman, Dan. *The Laws of Spirit*, A tale of transformation. Novato, California: HJ Kramer New World Library, 1995.

Millman, Dan. *Way of the Peaceful Warrior*. Novato, CA: New World Library, 1980.

Moning, Karen Marie. *Spell of the Highlander*. New York: Bantam Dell, 2005.

Montgomery, Ruth. *A Search for Truth*. Toronto: Random House, 1966.

Nelson, Miriam E, PhD and Lichtenstein, Alice H, D.Sc. *Strong Women, Strong Hearts*. New York, G.P. Putnam's Sons, 2005.

Newman, Dr. Laura. *Make Your Juicer Your Drug Store*. New York: Benedict Lust Publications, 1970.

Newman, Pauline. *Heartbeat Angels*, True Life spiritual experiences of personal angel encounters. Carvel, Alberta: Newman Publishing, 2001.

Null, Gary, Ph.D. and Null, Shelly. *The Joy of Juicing*, Creative Cooking with Your Juicer. New York: Penguin Putnam Inc. 1992.

O'Donohue, John. *Anam Cara*, A book of Celtic wisdom. New York: Cliff Street Books from HarperCollins Publishers Inc., 1997.

Olivotto, Ivo, MD et al. *The Intelligent Patient Guide to Breast Cancer, 4*[th] *ed.* Vancouver: 2006.

Pinkola Estes, Clarissa, Ph.D. *Women Who Run With the Wolves*. New York: Ballantine Books, 1992.

Pollan, Michael. *In Defense of Food*, an Eater's Manifesto. New York: Penguin Press, 2008.

Quinn, Gary. *May the Angels be With You*. A Psychic helps you find your Spirit Guides and your true purpose. New York: Harmony Books, 2001.

Raphaell, Katrina. *The Crystalline Transmission*, the Synthesis of Light. Santa Fe, N.M.: Aurora Press, 1990.

Regehr Clark, Hulda, PhD, N.D. *The Cure for all Cancers*. Chula Vista, Ca: New Century Press, 1993.

Sams, Jamie. *Sacred Path Cards*, the Discovery of Self Through Native Teachings. San Francisco, CA: Harper San Francisco, 1990.

Schoffro Cook, Michelle, DNM, DAC, CNC. *The Ultimate pH Solution*. Balance Your Body Chemistry to Prevent Disease and Lose Weight. Toronto: Harper Collins Publishers, 2008.

Somers, Suzanne. *Knockout,* Interviews with Doctors who are curing cancer and how to prevent getting it in the first place. New York: Crown Publishers, 2009.

Stein, Jess, editor. *The Random House College Dictionary*, revised edition. New York: Random House Inc. 1980.

Supernault, Esther. *A Warrior's Heart*. Edmonton, AB: Native Counselling Services of Alberta, 1995.

Supernault, Esther. *When We Still Laughed*. Edmonton: Scholastic Printers, 2002

Tolle, Eckart. *The Power of Now, a New Earth,* Awakening your life's purpose. New York: Penguin Group (USA) Inc., 2005.

Trudeau, Kevin. *The Weight Loss Cure*, What They Don't Want You To Know About. Illinois: the Alliance Publishing Group, 2007.

Van Praagh, James. *Ghosts Among Us*, Uncovering the truth about the other side. New York: Harper Collins Publishers, 2008.

Van Straten, Michael. The Healthy Food Directory. Burnaby, B.C.: New Millennium Books, 1999.

Virtue, Doreen, PhD. *The Lightworker's Way*, Awakening your spiritual power to know and heal. Carlsbad, CA: Hay House Inc. 1997.

Watson, Brenda, N.D., C.T. *Do You Suffer From Liver Problems?* Liver detoxification is vital for improving your health. Oakville, Ontario: Renew Life Canada. A brochure.

Weed, Susan S. *Breast Cancer? Breast Health!* The Wise Woman Way. New York: Ash Tree Publishing, 1996.

Weiss, Brian L. M.D. *Many Lives, Many Masters*. New York: Fireside, 1988.

Author Biography:

Esther Supernault, a nurse with a bachelor degree in psychology, finds inspiration from her Celtic/Aboriginal heritage and Mother Earth. An avid speed reader, she loves researching, science fiction and the paranormal, plus yoga, drumming, outrigger canoeing and hiking. Esther and her husband Cliff live on a sunny hillside acreage in Central Alberta near her beloved family and friends.